Also by Doug Dayton ·

Selling Microsoft

TOTAL MARKET DOMINATION

TOTAL MARKET DOMINATION

10 Steps for Supercharging Your Sales and Marketing

by
Doug Dayton

Adams Media Corporation
Holbrook, Massachusetts

ACKNOWLEDGMENTS

I would like to thank Ed Walters at Adams Media for his help with this project.

I would also like to thank each and every client that I have worked with over the last fourteen years. Without their help and guidance I would never have figured out how to keep it simple, stay on point, and take responsibility for moving business forward.

DEDICATION

This book is dedicated to Terry Lynn Smith, and to my family, friends, and clients who have encouraged me to write this book.

It's easy to develop a compelling marketing story, create an effective marketing strategy, and influence your customers' purchase decisions, *if you ask the right questions.* . . .

Published by
Adams Media Corporation
260 Center Street, Holbrook, MA 02343

ISBN: 1-58062-113-9

Printed in United States of America.

J   I   H   G   F   E   D   C   B   A

Library of Congress Cataloging-in-Publication Data
Total market domination / Doug Dayton.
p.   cm.
ISBN 1-58062-113-9
1. Sales management. 2. Marketing—Management. I. Title.
HF5438.4.D39   1999
658.8—dc21   98-52735
CIP

This publication is designed to provide accurate and authoritative information with regard to the subject matter covered. It is sold with the understanding that the publisher is not engaged in rendering legal, accounting, or other professional advice. If legal advice or other expert assistance is required, the services of a competent professional person should be sought.
— From a *Declaration of Principles* jointly adopted by a Committee of the American Bar Association and a Committee of Publishers and Associations.

Cover illustration by John Kleber.

This book is available at quantity discounts for bulk purchases.
For information, call 1-800-872-5627 (in Massachusetts, 781-767-8100).

Visit our home page at http://www.businesstown.com

TABLE OF CONTENTS

THANK YOU! x

PREPARING FOR CHANGE xi

    Step 1:   Assign an individual to be responsible for
               coordinating the sales evaluation process xiv

    Step 2:   Determine your objectives for implementing
               your Client-Centered™ sales evaluation. xiv

    Step 3:   Confirm your client's objectives before beginning
               your evaluation. xvii

**CHAPTER 1: DO YOU UNDERSTAND THE KEY FACTORS THAT
DRIVE YOUR CUSTOMERS' PURCHASE DECISIONS?** 1

Step 1: Describe your customer. 2

Step 2: Identify your customers' key purchase factors. 4

Step 3: Identify the business terms that are of greatest
         importance to your customers. 7

Step 4: Use your understanding of your customer's purchase factors
         to identify key customer benefits. 9

Step 5: Document your customer's purchase process. 10

Step 6: Identify any negative market factors that may impact your
         customer's purchase decision. 11

Step 7: Identify any emerging market factors that may impact your
         customer's purchase decision. 12

Step 8: Identify the purchase factors that your competitors
         are using to position their products. 14

Step 9: Evaluate your Marketing Information System. 15

The Bottom Line 18

CHAPTER 2: ARE YOUR COMPANY'S RESOURCES ALLOCATED IN A WAY THAT IS CONSISTENT WITH ACHIEVING ITS MARKETING OBJECTIVES? . . 19

Step 1: Evaluate your primary business objective. 20
Step 2: Evaluate your short- and longer-term business objectives. . . 23
Step 3: Evaluate your company's Value Equation. 26
Step 4: Evaluate where your company is in its business cycle. 27
Step 5: Evaluate your product sales. 31
Step 6: Evaluate your company's use of integration strategies. 32
Step 7: Align your marketing strategy with your
        company's objectives. 33
The Bottom Line 34

CHAPTER 3: HAVE YOU DEVELOPED A CLEAR, CONCISE, COMPELLING MARKET STORY? 36

Step 1: Identify the market factors that differentiate your
        company and your products. 37
Step 2: Evaluate your company's position in its market. 39
Step 3: Identify your company's most significant
        accomplishments. 41
Step 4: Evaluate your competitors' strengths and weaknesses. 42
Step 5: Evaluate your products' strengths and weaknesses. 44
Step 6: Define the elements of your marketing story. 45
Step 7: Map the elements of your marketing story to your
        customers' needs and concerns. 47
The Bottom Line 50

CHAPTER 4. DOES YOUR MARKETING PLAN PROVIDE THE FOCUS THAT YOUR COMPANY NEEDS TO LEVERAGE ITS SELLING EFFORTS? 52

Step 1: Develop a clear, concise, compelling marketing plan. 53
Step 2: Evaluate your marketing plan 61
Step 3: Evaluate your sales plan. 63
Step 4: Evaluate your sales kit. 65
Step 5: Evaluate your customer relationships. 73
Step 6: Evaluate your relationships with your business partners. . . 73
Step 7: Evaluate your distribution strategy. 75
Step 8: Evaluate your resellers. 84
Step 9: Evaluate your consultants and subcontractors. 87
Step 10: Evaluate your company's pricing strategy. 88
Step 11: Identify the most serious risk factors to your
        marketing plan. 95
The Bottom Line 97

CHAPTER 5: DO YOU HAVE EFFECTIVE PROGRAMS IN PLACE TO IDENTIFY PROSPECTIVE CUSTOMERS? 98

Step 1: Evaluate the prospecting methods that your company is
        using to generate leads. 98

Step 2: Evaluate your advertising and corporate
        communications plan. 106

Step 3: Review your advertising budget. 110

Step 4: Evaluate your corporate communications. 111

Step 5: Evaluate the effectiveness of trade shows, newsletters,
        user groups, and electronic bulletin boards. 114

Step 6: Evaluate your marketing department. 117

The Bottom Line 123

CHAPTER 6: DO YOU HAVE EFFECTIVE PROGRAMS IN PLACE TO QUALIFY PROSPECTIVE CUSTOMERS? 124

Step 1: Adopt a Client-Centered™ selling methodology. 125

Step 2: Evaluate your sales team's qualification process. 126

Step 3: Evaluate your product demonstrations. 131

Step 4: Evaluate your sales proposals. 133

Step 5: Evaluate whether your company is prepared to sell
        to major accounts. 135

Step 6: Evaluate whether team selling is an effective strategy
        for your company. 138

Step 7: Evaluate your Territory Plans. 140

Step 8: Evaluate your Account Plans. 142

Step 9: Evaluate your Account Review process. 145

Step 10: Evaluate your Sales Call Plans. 149

The Bottom Line 152

CHAPTER 7: IS YOUR SALES FORCE PREPARED TO REPRESENT YOUR COMPANY IN A PROFESSIONAL, CLIENT-CENTERED ™ WAY? 153

Step 1: Identify the key players in your sales and marketing
        organization. 155

Step 2: Describe your corporate culture. 157

Step 3: Review your company's personnel policies. 158

Step 4: Review your organization chart to identify teams that may
        be restructured or automated to improve productivity. ... 159

Step 5: Identify how and where your sales managers are
        spending their time. 162

Step 6: Define your sales manager's objectives and key results. ... 165

Step 7: Adopt a specific selling methodology. 166

Step 8: Evaluate your sales training programs. 167

Step 9: Evaluate the systems that you have in place for goal
        setting, motivation, and personnel appraisals. 168

Step 10. Evaluate your sales recruiting process. 170
Step 11: Evaluate your sales compensation plan. 180
Step 12: Evaluate your sales personnel. 189
Step 13: Evaluate your sales and marketing
　　　　department's workload. 197
Step 14: Evaluate your sales and marketing group's
　　　　overall effectiveness. 198
The Bottom Line 199

CHAPTER 8: IS YOUR COMPANY USING COMPUTERS AND COMMUNICATION TECHNOLOGIES TO LEVERAGE ITS SALES EFFORTS? 201

Step 1: Document your sales infrastructure. 202
Step 2: Identify areas of your sales infrastructure that should
　　　　be automated. 206
Step 3: Evaluate your sales automation system. 209
Step 4: Evaluate your customer information system. 216
Step 5: Evaluate your communication systems. 222
Step 6: Evaluate your accounting system. 230
Step 7: Evaluate your information systems support and service. . . 232
Step 8: Evaluate your use of the Internet and
　　　　network computing. 236
Step 9: Evaluate the total cost of ownership of your information
　　　　systems. 246
Step 10: Develop a budget for your sales automation project. . . . 248
Step 11: Evaluate your system suppliers. 249
Step 12: Costs and benefits—competitive advantage
　　　　and survival. 252
The Bottom Line 253

CHAPTER 9: DO YOU HAVE AN EFFECTIVE CUSTOMER SERVICE AND SUPPORT MODEL? 254

Step 1: Evaluate your service and support model. 255
Step 2: Perform a customer satisfaction survey. 257
Step 3: Identify any production issues that may
　　　　impact your business. 260
Step 4: Identify any quality control issues that may impact your
　　　　business. 261
Step 5: Evaluate your company's sales order process. 263
Step 6: Identify any order fulfillment issues that may impact
　　　　your business. 265
Step 7: Evaluate your sales and support facilities. 267
The Bottom Line 267

CHAPTER 10: DO YOU HAVE AN EFFECTIVE PROCESS FOR DEVELOPING SALES FORECASTS AND MARKETING BUDGETS? 268

Step 1: Evaluate your sales forecasting procedure. 269
Step 2: Create a sales forecast for your company based on your
  sales representative's monthly sales forecasts. 278
Step 3: Evaluate your marketing budget. 280
Step 4: Evaluate your financial systems and your
  management reports. 283
The Bottom Line 285

CHAPTER 11: IDENTIFY AND IMPLEMENT BEST CLIENT-CENTERED™ SALES PRACTICES 288

Step 1: Identify your company's critical success factors. 290
Step 2: Use the worksheets from your Client-Centered™ sales
  evaluation to identify your company's best
  sales practices. 295
Step 3: Develop an action plan, including objectives and key results
  (performance metrics), for each best sales practice that you
  plan to adopt within your company. 298
Step 4: Validate your company's best sales practices with your
  customers. 300
Step 5: Evaluate new marketing opportunities. 300
Step 6: Engineer creativity into your company. 303
Step 7: Develop a process for handling sales and
  marketing problems. 306
Step 8: Take responsibility for your company's success. 307
Ten Laws of Total Market Domination 309

A FINAL NOTE 311

APPENDIX A: SALES AUTOMATION SOFTWARE—EVALUATION GUIDE .. 312

APPENDIX B: LEADING SALES AUTOMATION COMPANIES 321

APPENDIX C: NON-DISCLOSURE AGREEMENT 323

INDEX 325

THANK YOU!

Before we begin—I would like to thank everyone who has supported my last book, *Selling Microsoft: Sales Secrets from Inside the World's Most Successful Company*.

It has been exciting to watch *Selling Microsoft* touch the lives of sales professionals from around the world. I have received telephone calls, letters, and e-mail from Client-Centered™ selling "converts" in Europe, Asia, Australia, and South America.

Here at home, the feedback has been just as positive. One reader wrote, "For the purchase price you have given away millions of dollars of consulting, and I greatly appreciate the time and effort you put into its writing." And another wrote, "I am now a card carrying, certified Client-Centered™ disciple." But perhaps the most heartfelt feedback came from a salesperson from the Midwest who wrote, "I purchased a copy of *Selling Microsoft*, which is now permanently in my briefcase as a reference manual, right next to my daily prayer book."

My sincere hope is that *Total Market Domination* will be as helpful to you as *Selling Microsoft*.

—DOUG DAYTON
Bellevue, Washington

PREPARING FOR CHANGE

Over the last fifteen years, I have helped hundreds of technology-driven companies develop business plans, marketing programs, and sales strategies. The most important lesson that I have learned is that the key to improving the effectiveness of your sales force is to adopt a Client-Centered™ attitude toward your customers and to develop a compelling marketing story, which explains exactly why a customer should do business with your company. Of course, making a statement like this is easy, the challenge, as Captain Jean-Luc Picard of the *Starship Enterprise* might point out, is to "Make it so."

Total Market Domination presents a step-by-step sales evaluation process that you can use to help you develop a clear, concise, compelling marketing story and improve your ability to influence your customers' purchase decisions. It's simple and straightforward, because the evaluation process is built around the ten questions that you need to answer to gain greater control of the selling process and build market momentum.

The sales evaluation process described in *Total Market Domination* is based on a Client-Centered™ approach to selling that I developed at Microsoft. And Client-Centered™ selling is based on the observation that you cannot help your customers move through their purchase process until you understand their needs and concerns. When you can see the world through your customers' eyes, you are in the best position to help your customers, and you can have the most influence in their purchase process.

Integrating a Client-Centered™ selling approach into your day-to-day sales operations will give you more control in each selling situation and will make the selling process easier. I call this "selling downhill." But before you can start selling downhill, you will have to evaluate every step of your selling process. And doing this takes a bit of work.

You will need to throw out many of your assumptions about how things are working in your company—and find out how they really work. And you will need to re-evaluate every sales and marketing activity that you are doing to verify that they are the most effective use of your marketing resources. Most importantly, you will need to verify that your marketing story is:

- ☐ *Clear*—if your customers don't understand your marketing story, it will not influence their purchase process;
- ☐ *Concise*—the more complex your marketing story is, the more difficult and expensive it will be to communicate; and
- ☐ *Compelling*—your customers will not make a purchase decision until you present a compelling reason for them to do business with your company.

THE QUESTIONS

The Client-Centered™ sales evaluation process is based on the ten questions that you must answer to help you achieve *total market domination*. Each question is covered in a separate chapter, which includes step-by-step instructions for implementing your evaluation.

1. Do you understand the key factors that drive your customers' purchase decisions?
2. Are your company's resources allocated in a way that is consistent with achieving its marketing objectives?
3. Have you developed a clear, concise, compelling marketing story that defines "who, what, where, when, and why" customers should do business with your company?
4. Does your marketing plan provide the focus your company needs to leverage its selling efforts?
5. Do you have effective programs in place to identify prospective customers?

6. Do you have effective programs in place to qualify prospective customers?
7. Is your sales force prepared to present your company in a professional, Client-Centered™ way?
8. Is your company using computers and communication technologies to leverage its selling efforts?
9. Do you have an effective customer service and support model?
10. Do you have an effective process for developing sales forecasts and marketing budgets?

In the process of evaluating your selling process you will compile the information that you need to evaluate and reengineer your organization's sales and marketing infrastructure.

SALES EVALUATION WORKSHEETS

Each chapter in *Total Market Domination* includes detailed worksheets that will help you define your business's objectives, position your products in your market, and analyze your business operations. The worksheets will also help you identify areas of your business that can benefit from new computer and communication technologies.

As you read through each worksheet, you should try to identify obsolete attitudes, practices, and procedures in your business, and visualize the changes that you must make to align your sales and marketing infrastructure with your strategic business objectives.

I have drawn on the experiences that I have had working at IBM and Microsoft and working with my consulting clients to help clarify each step in the sales evaluation process. And I have used a fictionalized version of my Client-Centered™ Training business to provide an example of the depth of response that is required to complete a thorough evaluation of your company's sales infrastructure.

Completing the worksheets may seem a bit overwhelming at first. But if you are patient and work through the process a step at a time, you will be able to literally *engineer* your marketing success.

Step 1: Assign an individual to be responsible for coordinating the sales evaluation process.

You may complete the Client-Centered™ sales evaluation worksheets for your own business or for a client's business. In either case, you may complete the sales evaluation worksheets yourself or have different worksheets filled in by the individual within your company who is directly responsible for the specific area of business who is addressed by the worksheet. Your sales manager, for example, might help you complete the worksheets on your company's sales objectives, and your sales support manager might complete the worksheets on customer service.

Blank copies of the sales evaluation worksheets are available on the author's Internet Web site at www.daytonassociates.com.

HONESTY AND OBJECTIVITY

Over the years, I have learned that the key to implementing a sales evaluation is to be as *honest* and *objective* as possible. Of course this is much easier said than done. Depending on your situation, you may need to "sell" the sales evaluation process to your coworkers before you can win their cooperation.

In any case, it is important to address any concerns that your coworkers have about being evaluated or judged during your evaluation. If people in your company are concerned about their jobs, or are afraid that their comments or suggestions will be used against them, they will become defensive and uncooperative.

I have found that the best way to overcome your coworkers' concerns is to be candid about your objectives, to encourage everyone to keep his or her answers as simple and direct as possible, and to encourage open communication if anyone feels that tough things need to be said.

Step 2: Determine your objectives for implementing your Client-Centered™ sales evaluation.

Most companies' primary objectives for implementing a sales evaluation are increasing sales revenues, controlling sales and marketing expenses, and evaluating new business opportunities. However, many other objectives may be addressed during the

General Information
Evaluator: (outside consultant if applicable) Mr. MBA
Date of Evaluation: 4/21/200X
Client Business/Organization: Client-Centered™ Training, Inc.
Address: 477 123rd Place NE, Bellevue, Washington 98005
Coordinator: Ms. Smith
Phone: (425) 451-1140
FAX: (425) 451-8505
E-mail: info@daytonassociates.com
Internet: www.daytonassociates.com
Company/Organization Founders: Doug Dayton and Terry Smith   Special interests or background: Doug Dayton and Terry Smith met at the University of Washington in 1976. Doug was interested in technology and marketing, and Terry was interested in law and administration. They formed a training company to leverage their experience and education.

How and when was your company formed?	Client-Centered™ Training was formed in 1985 after several consulting clients asked us to develop a custom training program for their sales personnel. Our seminars were well received, and we decided to resell them to new clients.
Describe your corporate organization: (Sole Proprietorship / Partnership / Limited Liability Corporation / Corporation / S Corporation / Joint Venture / Public Corporation / Other)	We are organized as a privately held corporation in Washington State.
What significant changes have occurred in your company's purpose and/or product focus since founding?	Originally we developed application specific training courseware. However, we soon realized that there was also an opportunity to provide executive level technology briefings and seminars on "emerging" technologies. After we began doing IT seminars, we developed a methodology for auditing our client's IT infrastructure.
Are any ownership changes planned?	We plan to issue key employees stock next year and would like to do an IPO in two years when our sales reach $10 million.
Are any Mergers or Acquisitions planned?	We have acquired the rights to Dayton Associates' Client-Centered™ Selling courseware. We want to use Dayton Associates' courseware as a basis for a new line of books and seminars on Strategic Business Planning.

evaluation process, such as identifying comarketing opportunities, evaluating customer service issues, and defining relationships with outside service providers, such as advertising agencies and fulfillment houses.

Your company's sales evaluation may be used to help you accomplish many different objectives:

- □ Prepare a business plan
- □ Create more effective marketing programs
- □ Organize and manage your sales organization
- □ Review your personnel
- □ Develop new product ideas
- □ Identify new markets
- □ Develop more effective sales strategies
- □ Evaluate your fundamental business model
- □ Evaluate merger and acquisition opportunities
- □ Help you re-energize your sales organization
- □ Identify your company's key success factors
- □ Identify best Client-Centered™ sales practices for your company

One way to identify your company's success factors is to explore how your business started and how it evolved.

Client-Centered™ Training's Key Objectives for Commissioning This Evaluation
1. Determine whether our marketing story is clear, concise, and compelling. (Chapter 3)
2. Evaluate whether our marketing budget is in line with other businesses in our industry. (Chapter 10)
3. Determine whether our company should enter any new markets. (Chapter 2)
4. Identify emerging market factors, such as online training, that may affect our business over the next three years. (Chapter 8)
5. Evaluate our sales training program. (Chapter 6)
6. Determine the most cost-effective way to use the Internet to market our services and provide customer support. (Chapter 8)
7. Determine whether our company's value equation is in balance. (Chapter 3)

Step 3: Confirm your client's objectives before beginning your evaluation.

In most companies, the individual who initiates a sales evaluation is usually a senior business manager, such as the President or Vice President of Sales and Marketing. However in some cases, such as when a Board of Directors initiates an evaluation, or when the evaluation is due diligence for a merger or acquisition, an individual who is outside of the company may be hired to facilitate the evaluation.

Most clients have three or four issues or concerns that have precipitated the evaluation process. However, some clients have difficulty articulating all of their objectives for their evaluation.

In any case, it is important to spend as much time as necessary with your client to identify its concerns and objectives before beginning your evaluation. If you don't understand your client's objectives, you will not know which areas of its business to focus on during your evaluation, and you will have less chance of helping your client identify and resolve its problems.

The primary benefit of the sales evaluation process is that it gives senior management an opportunity to look at their sales and marketing process from a fresh perspective.

WORKING WITH CONSULTANTS

Most business managers find it is very difficult to be objective about the ideas and programs that they have implemented, and about the personnel that they have recruited and trained.

An outside consultant can bring *objectivity* to your sales evaluation process. However, before hiring a consultant, you should find out about their previous experience, their success with other clients, and their ability to work cooperatively with your management team.

Most consultants know much *less* about their clients' businesses than their clients. The primary value that consultants can deliver is their objectivity, industry experience, and analytic skills. But different consultants, regardless of their previous experience, have different personalities and different working styles. It is wise to take the time to evaluate and interview several consultants to find one whose attitude, experience, and methods fit your needs and expectations.

THE CONSULTANT'S DILEMMA

The managers that bring consultants into an organization are often the *cause* of the problems that they are asking their consultants to help them resolve. This situation presents their consultants with an interesting dilemma. If they are honest and report that the managers who hired them are incompetent or have used bad judgment, they will most likely be fired, and they will not be able to help their client. And if they try to avoid this issue, they may not be able to present recommendations that will help their client solve its problems.

To resolve this dilemma, consultants learn to balance their responsibility to deliver a straightforward analysis of their client's situation with their self-serving desire to maintain a positive working relationship with their client. I believe that this is the main reason that consulting clients are so often given politically correct reports replete with trendy business maxims such as "thinking out of the box" and the "difficulty of managing change," rather than more straightforward insights and recommendations.

The fact that successful consultants are biased toward political survival is not necessarily a bad thing. Consultants who are brutally honest may be too difficult for many companies to work with. But the simple truth is that the problems most companies face are pretty straightforward, and the resolution to those problems is usually pretty obvious to a skilled, objective business consultant. It is the impact on specific individuals in the client's business that often obviates the possibility of ever resolving those problems.

Change *is* difficult to manage–because it affects people's lives. But it is easier to manage change when people are honest about their intent and their actions. When managers don't have the skills they need to do their jobs effectively, they must be trained. When managers don't understand their market, they must bring people into their organization who can articulate their customers' needs and concerns. And when managers want to build market share, they must be brutally honest about how well they have mapped their company's marketing story to their customers' needs and concerns.

KAYPRO CORPORATION

In 1984, Kaypro Corporation shipped over 100,000 Kaypro II PCs and become the fourth largest PC manufacturer in the world. Kaypro achieved its success by positioning itself as the "Volkswagen" of the nascent microcomputer industry—it supplied a high quality, portable PC at a very competitive price.

Kaypro raised $40 million dollars in a public stock offering and used most of this capital to improve its manufacturing facilities and ramp production. And for a while, it seemed Kaypro was unstoppable. But when IBM announced that it had developed a 16-bit PC that used Microsoft's new MS-DOS operating system, interest in less functional 8-bit systems, such as the Kaypro II, waned. Kaypro did not realize that 16-bit systems would be adopted by its customer base so quickly, and watched its sales revenues drop by about 50 percent over a twelve-month period.

At this point, in May of 1985, Kaypro turned to a young marketing consultant–fresh from Microsoft. When I arrived, I knew that Kaypro was already about six months later than its competitors in offering an IBM-compatible PC. But I didn't know that Kaypro's engineers were having such a difficult time reverse engineering IBM's PC architecture.

After several spirited meetings, during which I predicted market domination by IBM and aggressively priced PC clone manufacturers, I got permission from Kaypro's VP of Marketing to ask Kyocera Corporation to submit a bid to supply Kaypro with IBM-compatible PCs. It was clear to me that Kaypro's opportunity lay in reselling products through its loyal reseller channel rather than in attempting to become a low-cost PC manufacturer.[1]

The week after we received Kyocera's bid, Kaypro's engineers unveiled a prototype PC based on IBM's design, and scheduled a trip to Southeast Asia to source parts. Kaypro's President desperately wanted to believe that his company could build competitively priced PCs and supported his manufacturing staff's plan.

From my perspective, this was the turning point for Kaypro. Against my advice, my client decided to compete head-to-head

---

[1] Kyocera is a large Japanese electronics company that was manufacturing PCs for Tandy Corporation (Radio Shack).

against companies that had the resources and, more importantly, the expertise to bury them.

I recall thinking at the time that I had learned an important lesson: *People will do almost anything to convince themselves that they are acting in the best interest of their company if they feel threatened by change or are concerned about losing their jobs.*

To be fair, the Kaypro PC's design was competitive with products from most of the other IBM PC clone manufacturers. And Kaypro's managers realized that they needed to rebuild Kaypro's value-leader position in the market. But Kaypro could not drive its manufacturing costs down as rapidly as its competitors and it continued to lose market share.

I have learned many lessons about consulting since I left Microsoft. But the most important lesson I have learned is that building success and achieving total market domination is not just about developing great products or inventing new technologies; it is about people and about managing change.

Fifteen years ago I could not understand why Kaypro ignored my great advice. But today, I understand that business managers like to solve their own problems! When clients ask for "answers," they are really asking for someone to help *them* evaluate their problems and develop solutions that they can implement.

The most effective way to help clients is to guide them through an intuitive Client-Centered™ sales evaluation process that enables them to identify and prioritize their resources and their opportunities and to think "out of the box" about their problems.

CHAPTER ONE

DO YOU UNDERSTAND THE KEY FACTORS THAT DRIVE YOUR CUSTOMERS' PURCHASE DECISIONS?

In these days of escalating marketing costs and intense product competition, every market share point gained or maintained represents a hard-won marketing achievement.

— RENA BARTOS (1978)

The first step on the path to total market domination is to identify your customers' needs and concerns. Many companies make the mistake of thinking that their customers make purchase decisions based on one or two purchase factors that *they* think are key purchase criteria, such as price or product availability. But this is rarely the case.

Customers usually base their purchase decisions on a constellation of factors. And customers with similar requirements often base their purchase decisions on different purchase factors. One company, for example, may purchase a computer system because of its confidence in a trusted reseller, while another company in the same business might choose a different system because of its compatibility with its existing computer equipment or because of the availability of specific features.

Microsoft has developed best-of-breed applications in more categories than any other software company in the world. Microsoft is able to replicate its success because it has developed a coherent, step-by-step Client-Centered™ approach to marketing that ensures

1

that its product development and marketing strategies are aligned with its customers' needs and concerns.

Microsoft understands that there is no reliable way to predict which purchase factors will be important to its customers until it *qualifies* their need for its products and *verifies* their concerns about making a purchase decision. So before Microsoft develops a new product, it invests thousands of hours researching its customers' "view of the world."

Microsoft brings customer input into its product development process as early as possible, works with strategic business partners that have years of experience solving specific business problems, and confirms that its product's design will meet its customers' needs through extensive customer evaluation programs and focus sessions. This process helps ensure that Microsoft's marketing strategy is relevant and compelling to its customers and that Microsoft will maintain its position of total market domination.

Step 1: Describe your customer.

The better you understand your customer's business, the better prepared you will be to understand their needs and concerns. And the better you understand your customer's needs and concerns, the better prepared you will be to identify the key factors that drive their purchase decisions.

Customer Profile	Describe Your Typical Customer
Describe your typical customer.	Our typical training client is a division or business unit of a Fortune 5000 "technology-driven" company.
	Our principle seminar contact is a VP or Director of Sales
	Our typical client is a midsize company with between $15–250 million in revenues.
	60% of our clients are in the computer industry.
	Our principle consulting contact is the President/CEO, or VP of Marketing /Business Development.
Who in your customer's company makes the buying decision?	Training Programs—VP of Sales and Marketing, Sales Manager
	Consulting Services—Company's Board, CEO, President, VP Sales and Marketing, VP of information Technology

Describe a typical sales cycle for your products.	About 65% of our business comes from existing customers.
	About 25% of our business comes from referrals.
	We assign account managers to major accounts to prospect for new business opportunities.
	We also advertise, use direct mail, and use very selective telemarketing to invite prospective customers to free seminars.
	We make sure that our marketing seminars provide as much value as possible to invited attendees.
	We ask all contacts to describe their training requirements.
	In most cases we generate a proposal and make a sales presentation to address our prospective customers' concerns.
Initial contact	Clients who are referred to us by business associates that we have done work for often contact us directly.
Sales Process	If our prospect is interested in scheduling a program, we have a preliminary meeting where we discuss their objectives and requirements. Then, we schedule a second meeting where we review our proposed agenda.
Request for Information	If a prospect asks for information about our services, we send out a marketing packet and then follow up with a telephone call five working days later to be sure that they have all of the information they need.
	As soon as a prospect is prequalified, we schedule a meeting to discuss their training requirements and present our services.
Request for Proposal or Quotation	We usually respond to unsolicited Requests for Proposal. However, we always contact the client's RFP coordinator before any work is assigned.
	We specialize in custom program development, so we are not competitive with training companies that offer "prepackaged" seminars.
Problem Analysis	At our initial meeting we discuss our prospective customer's needs and provide samples of training materials.
	We also provide references on request.

Who is involved in the selling process from your company?	The account manager is the "quarterback" for our sales team.
	If custom training materials will be developed, we bring in one of our documentation specialists to review our client's requirements.
	We do not bring any of our subcontractors into our accounts.
Average time frame for each step of your selling cycle	Request for information to initial sales meeting: 1 to 3 weeks, depending on client's schedule.
	Initial meeting to contract: 2 to 6 weeks depending on our client's concerns and on the time needed to develop a proposal for them.
	Contract to delivery: 6 to 12 weeks depending on client's needs.
Typical purchase concerns	Price—can't afford custom program development
	Time frame for delivery
	Want application-specific training
	Want to interview our presenter
	Concerned that our material will be too advanced
	Client doesn't have time to "manage" a relationship with a training company
How can you shorten your customer's purchase cycle?	We need to schedule periodic meetings with our major accounts to learn about their training requirements and to seed new training opportunities.
	We are piloting a "training outsource" concept that will enable us to team an account manager and a training coordinator with our major clients to provide specialized services and to improve our understanding of our client's business.

Step 2: Identify your customers' key purchase factors.

Many of a customer's purchase factors are reasonable and logical, but some may be based on misinformation or personal bias. It is important to understand that regardless of how you feel about your customers' purchase concerns, your customers' conceptions and misconceptions will ultimately determine whether or not they purchase your products. So if you want to move your customers' purchase process forward, you must qualify *their* needs and verify *their* concerns.

Last year, Steve Ballmer, the President of Microsoft, used Phoenix, Arizona, as a test market for Microsoft's reseller programs. Microsoft could have relied on data published by independent research firms. But Steve felt it was important for Microsoft to get close to its resellers, and used this project to survey its reseller's concerns about Microsoft's channel programs. As a result of this survey, Microsoft committed additional resources to training its resellers on strategic products such as Microsoft's Small Business Server and made other changes to its reseller programs.

It is no accident that Microsoft's senior managers prioritize the time that they spend with customers. There is no other way for Microsoft or for your company to achieve or maintain total market domination unless you are prepared to get close enough to your customers to see the world from their perspective.

KEY PURCHASE FACTORS

Purchase decisions are influenced by *business* concerns, such as the ability of your product to help reduce operating expenses, and *personal* concerns. The most common personal purchase concern is the impact that a proposed product or solution will have on individuals' jobs in a customer's business. For example, if implementing your product will necessitate learning new skills, individuals in your customer's business may be concerned about losing their jobs to better-qualified workers.

Depending on the products or services that you are selling, your customers might base their purchase decisions on one or more of the purchase factors listed in the Customer Purchase Factors table.

Customer Purchase Factors*	1 (not very important) to 5 (very important)
Functionality and ability to solve problem	5
Confidence in consultant or system integrator	5
Reputation of manufacturer and supplier	4
Viability of supplier	3
Range of products available from supplier	2
Past experience with supplier	3
Reputation of supplier	3

Size and viability of supplier	3
Perceived quality of products	4
Specific capabilities or functionality	4
Quality of products	5
Perceived value	5
Utility of products	4
Style of products	3
Availability/delivery time	3
Compatibility with existing equipment	1
Availability of products	4
Quality of sales personnel/rapport	2
Quality of user support and training	3
Product maintenance schedules	3
Personal references	5
Sales presentations and demonstrations	3
Marketing message/advertising	2
Third-party support	3
Proximity to supplier and support	4
Warranty	3
Price of products	3
Financing terms	1
Other—Easy transition to new system	4
Other—Scheduling conflicts	5
Other	

° Average values may be computed from a customer survey to create a "typical" customer profile.

First Law of Total Market Domination

The easiest and most reliable way to learn about your customers' needs and concerns is to ask them.

The key to "seeing the world through your customers' eyes" is asking the right questions. And the key to asking the right questions is to make sure that your questions reveal all of your customers' needs and concerns.

Step 3: Identify the business terms that are of greatest importance to your customers.

After you have identified your customer's purchase factors you will need to qualify how important each factor is to your customer. The process of prioritizing your customer's purchase factors is an inexact science, and of course different customers will be concerned about different purchase factors. But as you gain more experience selling to different customers, you will be able to build a fairly accurate profile of your "typical" customer.

The time that you invest qualifying and prioritizing your customers' purchase factors will enable you to target your marketing story to the specific issues that your customers are most concerned about.

Customer's Purchase Factors	Priority in Decision Process	Client-Centered™ Training Customer's Specific Concerns
Product features	1	Must provide video training workshops and online courseware
Compatibility	5	Training videos must play on our salespeople's notebook computers
Cost (positive ROI)	4	$600 budget per salesperson
Service	8	Require customization of qualification module
Size (desktop cabinet)	7	Training must be available in half-day modules
References	6	Must have strong local references
Training for our personnel	9	Products must be easy to understand and use
Industry leader (supply all of our training needs)	3	We want to limit the number of training companies that we partner with
Personal factors	2	CEO's golf partner is very happy with Client-Centered™ Training's products and support

Client-Centered™ Training has worked with many customers and has developed a very detailed profile of its typical customer's purchase concerns. For example, some business terms, such as expedited shipping and quantity discounts are much more important to Client-Centered™ Training's customers than other business terms, such as accepting credit cards.

Business Terms	Importance to Client-Centered™ Training's Customers 1 (not important) to 5 (very important)
Credit Terms	2
Credit Cards	1
Returns	3
Refunds	3
Pick-up and Delivery	4
Expedited Shipping	5
Quantity Discounts	5
Bundled (Packaged) Pricing	5
Warranty	3
Select Principle Contact	4
Select Trainer	4
Other	-

ACTIVITY-BASED PLANNING

Microsoft and other companies that have a Client-Centered™ approach to marketing use activity-based planning to analyze how their customers use their products and which product features their customers are most concerned about.

Microsoft breaks down user tasks that its product supports into about twenty different "activities," such as creating a budget or sending a fax, that are the most important to its customers. Then, Microsoft's program managers map each activity to existing features in their product, to features in competitors' products, to different market segments, and to different customer profiles, such as novice and advanced PC users. When their activity-based analysis is finished, Microsoft uses its results to prioritize its development resources and to focus its marketing efforts on the activities that are most important to its customers.

Activity-based planning can enable your company to improve its products incrementally and to create new products that obsolete competitive products.

Step 4: Use your understanding of your customer's purchase factors to identify key customer benefits.

After you identify your customer's key purchase factors, you should be able to "map" each purchase factor to specific benefits that may be realized by purchasing your product. For example, if your customer is interested in tracking slow-moving inventory items, you might map this concern to your product's ability to generate an inventory report that covers product usage.

Focusing on customer benefits, rather than product features, will enable your marketing story to be more persuasive and will help you move business forward more easily.

Customer Need	Feature-Oriented Selling	Benefit-Oriented Selling
Broad range of training programs	We offer 6 different training programs.	Our programs address both sales and support issues.
Generate reports	Our product produces 6 different kinds of charts.	Our charts are easy to create and provide the detail your managers need to help them identify problems.
Control inventory	Our software generates an ABC Inventory Report.	Our ABC Inventory Report will help you identify slow-moving inventory items.
Versatile cutting capability	Our machine creates four different shapes.	We can reduce your milling costs by 35%.
Interface with standard protocols	Our product supports the IEEE 1394 specification.	We can interface with hundreds of multimedia devices.
Have 7/24 on-site service available	We have two hundred service and support personnel.	We have four-hour turnaround on all service calls made before 2:00 pm.

IF YOUR CUSTOMER DOESN'T UNDERSTAND IT, IT CAN'T HELP YOU SELL!

Many customers find it hard to distinguish one brand of PCs from another. But PC manufacturers have worked very hard to differentiate their PCs while remaining compatible with industry standards. For example, different PC manufacturers:

- □ Install faster microprocessors and more memory
- □ Use compact power supplies to reduce weight
- □ Include hardware features, such as modems
- □ Supply high-performance multimedia capabilities
- □ Bundle software applications, games, and educational materials

Each of these features provides a clear and obvious customer benefit. However, the speed of a PC's microprocessor and the amount of memory that is included with a system are the two most advertised features. This is not because they are the most important features; in fact, in some applications they have little impact on system usability, such as when a PC will be used to access the Internet. But processor speed and the amount of memory in a PC are features that a person who doesn't understand very much about computers can understand. And companies that achieve total market domination know that a product feature will not be perceived as a customer benefit until a customer understands the *value* of the feature to their business.

Step 5: Document your customer's purchase process.

The better you understand your customer's purchase process, the easier it will be for you to anticipate your customer's concerns and influence their purchase decision.

As you review your customer's purchase process, you should try to identify opportunities to influence your customer's purchase decision at each step of their purchase process. For example, you might advertise in a trade publication to help potential customers "anticipate or recognize need" for your products, and schedule a product demonstration at a trade show to help your customers "analyze and evaluate available solutions."

Put yourself in your customer's position and think about the things that you can do to move them through each step of their purchase process.

Typical 10-Step Purchase Process	Potential Marketing Process
1. Anticipate or recognize need.	Advertise in trade publications Participate in industry forums
2. Define specific characteristics of need.	Comarketing with industry consultants Customer focus groups
3. Search for supplier.	Advertise in trade publications Internet search engines
4. Qualify supplier.	Chamber of Commerce References ISO 9000 certification
5. Analyze and evaluate available solutions.	Demonstrate solution at trade show Competitive product comparison guide
6. Request proposals from suppliers.	Customer needs analysis Online product configurator
7. Analyze proposals.	Referrals Cost justification
8. Select supplier.	Guarantees Purchase options
9. Order solution.	Online purchasing Repeat order discount
10. Evaluate performance (feedback to purchasing).	Customer satisfaction forms Account review meetings

Step 6: Identify any negative market factors that may impact your customer's purchase decision.

It is important to identify and overcome any negative market factors that may impact your ability to achieve your sales objectives. For example, if economic conditions in your sales territory are poor, or if interest rates are very high, it may be difficult for your customers to obtain financing to purchase your products. In this situation, your selling success may depend on your company's ability to help your customers finance your products.

Similarly, if new competitors are moving into your market, new legislation is being proposed to regulate your marketing activities, or new technologies are changing how your customers manage their business, you will need to evaluate and respond to the impact that these factors may have on your customer's business.

Negative Market Factors	How will you overcome these obstacles?
Slowing economy	We provide 180-day terms to established clients with good credit history.
Rising cost of video production	We do not plan to raise prices on any of our courseware this year. We will bring video production in-house next year to contain costs and improve customer service.

THINKING OUT OF THE BOX

FasFax Corporation supplies point of sale (POS) systems to fast food stores, such as Burger King. In the early 1980s, the fast food industry went into a recession, and very few fast food stores were built. To generate sales revenues, FasFax developed a simple fine dining system based on its core POS technology that could be sold to restaurants that did not need to automate liquor sales. By repositioning its fast food POS system as a fine dining computer system, FasFax was able to generate additional sales and survive the economic downturn.

Step 7: Identify any emerging market factors that may impact your customer's purchase decision.

Anticipating emerging market factors, such as consolidation of suppliers and emerging technologies, can help ensure the viability of your business.

Emerging Market Factors That May Impact Your Business	What Are You Doing to Capitalize on These Factors?
How and when do you expect technological innovation to destabilize your market?	The Internet will enable companies to publish multimedia-training courseware as soon as faster Internet access—to stream (video) media—is available.
	We believe that training companies that are not publishing courseware on the Internet will be relegated to niche markets within ten years.
	According to IDC, the market for Web-based IT training will grow from 21% of the total IT training

	market in 1997 to over 32% in 2001. We expect a similar adoption curve for Web-based sales training programs as well.
	We are planning to use our Web server to publish courseware. And we would like to have this operational by next year.
	We are looking for a Web master to help us manage this process.
What is the time frame for your next technological "window of opportunity"?	We plan to offer our current products repackaged on CD-ROMs next year. This should give us a short window of opportunity (two years?) to recoup our investment in multimedia, before we move all of our courseware over to the Internet.
Other issues that may impact the market that you are selling into.	CC-T is concerned that the window of opportunity to take advantage of emerging Internet opportunities is very narrow.
	Some of our competitors are already developing interactive Internet courseware.
	Stanford just announced an MS degree in Electrical Engineering, available entirely through Internet courseware.
	And another university has announced the first online law degree.
Private and public educational institutions	Colleges and universities are beginning to target professional education.
	At this point, we are not too concerned about this trend. However, as these institutions gain experience with business professionals, they may be able to provide a compelling alternative to our Executive Training Seminars.
Multimedia / CD-ROM training	We are planning to acquire a multimedia company that has had experience working with companies in our business.
	We want to make all of our materials available on CD-ROM by the middle of next year.
Satellite broadcast training	We are evaluating the value of developing an infomercial to help us market our sales training program.
	We need to learn more about this technology.
Growing awareness of Total Quality Management and ISO 9000 certification.	We are evaluating the benefits of having our documentation ISO 9000 certified next year.
	We have begun searching for a consultant to help us work through the process, if we decide to become certified.

ACME Corporation (our largest client) is being sold to Big Sky Holding Company	We will meet with the President of Big Sky next month to sell our Client-Centered™ Training programs into their organization.

Second Law of Total Market Domination

Market-driven companies that stay close enough to their customers to anticipate what their customers must do to remain competitive and to react to market factors, which will impact their customer's purchase decisions, are the companies that will ultimately dominate their industry.

Amazon.com, the "world's largest" Internet-based bookseller, has obviated the need for its customers to visit bookstores, by promoting and reselling books on its Web site.

To compete with Amazon.com, the two largest retail booksellers, Barnes & Noble and Borders Books, have launched their own e-commerce sites. It is too early to know whether these sites will become as popular as Amazon.com's site, or whether Amazon.com's multibillion-dollar stock market valuation is justified. But it is clear that Internet storefronts will continue to win market share from physical storefronts as more people access the Internet for business and recreation.

Is your company exploring how it can use the Internet to help it achieve total market domination?

Step 8: Identify the purchase factors that your competitors are using to position their products.

By observing how your competitors position their products, you can identify the purchase factors that your competitors consider most important to their customers.

Purchase Factors That Competitors Emphasize	Training Instructors' Experience	Personal Video Workshops	Breadth of Training Program
Acme Training Corporation	No	Yes	Yes
Business Seminars, Inc.	Yes	No	Yes
Bellevue University	No	No	Yes
Business School	Yes	No	Yes
Client-Centered™ Training	Yes	Yes	Yes

All of Client-Centered™ Training's competitors emphasize the breadth of their training programs in their marketing materials. Client-Centered™ Training has verified that the breadth of its programs is an important purchase factor for its customers, and mentions this in its marketing materials. However, Client-Centered™ Training highlights its personal video workshops, which are only offered by one of its competitors.

Microsoft, like Client-Centered™ Training, strives to meet its competitor's capabilities, and then provide something extra. For example, Microsoft recently added Online Analytic Processing capabilities to its SQL Server database program. Supplying "something extra" that is of *value* to your customers is always compelling.

Step 9: Evaluate your Marketing Information System.

A *marketing information system* or MIS is a formal term for the process that a company uses to build a database of market information, and to coordinate, validate, and communicate marketing intelligence. Companies that dominate their market create robust marketing information systems to enable them to track their customers' needs and concerns, market trends, and competitive challenges.

It is not easy to create an effective MIS. But once a system is in place, your company can use it to help guide product and resource planning, prioritize research projects, support product development and production, and help evaluate the effectiveness of your company's sales and marketing programs.

The primary input to an MIS is intelligence from the sales force; however, in most companies, salespeople must stay focused on territory management and account development. So it is usually the marketing group's responsibility to gather, evaluate, and distribute this information from its sales force and from research companies, industry publications, financial analysts, and competitor's marketing communications.

Your company can use its MIS to provide the information that its managers need to make the informed decisions that will enable your company to achieve total market domination.

- □ *Corporate Communications*—Is your marketing message clear and effective? Is your company receiving complaints about its advertising from its distribution channel or from potential customers?
- □ *Sales Management*—Are your promotions continuing to generate customer interest? Are your competitors lowering bid prices? Are your sales forecasts accurate? Marketing should drive the implementation of new technologies that can leverage its sales and marketing programs.
- □ *Production*—Is quality improving, adequate, or lacking? Are you supplying the right mix of products?
- □ *Engineering*—What features are customers demanding? What modifications will enable new market segments to be penetrated?
- □ *Quality*—Is the number of your product defects increasing or decreasing? Are customers satisfied with your service? How many customer complaints were filed last month?
- □ *Research and Development*—What rumors have been heard about new technological developments?
- □ *Finance*—Are your accounts receivable policies in line with the rest of the industry? Do you have any collection problems with your key accounts?
- □ *Shipping*—Are your products arriving in good condition? Are your shipments timely? Are your shipments accurate?
- □ *Administration*—Have you received any complaints about how your phones are answered, or about how long it takes to return your customers' calls?
- □ *Legal*—Are your customers complying with the specific terms of their contract? Are your competitor's policies changing in regard to product usage, or indemnification?

□ *Senior Management*—Are your senior managers aware of new competitive facilities and new technologies that may impact your market? Are your senior managers aware of the impact that your marketing programs are having on your company's image?

Marketing Information System	Client-Centered™ Training's Resource
Do you maintain a Marketing Information System?	No—we communicate marketing information informally at our sales meetings.
Do you publish or distribute any information that compares your products to your competitor's products?	No.
Do you subscribe to any reports or periodicals that track developments in your industry?	We subscribe to trade magazines that focus on corporate training.
Do you have a process for evaluating and communicating marketing information gathered from industry publications and other public sources?	No—each salesperson is expected to keep up with competitors and industry trends.
Do you have a process for gathering marketing information from your sales team?	Our salespeople share competitive information (and rumors) on e-mail—but we do not have any formal process for managing this information.
Who is responsible for coordinating your MIS?	Our VP of Marketing collects competitive information in a file box.
Who is responsible for tracking industry developments?	Our VP of Marketing goes to industry trade shows and yearly meetings that help us keep up with new developments in our industry.
Who is responsible for tracking emerging technologies that may impact your company?	Our IS Manager keeps up with new computer technologies. We rely on our telephone company to inform us about new developments in voice and data communications.
Who is responsible for coordinating product development/engineering?	Our VP of Operations is responsible for managing all development projects—our President and VP of Sales meet with our VP of Operations to discuss project schedules and special customer situations twice a month.

The Bottom Line: Do you understand the key factors that drive your customers' purchase decisions?
The first step on the path to total market domination is identifying the key factors that drive your customers' purchase decisions. And the easiest way to do this is to follow the First Law of Total Market Domination, and simply ask them.

Taking the time to understand your customers' needs and concerns will enable you to "see the world through your customers' eyes" and will help your company develop products and services that are easy to sell.

Selling downhill—by addressing the constellation of factors that your customers will use to make their purchase decision—will enable you to market your products in a way that is both *relevant* and *compelling*. And *that* will help your company build the sales momentum that it needs to achieve total market domination.

If you feel that you understand your customers' needs and concerns, and that you understand every aspect of your customers' purchase process; it is time to take the next step on the path to total market domination. In the next chapter, you will review your company's short- and longer-term business objectives, evaluate your company's value equation, and confirm that your marketing strategies are aligned with your company's primary business objectives.

CHAPTER 2

ARE YOUR COMPANY'S RESOURCES ALLOCATED IN A WAY THAT IS CONSISTENT WITH ACHIEVING ITS MARKETING OBJECTIVES?

Intense competition in an industry is neither coincidence nor bad luck.

—MICHAEL E. PORTER

My old next-door neighbor is a very bright engineer who has spent the last fifteen years managing facilities and doing contract consulting work. A couple of years ago, he developed an ingenious idea for a computer program that could be used to manage large facilities, such as hospitals, that require detailed documentation of fire, water, security, electrical, and other systems.

My neighbor began spending his evenings and weekends developing his product. He hired a computer science major from the University of Washington to help him, but he quickly realized that the project was much larger than they could manage. And he decided to raise venture capital to hire the personnel that he needed to develop and market his product.

My neighbor discussed his business plan with me and asked for my advice. Since my neighbor had no experience running a software company, marketing a product, or working with financial people, I suggested that he recruit a senior marketing person, preferably with CEO experience, to help him raise capital and manage his company. But, against my advice, my neighbor decided to learn whatever was needed to "sell" his company himself.

My neighbor invested over a year of his life developing a prototype of his product and meeting with potential investors. But he failed to convince any of the investors that he met with to fund his company.

Companies that achieve total market domination have *all* of the resources, including the personnel, the products, and the vision that are necessary to develop a world-class business. And they have a detailed step-by-step plan of how they can use those resources to achieve their business objectives. My neighbor had a great product idea, and a world-class vision, but he did not have the management team that he needed to help him "sell" his company.

Step 1: Evaluate your primary business objective.

Providing all of the resources necessary to achieve total market domination is an obvious priority, but many factors may make it difficult for your company to do this. For example, if your company lacks the personnel resources that it needs to market all of its products effectively, it will need to *prioritize* the products and marketing activities that are most likely to help it achieve its sales objectives.

The first step in determining how to invest your company's marketing resources is to define your company's primary business objective or mission statement.

Your company's mission statement should reflect the *value* that your business provides to its customers. Many companies expand their mission statement to include the value that their company provides to its employees and shareholders. However, if a company publicizes its mission statement, it should emphasize the value that it provides to its customers. Customers are far more interested in the value that a company can deliver to them than in the value that a company can deliver to its own employees or shareholders!

Client-Centered™ Training's mission statement describes the value that it provides to its customers: "Client-Centered™ Training helps technology-driven companies increase their sales by providing training seminars and consulting services based on a Client-Centered™ approach to selling."

Client-Centered™ Training's mission statement is clear and concise and has proven to be compelling to technology-driven companies that are looking for an outside consulting firm to help them improve their sales performance.

YOUR MISSION STATEMENT IS A COMPASS

Client-Centered™ Training's mission statement is a useful compass for Client-Centered™ Training's management. Marketing resources that are invested in helping the company deliver "training seminars and consulting services based on a Client-Centered™ approach to selling" are well spent. Marketing resources that are invested in other business opportunities do not support the company's primary business strategy.

Last year I worked with a company that sold accounting systems to manufacturers and wholesale distributors. A quick review of my client's financial reports disclosed that my client was losing about $100 on every PC that it sold.

My client told me that it sold PCs because its customers expected it to deliver complete systems. I pointed out that my client was in the accounting system integration business, and that it could become more competitive and more profitable by focusing its marketing strategy on the value that it delivered to its customers. And I recommended that my client develop relationships with business partners, such as Dell Computers, that were able to supply competitively priced PCs directly to its customers.

My client agreed and was able to reduce its cost of sales and increase its profits by over 150 percent. The strategy was a winner for my client's customers as well. They could purchase higher-value PCs and have my client provide the on-site integration and support that they needed to manage their accounting systems.

Your company can use its mission statement as a reality check to determine whether specific business opportunities and marketing activities are consistent with its primary business objective.

Third Law of Total Market Domination

Your company's mission statement, like any other marketing communication, should be clear, concise, and compelling and should communicate the value that your company provides to its customers.

Since its inception in 1975, Microsoft's mission has been "to create software for the personal computer that empowers and enriches people in the workplace, at school, and at home." And, over the last two years, Microsoft has promoted Bill Gates's strategy to help its customers implement a Digital Nervous System or DNS. Microsoft's DNS is built upon a commitment to six principles: a PC computing architecture, all information is in digital form, universal e-mail, ubiquitous connectivity, common end-user productivity tools, and integrated business-specific applications.

It is no accident that Microsoft's DNS strategy and its product development plans are absolutely consistent with Microsoft's two primary business objectives—to ensure the viability of its Windows product family and to enhance its position as an Internet technology company.

If it takes more than one sentence to describe your company's primary business objective, your company probably does not have the focus that it needs to dominate its market.

Business Objectives	
Company's Mission Statement (one or two sentences)	Client-Centered™ Training, Inc. helps technology-driven companies increase their sales by providing training seminars and consulting services based on Client-Centered™ Selling.
What product(s) does your company manufacture or resell?	Client-Centered™ Sales Seminars Client-Centered™ Selling Guides and Books Client-Centered™ Selling Newsletter
What service(s) does your company provide or resell?	Sales, Marketing, and Technical Communications Consulting Custom Program Development Services Seminars on emerging Information Technologies
Does your company finance your product sales?	We provide 30-day terms to customers in good standing.
Does your company provide indirect services such as warehouse, transportation, distribution, information processing?	N/A

Step 2: Evaluate your short- and longer-term business objectives.

The next step in determining how to invest your company's resources is to evaluate your company's short- and longer-term business objectives.

You can use the process of defining short- and longer-term business objectives to help you identify your company's priorities, evaluate its strengths and weaknesses, and make more informed decisions about where and when to invest its marketing resources. But before you can develop a marketing plan for your company, you will need to define your objectives and specify the goals and key results that you will use to monitor your selling success.

Client-Centered™ Training's Financial Objectives for June, 30 200X	Goal / Key Result
Sales Volume	$1.8 million in sales
Market Share	16% market first year
Profitability	Increase training seminar profits by 35%
Number of Customers	Close 25 new customers this year
Size of Customers	Close at least two Fortune 100 accounts
Number of Employees	Hire 15 new employees next year
Market Capitalization	$31 per share valuation (prepare for IPO in three years)

Client-Centered™ Training Short-term Business Objectives	Time Frame: Next Six Months
Profit	Increase profit by 8%
Markets	Open Europe
Products or Services	Launch Client-Centered™ Trade Show Selling seminar
Production	Improve production turnaround
Sales/Distribution	Evaluate Asian representative
Training/Support	Train sales force on how to present our company's capabilities
Research and Development	Evaluate Dayton Associates Web site
Financial (IPO etc.)	Interview investment bankers

| New Businesses | Roll out new advertising campaign in Northwest region |
| Company Involvement | Support local charity |

Client-Centered™ Training Longer-term Business Objectives	Time Frame: Six to Twelve Months
Profit	Increase profit by 20%
Markets	Open Asian market
Products or Services	Launch "Market Focus = Market Success" Training Program
Production	Lease a new color laser printer
Sales/Distribution	Concentrate sales effort on Southwest territory
Training/Support	Schedule "The Zen of Paying Attention" leadership program

Train our support personnel on after-sale "value added" selling |
Research and Development	Develop courseware based on Dayton Associates materials
Financial (IPO etc.)	Schedule outside financial audit
New Businesses	Work with European representative
Company Involvement	Sponsor local charity's Annual Fund Raiser

Client-Centered™ Training has made an effort to develop both short- and long-term business objectives. However, most small companies and many mid-sized companies do not invest the time to do long-term planning.

If your company does not develop long-term business objectives, it will not have a compass to help it make decisions that will have a long-term impact on its growth and success, such as leasing new facilities, purchasing capital equipment, developing new products, and establishing relationships with business partners.

Client-Centered™ Training Longer-term Business Objectives	Time Frame: One to Two Years
Profit	Maintain profitability
Markets	Grow International sales
Products or Services	Launch at least one program each quarter
Production	Bring seminar guide production in house
Sales/Distribution	Schedule U.S. Sales Conference in St. Martin
Training/Support	Schedule all employees for "The Zen of Paying Attention"
Research and Development	Produce courseware based on Dayton Associates materials
Financial (IPO etc.)	Prepare for IPO
New Businesses	Acquire a multimedia production company
Company Involvement	Continue to sponsor a local charity

Client-Centered™ Training Longer-term Business Objectives	Time Frame: Two to Five Years
Profit	Maintain profitability
Markets	Grow International sales—focus on Asia and Western Europe
Products or Services	Launch at least one new program each quarter
Production	Bring all seminar guide production in-house
Sales/Distribution	Schedule first International Sales Conference in Venice
Training/Support	Select VP for Customer Service Department
Research and Development	Internationalize courseware based on Dayton Associates materials
Financial (IPO etc.)	Complete IPO
New Businesses	Acquire a multimedia production company
Company Involvement	Sponsor a local charity and the United Way

Client-Centered™ Training Longer-Term Business Objectives	Time Frame: Five to Ten Years
Profit	Maintain profitability
Markets	Diversify into additional markets by localizing programs using native translators
Products or Services	Launch two training programs each quarter Publish 4 books each year
Production	Bring multimedia production in-house
Sales/Distribution	Move all products to internal Intranet server
Training/Support	Develop a Train-the-Trainer program for Client-Centered™ Selling Seminar
Research and Development	Schedule first yearly Personal Growth retreat
Financial (IPO etc.)	Consider merger and acquisition opportunities
New Businesses	Acquire additional multimedia production companies
Company Involvement	Sponsor a local charity and the United Way

Step 3: Evaluate your company's Value Equation.

The primary objective of your company's management team is to increase shareholder value. And the most effective way to do this is to maintain a balance between customer requirements, employee demands, and shareholder expectations.

When your company's "value equation" is in balance, its shareholders are getting a fair return on their investment, its employees are being compensated at or above market wages, and its customers are receiving fair value for the products and services that they purchase.

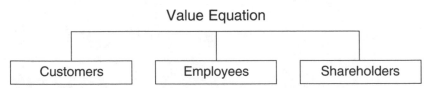

Value Equation

Customers | Employees | Shareholders

Balancing your company's value equation can be very challenging as your company grows and enters new markets. But if your company does not provide a reasonable return on its shareholders' investment, its managers will be held accountable. If your company's compensation program is not competitive, it will suffer high employee turnover. And if your company's customers are dissatisfied, it will lose market share to its competitors.

The "Stakeholder Value" table illustrates how Client-Centered™ Training balances its value equation.

Stakeholder Value	Value to Client-Centered™ Training's Stakeholders
Customers	We provide the highest quality sales training available.
	We provide custom sales training programs with fast turnaround.
	We provide books and training guides to support our programs.
	Our consultants and trainers have extensive industry experience.
Employees	Dynamic, interesting workplace.
	Freedom to be creative and achieve recognition for contributions.
	Top 25% of industry compensation.
	Opportunity to advance with rapidly growing company.
Shareholders	Our sales revenues have grown 35% every year since our company was founded.
	Corporate profits are retained to finance growth.
	We anticipate offering an IPO in two years.
	Our principles are satisfied with their ROI.
Is your VALUE EQUATION in balance?	Yes. If we can maintain our profit margins and meet our revenue forecasts, our Value Equation will remain in balance.

Step 4: Evaluate where your company is in its business cycle.

Markets evolve over time. Identifying where your market, your company, your products, and your competition are in their business cycle will help you anticipate market trends and position your company to take advantage of new market opportunities.

Market Start-up/Product Introduction—Markets at this stage are often monopolistic, with one supplier producing one product. Suppliers usually select a narrow, nonoverlapping distribution plan and use skimming or penetration pricing strategies to build market share and to recoup product development and other start-up expenses.

Market Growth—As product sales increase, markets are typically characterized as having monopolistic competition. Although there are usually a few key suppliers, other suppliers may be attracted by the lure of high profitability and rapid market growth. Suppliers differentiate their products and build market share with innovative products, high-profile promotions, and competitive pricing strategies.

Market Maturity—As the number of suppliers in a market increases and standardized products become available from numerous sources, markets are characterized as moving from monopolistic competition to pure competition (oligopolies). As products become more directly competitive, pricing often becomes very aggressive, resulting in price wars, and suppliers move toward more intensive distribution strategies with smaller profit margins. Late entrants into the market often wish that they had chosen an earlier, more profitable time to jump into the market.

Figure 2-1
Typical Sales and Profit Life Cycle

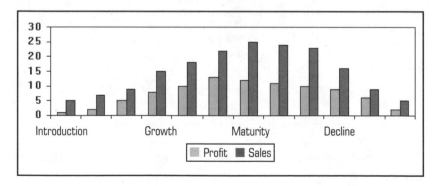

Market Decline—As markets decline, suppliers often expand distribution to the maximum saturation level that the market will bear in an attempt to maximize their profits. However, the move toward intensive distribution usually reverses when suppliers realize that overdistribution of their products is putting their company at a competitive disadvantage against competitors that have more controlled distribution. When customer demand declines, weaker products begin to lose market share, and many companies get out of the market because they can no longer justify the manufacturing and distribution resources needed to compete profitably.

Client-Centered™ Training's primary market—the sales seminar business—is in its growth phase. Client-Centered™ Training competes for its client's business with many other companies that are attempting to build market share by developing innovative products, using high-profile promotions, and employing competitive pricing strategies.

	Business Cycle			
Business Unit	**Start-up**	**Growth**	**Maturity**	**Decline**
Sales Seminar Business		X		
Client-Centered™ Training, Inc.		X		

The markets for Client-Centered™ Training's Strategic Products are in various states of development. For example, the Emerging Technology Seminar business is a start-up business, with no dominant players and market demand far exceeding supply. However, several well-established companies, which offer high-quality products at competitive prices, dominate the market for business development seminars.

Client-Centered™ Training's Strategic Products	Start-up	Growth	Maturity	Decline
Consulting Services		X		
Emerging Technology Seminars	X			
Business Development Seminars			X	
Sales Training Books		X		
Sales Training Guides		X		
Multimedia Training Materials	X			
Internet Publications	X			
Emerging Technology Newsletter	X			

Worldwide Market Sales Seminars	Start-up	Growth	Maturity	Decline
U.S. Fortune 200			X	
U.S. Fortune 5000		X		
Europe	X			
Asia	X			

Client-Centered™ Training competes directly with regional training firms, management consultants, and local colleges, which are investing their resources to gain market share in the sales training market. However, Client-Centered™ Training is less concerned about competing with universities, which are targeting candidates who are interested in earning post-graduate degrees.

Major Competitors in the Sales Seminar Market	Start-up	Growth	Maturity	Decline
Local Colleges			X	
Universities				X
Regional Training Firms			X	
Management Consultants		X		

To achieve total market domination, your company must adjust its marketing strategy to leverage its position in its market. For example, if your company is introducing a product into a mature market, it may need to set very aggressive prices to build market share. But if your company is entering a new market, it might need to use a penetration-pricing strategy to help it build market share.

Step 5: Evaluate your product sales.

Gaining market share is an important step on the path to total market domination. A difference of ten percentage points in market share is typically accompanied by a difference of about five points in return on investment. So the average rate of return for business units with shares of more than 40 percent is two and a half times the average for those with shares of 10 percent or less. However, increasing sales is not a foolproof path to success. Many companies increase their sales at the expense of their profit margin. And that can be a path to bankruptcy. [1]

Figure 2-2
Relationship Between Market Share and ROI

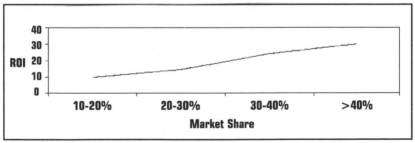

---

[1] Return on Investment (ROI) is the ratio between the profit for your company after tax and its assets employed in its operations. Table Source: Robert D. Buzzell, Harvard Business Review, from the Profit Impact of Market Strategies (PIMS) project at the Marketing Science Institute.

PRODUCT PERFORMANCE

Is the sales volume of your product rising, remaining constant, or falling? Most products have a product life of five to twenty years. If a mature product's sales are on a downtrend, it is usually wise to invest as little of your company's marketing resources as possible to maintain your products' market share. And if your product is losing money, it is usually wise to stop marketing the product as soon as possible. However, when your product's sales are increasing, your company may benefit from investing additional marketing resources to increase its product's market share.

Do you have a process in place to weed out unprofitable products? It is easier for companies to launch new products than to kill existing products because most companies have no systematic procedure for identifying and eliminating products that have failed to gain market momentum or that are only marginally profitable.

Continuing to market unsuccessful products can depress your company's overall level of profitability, tie up limited resources, and hinder your company's ability to pursue new business opportunities. Nevertheless, most companies continue to increase the number of products that they sell until they run into financial problems.

Are you maximizing your company's profits? Your company should test the prices of its products periodically to ensure that your company maximizes its profits. Salespeople rarely believe that their company can raise prices without "destroying" their product's marketability. However, customers are often willing to pay premium prices for quality products.

Step 6: Evaluate your company's use of integration strategies.

As markets mature, companies often implement product and marketing integration strategies to help them leverage their competitive position.

☐ *Forward product integration* refers to integrating the components or products that your company builds into a larger system that can enable it to address new markets.

Client-Centered™ Training seminars comprise individual modules that can be modified to support specific customer requirements. Client-Centered™ Training has integrated its Time Management and Territory Management modules into a new Major Account Selling Program.

□ *Backward product integration* refers to producing components or subassemblies that can alternately be purchased from other suppliers. Backward integration can enable your company to increase the value that it adds to its products, but it can lead to a loss of the specialization that differentiates your company and may be part of its competitive advantage.

Client-Centered™ Training plans to reproduce its CD-ROM training programs in-house next year. This capability will enable it to increase its profit.

□ *Forward marketing integration* refers to eliminating external distribution and support channels.

Client-Centered™ Training plans to replace its independent sales representative in Europe after it opens its new office in London next year.

□ *Complete or "turnkey" solutions* can help your company gain a competitive advantage by making it easier for your customers to solve their problems.

Client-Centered™ Training offers a Sales Conference Management program through its Special Services Coordinator that enables it to manage every aspect of its client's training events. Client-Centered™ Training calls this its "Turn-the-key to Success" strategy.

Step 7: Align your marketing strategy with your company's objectives.

Companies that fail to develop clear marketing objectives often develop complicated or prohibitively expensive marketing strategies that are difficult or impossible to implement. And companies that fail to track the success of specific marketing strategies often create new marketing strategies that are as unsuccessful and short-lived as the strategies that they are replacing.

The only way to avoid these problems is to invest the time needed to develop clear marketing objectives, to track the outcome of each marketing strategy, and to take any corrective action that is necessary to re-engineer unsuccessful marketing strategies to achieve your sales objectives.

REAL WORLD PROBLEMS

Although it is of obvious value to align your marketing strategy with your corporate objectives, it may actually be very difficult to realize this goal.

- □ *You may not have access to the market intelligence you need to make informed decisions.*

  Many companies, for example, do not have a marketing information system in place to track market trends and competitors' strategies.
- □ *You may assume incorrectly that your market or distribution channel is stable or is changing in a particular direction.*

  Many companies fail to stay abreast of emerging technologies that will impact their market. For example, many distribution companies do not have an Internet strategy.
- □ *You may assume incorrectly that your views or policies are shared and are being implemented by all of the personnel in your organization.*

  Many senior managers, for example, have little or no contact with their company's sales representatives. They don't know what they are thinking about, they don't know what they are feeling, and most importantly, they don't know what they know about their products, their company, and their market.
- □ *You may distribute your company's resources evenly between different marketing groups, distribution channels, or production teams, rather than allocating your resources where they will maximize your company's profitability.*

  Many companies, for example, espouse a philosophy of rewarding their most productive employees but base employee advancement and compensation on seniority rather than productivity.

The Bottom Line: Are your company's resources allocated in a way that is consistent with achieving its marketing objectives?

If your sales and marketing team does not have all of the resources that it needs to move business forward, it will waste time and it will lose business to better-prepared competitors.

By identifying your company's short- and long-term objectives, you can develop strategies that enable your company to allocate its marketing resources wisely. And by evaluating where your company's products are in their life cycle and using market and product integration strategies, you can position your company and your company's sales strategies to win market share.

In the next chapter, you will learn how to create a clear, concise, compelling marketing story that will put your company on the path to total market domination.

CHAPTER 3

HAVE YOU DEVELOPED A CLEAR, CONCISE, COMPELLING MARKETING STORY?

There is no such thing as a commodity. All goods and services are differentiable.

—THEODORE LEVITT

Whether you are a sole proprietorship or a Fortune 500 company, you have the same job to do. You must develop a clear, concise, compelling marketing story that addresses your customers' needs and concerns. And you must use the elements of your marketing story to help you create interest for your products, move business forward, and close sales.

Customers rarely spend more than a few minutes identifying companies that they would like to do business with. If your company's marketing story is not clear, concise, and compelling, it will not attract customers' interest, and it will not enable your customers to understand why they should do business with your company. And if it is difficult to explain why customers should do business with your company, your company will be selling uphill.

When venture capitalists consider making an investment in a start-up company, the first question that they usually ask is, "What's the company's story?" The answer to this simple question can be as revealing about the potential success of a new business venture as an in-depth market analysis.

INTEREST, INFORMATION, AND PREFERENCE

Your sales force can use your marketing story to help them move business forward with your customers by arousing interest in your products, providing the information your customers need to make informed purchase decisions, and creating a preference for your products.

Investors like to bet on companies that have the best chance of achieving total market domination. And companies that achieve total market domination communicate the value that they provide to their customers in a clear, concise, compelling way.

Marketing Story Objectives	Example
Arouse Interest	Advertise success Demonstrate product Point-of-sale promotion
Provide Information	Discuss product features Discuss product benefits Present needs analysis Propose solution
Create Preference	Describe past successes Introduce referrals Present competitive analysis Propose cost effective solution

Step 1: Identify the market factors that differentiate your company and your products.

Anything that your customers need or care about may be used to define a new market segment or differentiate your company's products from its competitor's products. Your company may, for example, differentiate itself from its competitors by focusing on functionality, service, price, style, warranty, or any of the other factors listed on your "Customer Purchase Factor" worksheet.

Understanding the factors that impact your customer's purchase decisions will enable you to respond effectively to competitive challenges. For example, customer demand for rapid turnaround has segmented the printing business between while-you-wait copy centers and longer-turnaround print shops. Many customers are willing to pay a premium and accept fewer printing options to get their order delivered on the same day they place their order.

Client-Centered™ Training's Market	
Type of Business	Training, Consulting, and Publishing
Industry Specialization	Professional Education and Business Consulting
What geographic markets have you targeted for your marketing efforts?	North America—expanding into Europe, Asia, and South America
User Type or Classification (e.g., SIC code)	We would like to focus our telemarketing on technology-driven companies that have a direct sales force.
Why did you target these markets?	We are well established in the United States. Europe and Asia are just beginning to appreciate the need for postacademic professional education. We believe we can position our company as the leading (international) management training organization by being an early market participant. We feel multimedia titles will enable us to take advantage of the Internet.
What is the history of your market?	Our market has been growing at about 9% per year for the last twenty-five years.
Why and how has your market grown?	As the costs of doing business increase, it becomes more cost effective for companies to leverage their personnel's capabilities with training seminars and workshops.
How stable is your market?	General economic factors may impact our sales; however, over a 6-month recession our market has been surprisingly stable.
What is the size of your market? (A procedure for estimating the size and revenue potential of your market is provided in Chapter 10.)	Approximately 500,000 businesses with annual sales over $10 million are prospects for our training services. Over one million businesses with annual sales over $2 million are prospects for our consulting services.

Number of units per year?	No estimate available.
Revenue per year?	We estimate the market for our products to be about $850 million.
What percent (share) of your market do you control?	Less than 1%
Have any of your competitors been forced out of business recently? If so, why?	The Brain Trust went out of business last month. We think their problems began when they lost their two best salespeople and their program development manager.
Are there any major obstacles that may prevent you from realizing your market objectives?	It is very difficult to find qualified employees. We need employees who understand our business and who are professional, entrepreneurial, and self-motivated.

Step 2: Evaluate your company's position in its market.

Establishing a strong market position, such as "value leader," will help your company build brand awareness and customer acceptance of your products. But it is important to understand that every market position has advantages and disadvantages.

If, for example, your company is a value leader, it will not be able to provide the service level that competitive companies that target less price sensitive customers can afford to deliver. And if your company markets to prestige shoppers, it may not be able to offer less costly products that appeal to a broader customer base without denaturing its exclusivity.

In any case, your marketing strategy should capitalize on your company's strengths but remain flexible enough to address changing market factors. Compaq Computers, for example, has developed a reputation for providing the highest-quality business computers. However, Compaq has repositioned its entry-level PCs to capitalize on the huge demand for low-cost home computers.

Market Strategies and Barriers to Market Entry	Client-Centered™ Training's Market Position
Cost leadership	We do not attempt to compete on price.
Differentiation (design or brand image, technology, distribution, features, customer service)	We have secured a position in our market as a leading supplier of custom training programs.
Focus (on a particular buying group, product segment, or geographic area)	We target Fortune 5000 customers.
Broad product base	We do not have the resources to be all things to all customers. So we focus our product development and marketing efforts on the in-house training needs of sales and marketing departments in mid- to large-sized companies.
Entry factors/Start-up costs	Our clients expect us to provide the highest-quality multimedia courseware. We have invested over $1 million in courseware development over the last 18 months.
Threat of substitution	We are concerned that public and private colleges and universities may become more aggressive in pursuing professional training opportunities.
Bargaining power of buyers (For example, customers can play competitors against one another to "bid-down" prices.)	Our clients are usually much more concerned with the quality of our deliverables than our fees. Our primary "competition" is ongoing business activities that make it difficult to schedule training programs.
Bargaining power of suppliers (For example, suppliers can raise prices to reduce industry profitability.)	Our suppliers are continually raising prices. However, at this time we do not anticipate that this will significantly impact our profitability. Margins on our books and training guides may be impacted next year if the cost of paper continues to escalate.
Rivalry among current competitors (see "Competitive Strategies" table)	We compete primarily with our client's internal training groups. However, most companies view our programs as complementary to their internal training programs. We do not think our market has a high enough profile to attract the interest of large companies in related industries that are looking for expansion opportunities.

Step 3: Identify your company's most significant accomplishments.

Most companies that dominate their market are successful because they do a few things very well. Identifying your most significant accomplishments can help you understand how, when, and where your company provides value to your customers, employees, and shareholders.

One of the most common reasons why companies lose momentum is that they lose focus on the key factors that were responsible for their initial success.

Area of Company	Client-Centered™ Training's Significant Accomplishments
Personnel/Organization	Our most significant organizational achievement was building a network of freelance consultants that we utilize on projects that are too big for us to handle ourselves.
Product	Our new "Information Technology Audit Handbook" enables us to bring our IT Audit methodology to a much larger audience, and to provide this information at an extremely competitive price.
Service	Our Internet Web site's feedback page enables us to provide faster customer response and helps us stay in touch with our customer's evolving training requirements.
Sales/Marketing/Distribution	We are using our Internet Web site to help us generate international sales.
Finance	We have a $500,000 line of credit with Big Bucks Bank. We have engaged the Don't-Go-Way Credit Company to provide financing for our key accounts.
Technology	Our Internet service provider has a T1 connection that enables us to distribute multimedia materials.
Public Service	We recently donated over $25,000 of our surplus office equipment to charities.

Step 4: Evaluate your competitors' strengths and weaknesses.

Most businesses have both *direct* and *indirect* competitors. Direct competitors are in the same business and provide similar solutions; indirect competitors compete for business by providing alternative solutions. For example, Client-Centered™ Training has direct competitors such as other sales training companies, and indirect competitors such as local colleges that offer business classes.

Identifying the advantages and disadvantages of doing business with your company and with your competitors will enable your company to re-engineer areas of its business that need improvement, and to develop a marketing story that highlights its strengths.

Client-Centered™ Training's Competition

Major Direct Competitors
Acme Training Systems
Sales Seminars, Inc.
Positive Force Learning

Major Indirect Competitors
Seattle Community College
Big Sales Workbook and Training Guide
Sales Today magazine

Product/Service: Marketing and Technical Communications Consulting
Accounting companies' management consulting groups
Independent industry-related consultants
Research firms
Trade press / Analysts / Gurus

Product/Service: Client-Centered™ Training Seminars
Academic institutions
Regional training companies
Internet-based training companies
Multimedia training companies

Product/Service: Training Books and Guides
Part-time MBA programs
Video seminars / Executive briefings
Other business publications
Newsletters

Advantages of Doing Business with Your Company	Advantages of Doing Business with Your Competitors
Our seminars are custom tailored to our customer's requirements.	Less expensive "seminar in a box" programs.
Highest quality product available.	Standard products are available off the shelf.
Custom training materials are available.	Basic courseware is good.
Highest quality presenters.	More readily available presenters.
Will work with customer to tailor product.	Does not require management's attention.
Depth of industry insight.	May have access to better market research.
Provide coverage in U.S.	Provide global coverage.
Provide high-quality books to back up seminars.	Provide multimedia-training materials.

COMPETITIVE INTELLIGENCE

There are many places to gather "intelligence" about your competitors. If, for example, your competitor's stock is publicly traded, you can access copies of their annual report and their 10-K on the Internet. However, the most effective way to get information about your competitors is to stay close to the market you are selling into by working closely with customers and reading relevant trade publications.

Sources of Competitive Information	
□ Personal Contacts	□ Trade Publications
□ Company Resources	□ Trade Associations
□ Customers	□ Chamber of Commerce
□ Past Employees	□ Annual Reports / Stock Prospectus
□ Job Seekers	□ Bank / Credit Report
□ Suppliers	□ Brokerage Firm
□ Local, Regional, and National Newspapers	□ Academic Institutions
□ Business Publications (*Business Week, Forbes*, etc.)	□ Government Publications
	□ Census Bureau's Standard Industry Classification Manual and Demographic Reports

□ Internal Revenue Service's Statistics of Income	□ Forbes Annual Report On Business
□ Standard & Poor's Corporate Record and Industry Surveys	□ Encyclopedia of Business Information Sources
□ Dun & Bradstreet Reference Book of Corporate Management	□ Private Consulting and Research Firms
	□ Trade Shows
□ Moody's Industrial Manual	□ Online News Sources
□ Thomas Register of American Manufacturers	□ Internet search engines, such as AltaVista, Infoseek, and Excite.

Step 5: Evaluate your products' strengths and weaknesses.

Defining the strengths and weaknesses of your products will help you create an action plan for improving your competitive position in your market.

After you have identified your products' strengths and weaknesses, you can map your products' strengths to specific elements of your marketing story and evaluate what your company can do to overcome its products' weaknesses. For example, Client-Centered™ Training could partner with a computer-based training company to help its consulting group address its customers' online training needs.

A Client-Centered™ approach to product development—focusing on customer needs and concerns—is the best way to ensure the long-term viability of your company.

Client-Centered™ Training's Products	Features	Benefits	Limitations
Training Seminars	Customized Modular	Meet specific client's needs	Time to develop custom programs Higher cost
Consulting Services	Depth of industry experience Evaluation program	Predictable outcome Can be done in phases	More expensive than training in-house personnel No computer-based training services
Books and Training Guides	Concise, up-to-date Attractive format Inexpensive	Compelling to read Easy to understand Useful information	Not as effective as a live presentation

LEMONS AND LEMONADE

Early in my consulting career, I worked with a software company called NBI, which had developed a Windows-based word processor called Legacy. Legacy competed with word processors from Microsoft, Lotus, and WordPerfect—the three most successful companies in the PC software business. It was clear that NBI did not have a compelling marketing story for Legacy, and that there was no compelling reason to purchase their word processor rather than one of their competitor's products.

I recommended that NBI reposition its word processor as an easy-to-use desktop publishing tool for business users. But NBI didn't like my advice, and they hired another consultant who advised them to promote Legacy through an expensive direct-mail campaign. Eight months later, NBI went out of business. And about a year later, Microsoft targeted this opportunity with Microsoft Publisher, which has been extremely successful.

We will never know whether Microsoft would have taken the sugar out of NBI's lemonade.

Step 6: Define the elements of your marketing story.

When you create your marketing story, you should start with all of the facts that a journalist would include if they were writing up a news event. You will need to describe who you are, what your mission is, where a customer can purchase your products, when your products will be available, why a customer should purchase your products, and how your products can help your customers save money, increase profits, or develop new business opportunities.

I used this template at Microsoft to create marketing stories for our OEM products:

Marketing "Story" Elements	Client-Centered™ Training's Marketing Story
Who?	We are the leading suppliers of professional sales and marketing training programs.
What?	We supply seminars and publications based on Client-Centered™ Selling.
Where?	Our products are available throughout the United States and Canada.

When?	Client-Centered™ sales training is available now. Our new "Selling Up!" seminar program will be available next quarter.
Why?	Our training methodology helps our customers reduce training costs by over 25% and increase sales by at least 15%.
How?	Client-Centered™ Selling is based on proven step-by-step selling techniques that ensure a consistent, winning performance by every sales and marketing person in your company.

The specific elements of your marketing story that are empha-sized during a sales call or in a specific marketing communication, such as an advertisement or a marketing brochure, will depend on your business objectives. But in any case, your marketing story should provide all of the information about your company's prod-ucts that a prospective customer needs to know to make an informed purchase decision.

Be honest about your capabilities.

Prospective customers will not ask for your help unless it is obvious who you are, what you do, and how you can help them. And customers will not ask for your recommendations unless they trust you and believe that you—and your company's products—are capa-ble of helping them solve their problems.

Scale your marketing story to fit the reality of your com-pany's capabilities.

If your company has an operating budget of $150,000, has just hired its third employee, and sells cleaning products door-to-door to customers in Boise, Idaho, your marketing story should focus on the value that your company delivers to its customers in Boise. But if your company has established a virtual store on the Internet and exports cleaning products to customers around the world, your company should create a marketing story that is compelling to all of its customers.

Be enthusiastic but eschew perfection.

It is easy to be enthusiastic about your products when you are confident that they provide good quality and value. But there is no "perfect" marketing story, because there is no perfect product for every customer's needs. For example, most customers must trade off some level of performance or quality against their desire to solve their problem as inexpensively as possible.

The only "perfect" marketing story is one that addresses your customers' needs and concerns!

Evolve your marketing story as you gain market experience.

It is very difficult to develop a compelling marketing story until you have had an opportunity to work with many different customers. In complex selling situations it can take many months of interaction with your customers to fully understand their needs and concerns. And in high-tech markets, customers' product choices and expectations may change on a monthly basis.

Step 7: Map the elements of your marketing story to your customers' needs and concerns.

No matter how compelling your marketing story is, it can only provide the framework for the information that is presented to a specific customer. And, depending on the logistics of a specific selling situation, it may only be possible for you to present a few elements of your marketing story.

One of the most difficult decisions for a company to make is deciding which elements of its marketing story to communicate to its customers. For example, if your company manufactures a product and is trying to recruit new resellers, it might focus on its leadership position in the industry (who) and the fact that its products offer a significant competitive advantage over other suppliers (how). If your company's primary objective is the announcement of a new product, your marketing story might focus on the availability of your product (when), and your product's features and benefits (why).

In any case, your sales force must position and present the elements of your marketing story in a way that is in *sync with your customers' purchase process*. If customers do not have the background to understand the value of your products, or if they have not moved far enough through their purchase process to be able to evaluate your marketing story in the context of their needs and concerns, your communication will not be effective.

Story Elements	Client-Centered™ Training's Marketing Story	Customer Benefit
Who?	We are the leading suppliers of sales training programs for technology-driven companies.	It is less risky to work with a successful, well-established training company.
What?	Our programs comprise individual modules that are easily tailored to our clients' specific requirements.	Our flexibility ensures that our clients receive the exact training experience that they need to achieve their sales objectives.
Where?	Our seminars and workshops are offered at our clients' site.	Delivering programs at our clients' site helps reduce our clients' training costs.
When?	Client-Centered™ Training can be adapted to fit into our clients' training schedule.	We deliver a broad range of programs—from a 1-hour keynote to a five-day interactive workshop.
Why?	Client-Centered™ sales training has helped many of our clients increase sales by over 25% within three months.	Client-Centered™ sales training is cost-effective and provides a rapid return on our clients' investment.
How?	Client-Centered™ sales training is a proven, step-by-step approach to building selling success.	Client-Centered™ sales training helps our clients gain a competitive advantage over companies that employ less effective selling methodologies.

Companies that achieve total market domination do not overwhelm their customers with product information before they are ready to use that information to move their purchase process forward.

Let your customers help you understand the value of your products.

In the music business it is not uncommon for "B" sides to rise to the top of the charts. If the people in the music business really knew everything about their customers' preferences, this would never happen.

Listen to your customers. When they get excited about a specific component of your marketing story, use that information as a data point to help you re-evaluate the value that your products provide.

AMBREX ACCOUNTING SOFTWARE

One of my first consulting clients was an entry-level accounting software company based in Vancouver, BC. My client's system handled multiple currencies as well as many high-end accounting systems, but its reporting capabilities were very limited.

I told my client that it would have difficulty selling its system in the United States because companies that would be interested in an entry-level accounting system rarely accept any currency other than our own greenbacks. And larger companies, which would benefit from this feature, would not be satisfied with the program's limited reporting capabilities.

If your product's "compelling" features do not map to your customers' concerns, your sales force will be selling uphill. And when your sales force is selling uphill, it will be expensive to communicate your marketing story, it will be difficult to win repeat business and referrals, and it may be impossible for your company to achieve the market momentum that it needs to achieve total market domination.

"WE DON'T HAVE TIME TO TEST OUR MARKETING STORY"

Several years ago I was retained by a start-up software company that had just spent over 70 percent of its marketing budget on a direct-mail campaign to launch its new product.

My client's mailer was one of the worst that I have *ever* seen. It was *not clear* what my client's product did or how a customer could benefit from using my client's product. The mailer was *not concise*, which meant it was very expensive to produce and mail. And the mailer was *not compelling*; the price of my client's product was eight times greater than subsequent market testing indicated its customers were prepared to pay for it.

My client's marketing team did not test its campaign because it wanted to bring its product to market as quickly as possible. And my client was devastated when its response rate was less than one-tenth of one percent.

At our first meeting, it was pretty obvious that my client had two choices: it could go back to its investors to raise additional capital to relaunch its product, or it could sell the rights to its product to another company. My client was thrilled when a software company that wanted to purchase its product made a reasonable offer.

Fourth Law of Total Market Domination

Don't roll out your marketing program until you have tested your marketing story.

If a market survey produces unreliable results, or a pilot test fails to confirm your expectations, slow down. Do more research and more market testing before your company becomes too committed to its marketing strategy.

If your marketing programs are implemented in stages and your company's resources are phased into a project, it will be less costly to redirect your company's marketing efforts if your company fails to meet its marketing objectives, or if other, more profitable business opportunities arise.

The Bottom Line: Have you developed a clear, concise, compelling marketing story?

Salespeople are storytellers. So it is easy to see why creating your marketing story is such an important step on the path to total market domination.

The rewards for developing a compelling marketing story can be great, but the risks of presenting a less-than-compelling story are also great. If your marketing story is not *clear*, your customers will not understand it; if your marketing story is not *concise*, it will be very expensive to communicate; and if your story is not *com-*

pelling, it will not motivate your customers to do business with your company.

After you have developed a compelling marketing story, and mapped the elements of your marketing story to your customers' needs and concerns, you will find yourself selling "downhill" in every selling situation. And *that* builds sales momentum and makes selling fun!

In the next chapter, you will learn how to develop a marketing plan that will help you allocate your marketing resources and achieve total market domination.

CHAPTER 4

DOES YOUR MARKETING PLAN PROVIDE THE FOCUS THAT YOUR COMPANY NEEDS TO LEVERAGE ITS SELLING EFFORTS?

As products and product lines increase numerically, the range of management problems seems to grow geometrically.

—PHILIP KOTLER

You can manage your business by the seat of your pants, or you can use objectives, key results, and a structured planning methodology to *engineer* its success. Microsoft's investment in strategic planning activities has enabled it to engineer its market dominance by focusing on the *value* of the products that it delivers to its customers.

Fifteen years ago, Microsoft realized the *value* of a graphic user interface and invested hundreds of millions of dollars to develop Windows-based software that supported this emerging technology. Today, Microsoft is employing the same strategy—this time betting on the *value* of the Internet—by incorporating emerging Internet standards into its Windows operating system, development tools, and office applications.

It is unlikely that Microsoft will be able to achieve as dominant a position in the Internet software market as it has in the PC software market. But it is clear that Microsoft's investment in strategic planning has enabled it to identify a break point and to refocus its marketing strategy to leverage the value that the Internet can provide to its customers.

ENGINEER YOUR SUCCESS

The Client-Centered™ planning process that I used at Microsoft is a simple step-by-step process that begins with defining your company's primary business objectives. These objectives provide the basis for a marketing plan that defines the strategies, tactics, and resources that your company can use to help it achieve its business objectives.

Step 1: Develop a clear, concise, compelling marketing plan.

A marketing plan is a written statement that defines the strategies, tactics, and resources that your company will employ to reach its business objectives. Put more simply, your marketing plan is the "why" behind whatever your company plans to do to achieve its sales objectives.

A marketing plan has two key objectives. It can serve as a reality check to help you determine the likelihood of achieving your marketing objectives. And it can serve as a communication vehicle to help you sell your ideas internally, to senior management and to your sales team, and externally, to potential investors.

MARKETING PLAN TEMPLATE

The process of developing your marketing plan can help your company allocate resources, organize operations, prioritize activities, evaluate different marketing activities, think creatively about problems, and identify new business opportunities.

If you take the time to communicate clearly and concisely, you can communicate many of the following sections in one or two sentences.

I. Executive Summary

The executive summary is the most important section of your marketing plan. It should summarize the main points that you have made in each section of your marketing plan and should restate the reasons that you believe your business strategy will be successful.

Try to keep your executive summary to a manageable length; it should take an average reader no more than five to ten minutes to read. And keep in mind that your executive summary should—like every communication—be clear, concise, and compelling.

1. *Describe your product or service.* The description of your product should be as specific as possible. Include pictures or diagrams if they help describe your product. Include samples of output if they are relevant. If your product is unique, explain why this matters. Explain the primary purpose, utility, or advantage of your product. Describe what your product can do for your customer.

2. *Discuss your target market.* Specifically what and/or where is your target market? Are secondary markets being considered? Will modification of your product allow it to address other markets' needs? Will declining manufacturing cost over your product's life cycle open new markets?

3. *Describe your product's strategic advantage.* If your product is "revolutionary" discuss how current market needs are being satisfied. Explain what differentiates your product from competitive products that are already available.

4. *Specify dates that have been set as goals for product availability and shipment.* When will your company complete its research,

release a fully functional prototype, make its first customer shipment? Be optimistic, but be realistic.

5. *Describe any special skills or proprietary technology that provide a competitive advantage.* If your team has specific skills or if a specific technology has been developed that relates directly to your product, explain what or who is involved. Describe relevant patents or copyrights.

6. *Specify what investments or other resources are required to implement your plan.* Be specific, detail who will be involved and when additional financial resources must be committed to your plan.

7. *Summarize projected sales and revenue forecasts.* Define your expectations for product sales and market penetration. Explore future business opportunities.

8. *Briefly describe your reason for implementing this product strategy*: Explain why you developed this product and what other product strategies were considered.

9. *Outline your objectives and key results.* Your executive summary should distill the totality of your marketing plan in a concise, positive statement of your primary objectives and key results.

10. *Describe your exit strategy for potential investors.* If your marketing plan is being presented to investors, it should explain how and when they would profit from their investment. In most cases this will be through a public stock offering or the sale of your company.

II. Market Information and Competitive Strategy

Provide enough information about your market to enable your reader to understand why you have decided to address this business opportunity.

1. *Describe your market.* Examine both historical and current market data to describe the factors that you feel will influence your customers' purchase decisions.

2. *Describe your typical customer.* Discuss your customers' needs and concerns. Describe the psychology of your typical customer.

3. *Describe market trends that may influence your customers' purchase decision.* Provide enough information to enable your reader to understand how your product fits into your market.

4. *Describe competitive solutions.* Explain how competitive solutions are being used to address your customers' needs.

5. *Describe any social or cultural factors that may impact your marketing plan.*

6. *Describe any economic or business conditions that may impact your marketing plan.*

7. *Describe any political issues, laws, or regulations that may impact your marketing plan.*
8. *Describe any market research that you have done to validate your marketing plan.* Provide a brief analysis of your target market, including demographic, geographic, life style, and other data that will help your reader understand how and why your company has targeted this business opportunity.

III. Product Strategy

The intent of this section is to describe your product thoroughly enough so that your reader can understand "who, what, where, when, and why" a customer would benefit from purchasing your product.

1. *Define your product.* Include a complete product specification that describes the benefits of your product.
2. *Describe how your product works.* Include a detailed description of how your product works. Focus on the specific factors that differentiate your product from competitive products in terms of performance and design. Describe modifications or additions that are planned or that could be implemented in the future to improve or differentiate your product.
3. *Describe how your product is different from other products.* Include a competitive analysis to help your reader understand how your product compares to and is positioned against competitive products. Explain why you think your product strategy will be successful against your competition.
4. *Describe any innovations that enable your product to help your customers increase profits, decrease expenses, or enter new markets.* If this information is confidential explain how and when this information can or will be revealed, e.g., at product launch or when a prospective customer has executed a nondisclosure agreement.
5. *Describe the product strategies your company will employ to establish and maintain market leadership.* Describe your product strategy. When will new products be released? How will these products help your company increase its market share and profits? Will any of your business partners be able to help your company develop innovative products?
6. *If your product is "revolutionary" and has no competition at this time, describe new technologies that may spawn competition in the future.* Include reports and research from market research firms, trade publications, and other objective information sources.

IV. Distribution, Pricing, and Promotion Strategy

This section should explain how you plan to price, promote, and distribute your products.

1. *Describe the distribution channels that will be used to market your product.* If you plan to build a direct sales force, explain how and why you are doing so. Describe your company's existing reseller relationships. Describe your plan for recruiting new resellers. Will your company develop separate sales channels to handle the needs of different customers, such as national accounts, educational institutions, and government agencies?

2. *Describe your plan for training, supporting, and motivating your sales force.* Describe how you will prepare your sales force and your resellers' sales force to represent your products in a professional Client-Centered™ manner. Describe your sales and marketing infrastructure, including sales automation and order processing systems. Describe your compensation plan for motivating your sales force and your resellers.

3. *Describe your pricing plan.* Summarize any market research that you have done to determine the cost of manufacturing and distributing your product. Include a preliminary price list if it is available. Include a comparative pricing guide if it is applicable.

4. *Advertising plan.* Describe your advertising plan and budget.

5. *Special promotions.* Describe your product launch plan and any introductory promotions that you have planned. Specify your objectives for your product launch.

6. *Corporate communications plan.* Describe your plan for working with the press and with industry analysts. Include copies of all product reviews and press announcements.

7. *Franchise plan.* Describe your plan for licensing or franchising your products and your technology to other companies (if applicable).

V. Operations

Your operations plan should be detailed enough to enable your reader to understand in general terms how your business is managed and should describe any factors that may impact your company's ability to achieve its marketing objectives.

1. *Describe your production schedule.* Specify the date that you will have a working prototype. Specify when beta-test units will ship to selected customer sites. Describe how you will support your beta-sites. Specify the date for your first product shipments.

2. *Describe your production capabilities.* Describe your manufacturing operation. Describe your product distribution operation. Describe strategic relationships with third-party service organizations. How quickly do you expect demand for your product to ramp? Do you have plans to outsource production if product sales increase more rapidly than expected? What processes or tasks can your company outsource? Are alternate suppliers available for raw materials and subassemblies?

3. *Describe your plan to service and support your products in the field.* Do you plan to support your products directly, through resellers, or through a third-party support organization?

4. *Describe your staffing requirements and hiring plan.* Do you have all of the production and support personnel in place to support your marketing plan? Do you have a budget to hire additional personnel? How long will it take to train new employees?

5. *Discuss your company's short- and long-range objectives.* Are your objectives and key results overly aggressive, or are they conservative?

VI. Risks

1. *Describe any potential problems that may impact your marketing plan.* If you cannot envision *any* potential problems, you are not being objective or realistic.

2. *Identify the assumptions that you are making in your marketing plan about your customers' requirements and purchase factors.* Explain how you have tested your assumptions about your customers' requirements and purchase factors.

3. *Summarize any market research that you have done.* Use customer focus groups and meetings with consultants and industry analysts to verify elements of your marketing plan and help you evaluate any assumptions that you have made about your customers.

VII. Financial Statements—Budgets and Revenue Forecasts

1. *Include pro forma budgets for start-up and production costs, cost of sales, overhead, and forecast revenues.*

2. *Include a Breakeven Point analysis and describe your expected Return on Investment.*

3. *Include a marginal cost and revenue analysis if these are applicable.*

4. *Include a projected cash flow analysis.* Specify what sales revenues will need to be generated to stay on plan for the first twelve to thirty-six months of operation.

5. *If your marketing plan will be presented to outside investors, it should include a complete set of audited financial statements.* Feel free to include explanations or expand on the information that is included in your financial reports if it will help your reader understand your business situation.
6. *Compare your assumptions and projections with published industry averages for similar types of businesses.* If your figures are out of line with the rest of your industry, explain why your numbers are different.

VIII. Management Team

1. *Include information on staffing requirements.* A good way to present this information is in a standard organization chart. Clear, concise job descriptions will give your reader a good indication of where personnel will be required and what they will be doing to facilitate your plan.
2. *Include resumes and biographies of the key people who are involved with the venture.*
3. *If your marketing plan is targeted at investors, you should be prepared to discuss your principle's personal motivations for starting a new business.* If, for example, your company's founders have given up successful careers with another company or have invested their own money in their new venture, you can "sell" their motivation and commitment.

Reality Check

Some of the heuristics that you can use to test your marketing plan are:

- □ *Simplicity*—The simpler your plan is, the easier it will be to implement.
- □ *Clarity*—If your plan is hard to read, it is probably unnecessarily complicated.
- □ *Reasonableness*—Unreasonable plans are usually based on one or more incorrect or overly optimistic assumption that will obviate your chance for success.
- □ *Time frame*—The longer your plan will take to implement, the less likely it is that it will proceed as planned or produce its anticipated results.
- □ *Delayed return on investment*—The longer it will take to realize a positive return on your investment, the greater the possibility

that unexpected factors will prevent your company from achieving its objectives.

☐ *Number of people affected*—The more people who are impacted by your plan, the less likely it will be for your plan to stay on schedule or achieve its objectives.

☐ *Untested assumptions*—Untested assumptions about customers' needs and concerns signals that your company has not been taking a Client-Centered™ approach to marketing its products.

☐ *Personal gain or loss*—Business managers often develop complex marketing strategies when they fear that a simpler strategy will reveal the weakness of their business plan and hurt their career.

SELLING YOUR STORY

Over the last ten years, I have reviewed scores of business plans for start-up technology companies that were seeking investment capital. In *every* case, the companies' plans forecast meteoric sales, total market domination, and a public stock offering . . . usually within five years.

Of course, very few companies ever achieve total market domination. And it is almost impossible to predict early in a company's life cycle what its capitalization value will be in five or ten years. Nonetheless, everyone plays—technology companies pitch their "story," and venture capitalists try to pick the next Microsoft.

Most companies exaggerate their sales projections in their business plan because they anticipate that the venture capitalists who review their business plan expect them to do so, and that the investment bankers will cut any projection that they make in half, regardless of how conservative their forecast is! But most venture capitalists are not as concerned with the actual numbers in the forecast as they are in the *logic* behind those numbers. For example, if a company claims that it will be able to triple its sales without adding additional sales or support personnel, a venture capitalist might think that its management team is taking too many vitamins.

Most venture capitalists select investments based on two key factors: a company's management team and the revenue potential for the market that the company is planning to dominate. If the market opportunity is large enough to generate a large payback or "upside," and the company's management team has developed a compelling marketing story and has the ambition and the tenacity to drive their company to success, the company will be an attractive investment opportunity. And the further along toward achieving total market domination that a company is, in terms of developing, launching, and selling its product, the more valuable and the less risky an investment in the company will be.

Most companies that achieve total market domination must work through many problems before they build the market momentum to achieve their business objectives. And the ability to work through those problems ultimately depends on its manager's vision, business aptitude, and ambition. Which is why many successful venture capitalists don't "bet on companies," they search for those rare individuals who can lead their business to great success.

Step 2: Evaluate your marketing plan.

Markets change over time, and marketing strategies that have worked in the past may or may not produce the same results when they are repeated. This is why it is so important to evaluate your company's short- and longer-term marketing strategies periodically to determine whether they will enable your company to achieve its marketing objectives.

Evaluate Current (Short-Term) Marketing Objectives	Client-Centered™ Training's Marketing Plan
Marketing	We are using the Internet to help us attract and communicate with potential clients.
Sales/Distribution Channels	We target Fortune 5000 companies.
Product Line	We provide leading-edge training opportunities, courseware, and books for successful professionals. We also provide strategic marketing consulting services.
Manufacturing	We currently outsource almost all manufacturing. We outsource all color print services. We can manufacture new training guides in eight to ten working days.

Target Markets	We target "technology-driven" Fortune 5000 companies that demand the highest quality training services. We plan to target manufacturing companies next year.
Service/Support	We provide custom training programs that are designed to meet our client's specific needs and concerns. We provide an unconditional guarantee that our training experience will match or exceed our program description as described in our marketing brochure and sales presentations.
Purchasing	We have relationships with several low-cost international suppliers. We plan to reduce our dependence on outside printing services.
Research and Development	We work with outside subcontractors, which enables us to reduce our overhead and to be responsive to customers that have larger projects than our in-house staff can manage.

Evaluate Longer-Term Marketing Objectives	Client-Centered™ Training's Marketing Plan
What new products or services would you offer if you had the capital to finance new ventures?	Multimedia products Video training seminars Prepackaged technology audit guides
What new projects do you have planned?	Review and repackage Dayton Associates' training materials Evaluate multimedia opportunities Develop an Internet banner advertisement
Do you plan to release any new products in the next five months?	Book on client-centered selling Book on trade show selling Book on time management
Do you plan to release any new products in the next six to twelve months?	CD-ROM-based training materials Executive technology briefing on the Internet Executive technology briefing on network computing
Do you plan on starting up a new business?	We plan to acquire a multimedia production company and bring all print services in-house.
Do you plan on opening new markets?	Europe Asia

What advertising or press-related activities do you have planned for the next six months?	Print advertising in industry periodicals. Press tour to promote Technology Audit Workbook program.
What marketing materials, such as product brochures and white papers, do you plan to create over the next six months?	Client-Centered™ Training Programs brochure Client-Centered™ Selling Workshop Guide Client-Centered™ Trade Show Selling Guide White paper on the Technology Audit Process Executive Technology Briefing brochure
What seminars, trade shows, or other promotional activities do you plan to attend or sponsor over the next six months?	National Business Conference Internet conference Manufacturer's Trade Symposium National Training Association Conference
Do you have licenses or agreements in place to manufacture, distribute, market, or resell any other company's products or services?	Yes. We have entered an agreement to publish and distribute Dayton Associates' training materials.
Are you involved in any joint ventures? Describe these joint ventures.	Yes. We plan to enter into a joint venture with our European distributor. They will localize and resell our products.
Are you working with any outside product developers or testers?	Yes, we use subcontractors to help develop custom materials.
Do you work with any outside training organizations?	No.

Step 3: Evaluate your sales plan.

Sales plans describe the "tactical" details behind a marketing plan and provide a road map to the specific sales objectives that you have specified in your marketing plan. A sales plan typically describes:

- Size, organization, and geographical distribution of the sales force
- Distribution channels
- Territory assignments
- Sales priorities (how resources are focused to maximize sales)

- Recruiting plan for territory managers, sales representatives, and sales support personnel
- Compensation plan for sales representatives and sales support personnel
- Reseller agreements
- Pricing and terms of sale
- Sales training, motivation, and coaching
- Use of independent marketing resources and outside consultants

If your company has developed a reasonable marketing plan, it should be relatively easy to formulate your sales plan. But if your company's marketing plan is based on flawed assumptions, such as not addressing one or more of your customers' key purchase factors, it is unlikely that it will ever be able to create a sales plan that will enable it to achieve its business objectives.

Sales Plan Evaluation	Client-Centered™ Training's Sales Plan
Define size, organization, and geographical distribution of the sales force.	Our sales force comprises a VP Sales, two account representatives, and a marketing assistant based in Bellevue, WA; and a VP Sales and a sales assistant based in Victoria, BC, Canada.
Define alternate sales and distribution channels (including joint-marketing partners such as independent sales representatives and mail-order companies)	Our company works with national speakers bureaus such as Leading Authorities, Inc.
Define all sales territory assignments.	Our sales territories are based on three geographical regions: U.S. East, U.S. West and Canada.
Who is responsible for allocating and managing your marketing resources?	Our Sales VP in Canada handles all direct mail promotions. Our marketing assistant coordinates all RFPs. And our Director of Marketing manages our PR budget.
Detail your recruiting plan for territory managers, sales representatives, and sales support personnel.	We hire sales personnel who have had previous experience selling seminars, training programs, and consulting services.

Review your compensation plan for sales representatives and sales support personnel.	Everyone in our company has a performance review every six months.
Describe pricing and terms of sale. Are these competitive in your target market?	Our prices are in the custom-program range. We are competitive with other professional services companies that work with Fortune companies.
Describe specific plans for sales training, motivation, and coaching.	Our "open registration" seminars are open to all of our personnel.
Describe relationships with outside marketing resources and consultants.	We work with an outside video production company that handles some of our press relations. We refer clients to a small group of consultants who provide services that we do not provide. These consultants refer their clients to us when there is a good fit for our services.

Step 4: Evaluate your sales kit.

The easiest way to communicate your company's sales plan to your sales force is with a sales kit that contains all of the information that your sales force needs to communicate your marketing story and address all of your customers' questions about your company's products, services, and policies.

ASSEMBLING A SALES KIT

In most companies, the marketing department develops portions of the sales kit, such as price sheets and materials that help the sales force position the company's products. And the sales manager develops other portions of the sales kit, such as each account representative's or reseller's territory assignments. In any case, the effort spent producing your sales kit will be leveraged many times, as each sales representative confidently presents your company's marketing story to your customers.

The key to putting together an effective sales kit is to think though each step of your sales process and then to assemble all of the information that you will need to address your customers' concerns about your products and services.

For example, if you are in the computer business, your sales kit might contain the materials listed in the "Computer Network Sales Kit," and an automated network configuration guide. The network configuration guide might be a program running on a salesperson's PC, or it might be a program stored on an Internet server that your sales representatives could access with a portable computer in your customers' office.

Example of a Computer Network Sales Kit

- Company information
- Company history (marketing story)
- Company's mission statement (business plan)
- Success stories (applications)
- Customer references
- Company policies and procedures (administration and finance)
- Product information (This could be published on a Web site.)
- Pricing
- Availability
- Delivery and installation information
- Equipment leases
- Contracts and other forms

- Your business calendar (This could be automated.)
- Sales brochures
- Demonstration materials (e.g., auto-demo on Web site)
- Technical reference guides
- Product samples
- Competitive information
- Customer interview (requirements / analysis) form
- Calculator, tape measure, or other tools
- Personal information
- Other information (e.g., a network configuration program)

SALES KIT TEMPLATE

You can use the following template, which includes the resources that I put into Microsoft's OEM account manager's sales kits, to help you develop a sales kit for your own sales force.

I. Market Information

The more information that your sales force has about your company's marketing objectives and strategy, the more effective it can be when facing competitive situations in the field.

This section should clarify which markets your company has targeted and explain why they were chosen.

- ☐ How and why did your company choose its market?
- ☐ What value does your company bring to its customers?
- ☐ What is your company's mission statement?
- ☐ What are your company's primary business objectives?

II. Prospecting Information

Your prospect list should map to the target market that you have identified in your marketing story.

- ☐ Who are the best prospects for your products?
- ☐ How can your sales representatives contact the decision-makers in these companies?

III. General Product Information

This section should provide a top-down description of your product, written at a level that a general business reader can understand.

At Microsoft we organized our training materials so that they made as few assumptions as possible about our readers' prior knowledge or experience. We also made an effort to target our sales brochures and other marketing communications to the appropriate audience. For example, our OEM customers' engineers were not impressed with glossy brochures that listed features and benefits. And our OEM customers' business managers did not want to take the time to read detailed technical bulletins.

- ☐ What products does your company supply?
- ☐ What do your products do?
- ☐ Why do customers need your products?

IV. System Functions

This section should present the features and benefits of your product from your customers' perspective. Whenever possible, this section should include specific examples of your product's performance and utility.

It is helpful to include supporting documentation from objective sources for any claims your company makes about its superiority over competitors' products or technologies.

It is usually best to present product comparisons and benchmarks at a simple executive-summary level, and then provide detailed technical information in an appendix or a separate document.

As a rule, when your message is too complex to summarize in a few simple graphs, or to describe with six or seven bullets or summary points, it is too complicated for an executive audience. Of course "executive audience" in many selling situations is synonymous with "decision-maker"! Remember the salesman's maxim, *"Keep it short and simple."*

V. System Architecture

This section should cover whatever information is necessary to enable your reader to get an overview of how your product or system works and how it interfaces to other products or systems that your customer may be using.

- □ How does your product work?
- □ Describe any new technologies that enable your product to work.
- □ How does your product work with other products or systems?
- □ What interfaces or connections are available to expand your system?

The easier it is for your customer to visualize how your product works, and how it will work with their existing systems, the easier it will be to convince your customers that the advantages of implementing your product outweigh any potential risks.

VI. Product/Technical Specifications

Technical information is usually provided in technical reference manuals, help systems, service and support guides, installation guides, and technical papers.

Many technology-driven companies are developing online documentation and providing customer support through Internet Web sites. This investment is enabling these companies to reduce their reliance on customer support personnel, making it easier and more profitable for resellers to represent their products, and making it more cost-effective for customers to install, implement, and support their solutions.

VII. Accessories and Ancillary Products

This section should describe all ancillary products and accessories that will be tied to key products.

- □ What accessories are available?
- □ Are customization services available?
- □ Is any product enhancement available?

VIII. Third-Party Suppliers

Third-party suppliers supply accessories or enhancement products that increase the functionality or appeal of your company's products.

- What accessories are available from third-party suppliers?
- What enhancement products are available from third-party suppliers?

IX. Summary of Expansion Capabilities

This section should describe how your company plans to enhance its product in the future.

- What new features will be added to your product?
- When are enhancements or product updates going to be available?
- Will any new markets be targeted?

Many companies withhold information about new products from their sales force because they are concerned that this information will make it difficult for their sales representatives to sell the remaining inventory of their current product or that it will delay their customers' purchase decisions. This policy makes it easier for sales representatives to tell their "old" marketing story, but it can alienate customers that purchase discontinued or obsolete products.

In most situations, companies can avoid this problem by planning product transitions carefully and by offering their customers discounts or other incentives to purchase their old products.

Developing win-win product transition strategies will enable your company to maintain a straightforward Client-Centered™ relationship with its customers and build customer loyalty.

X. Configuration Information

This section should provide the information that your sales force needs to configure your product to meet your customers' needs.

- Which products work together?
- Which products don't work together?
- Which products require additional products to work at all?

Avoid making assumptions about what your sales representatives know about your company's products. If you include very basic information in your sales kit, your sales representatives can skip over any information that they already know.

XI. Support Strategy

This section should provide all of the information that your sales force needs to address your customers' concerns about product support and service:

- How will your products be supported?

- Will any service or support engineers be assigned to specific customer accounts?
- What is your policy on product warranty?
- Who handles warranty repairs?
- How will service be handled after the warranty period?
- What supplies should be ordered?
- Are service contracts available?
- What third-party support is available?

XII. Implementation/Conversion Strategy

This section should provide all of the information your sales force needs to answer your customers' questions about the process of installing and implementing your company's product. This section can also address what has been done to simplify or expedite the installation, upgrade, or conversion process and identify any known installation problems.

- How long will the installation, upgrade, or conversion take?
- How can customers prepare to implement your product?
- Have special utilities been developed?
- How much time should be budgeted for data conversion?
- Are third-party contractors or consultants available to help with customer implementations?

XIII. Sales Training

This section should address any questions that your sales force has about the programs and resources that are available to prepare them to present your company's products with a professional Client-Centered™ approach.

- Does your company provide training on new products?
- Will your company reimburse a sales representative's outside training expenses?
- How much time should your sales representatives allocate to learn about a new product line?
- Does your sales representative or reseller need to become licensed or certified to represent your product?

XIV. Customer Education

This section should specify any education, training, or previous experience that is necessary for your customers to install, implement, and support your product.

- What training programs are available?
- How long is the program?
- When are your training classes offered?

- How much money should your customer budget to train its staff?
- Do you recommend any third-party training companies?
- Does your company offer on-site training?
- Does your customer need to become licensed or certified to use your product?

XV. Competition

Competitive intelligence can provide the edge that your sales force needs to build market momentum.

- Who are your major competitors?
- What are your competitors' strengths and weaknesses?
- How do your competitors' products compare with your company's products?
- Do you have reference accounts that have experience with your competitors' products?
- Do you have testimonials and references from former competitive accounts?

The easiest way to communicate information about your competitors is in a comparative product guide that summarizes your competitors' strengths and weaknesses. However, disseminating out-of-date competitive information can damage your sales representatives' credibility and cost your company sales. Always *verify* comparative product information *before* providing it to your sales force.

Most companies collect competitive product information at trade shows and from published product reviews. But the easiest way to develop a competitive product guide is to use a competitor's product guide as a template. You will need to confirm the information that your competitor has published, but this approach can save you a great deal of time.

XVI. Product Ordering and Distribution Information

This section should outline all of your company's procedures and policies for ordering products and services. It should also explain how orders are placed, tracked, and fulfilled.

- Procedure for placing an order
- Order acknowledgement policy
- Order status and tracking options
- Product availability and back order policies
- How can customers establish a line of credit?
- How are orders prioritized?
- Who is responsible for ensuring prompt delivery?
- Can customers track their orders on the Internet?

XVII. Terms and Conditions of Sale

This section should contain all information on terms and conditions of sale.

- □ Price list
- □ Service fees
- □ Additional fees such as freight charges, restocking fees, and finance charges
- □ Volume discounts
- □ Rebates
- □ Class of customer discounts (reseller, distributor, major account)
- □ Other discounts
- □ Trade-in offers
- □ Financing terms

XVIII. Distribution Support

This section should contain all of the information that your resellers need to understand your company's policies and procedures for working with its resellers and distributors.

- □ Lead referral programs
- □ Major account sales programs
- □ Special marketing programs
- □ Business partner discounts
- □ Discounts for reseller's sales personnel
- □ Demonstration product pricing
- □ Advertising plan
- □ Advertising tear sheets
- □ Marketing co-op
- □ Promotional materials
- □ Special programs, e.g., government or education marketing programs.
- □ Introductory offers
- □ Initial purchase specials

XIX. Employee Programs

- □ Employee discounts
- □ Family and friends discounts

XX. Product Availability and Delivery Schedules

This section should specify when, where, and how new products will be available.

- □ What marketing plans will be implemented?
- □ What advertising will be done?
- □ Are any special promotions scheduled?

Preannouncing products can generate customer interest, but missing product release dates will erode your company's credibility and good will.

Step 5: Evaluate your customer relationships.

Your existing customers are your best prospects for new products and services, so it makes sense to map your company's new products to your customers' emerging needs.

Companies that achieve total market domination leverage their customer relationships by selling products *horizontally*, across their customers' companies, divisions, and workgroups, and *vertically*, within the company, division, or workgroup that they are selling to.

The "Customer Relationships" worksheet describes how Client-Centered™ Training is using horizontal and vertical solutions to leverage its customer relationships.

Customer Relationships	Client-Centered™ Training Sales Opportunity
Map new product to emerging customer need.	We should be able to sell our new Emerging Technology seminar program to companies in retail financial services markets.
Horizontal solution	Acme's Consulting Division has standardized on Client-Centered™ Selling. We should try to sell a Client-Centered™ Sales Seminar to Acme's System Integration Division.
Vertical solution	We have presented our Client-Centered™ Sales seminar to Acme's Consulting Division. We should propose delivering a Client-Centered™ Presentation Skills workshop next quarter.

Step 6: Evaluate your relationships with your business partners.

The most effective way to leverage a limited marketing budget and "expand" your sales force is to join forces with one or more business partners. Business partners can provide access to specific customers, product promotions, financing, technical expertise, and other resources that you can use to help you market your products.

Several years ago, Microsoft and Hewlett-Packard teamed up to promote Hewlett-Packard's Laser Printer and Microsoft Word. The "Set your laser on stun ..." alliance profited both companies. Microsoft was able to demonstrate its support for H-P's new laser printer, which positioned its word processor as a leading-edge "corporate" word processor. And Hewlett-Packard was able to demonstrate the ability of its laser printer to do complex desktop publishing tasks, and advertise the endorsement for its proprietary technology from a leading word processing software developer.

Always be on the lookout for creative comarketing opportunities. Once you start to consider the possibilities, it may be difficult to decide which ones to go after first!

Marketing Partner	Potential Strategic Advantage
Retailers	□ Access to customers □ Promotion
Value added resellers	□ Technical expertise □ Access to customer base
Independent sales representatives	□ Commission sales □ Extremely motivated
Wholesalers and distributors	□ Help finance distribution □ Inventory management
Consultants	□ Provide leads □ Third-party expertise
Manufacturer's representatives	□ Extremely motivated □ Good contacts
System integrators	□ Technical expertise □ Access to customer base
Brokers	□ Contacts □ Expertise
National buying services	□ High volume □ Close-out specialists
Mail order companies	□ Low-cost distribution □ Pilot new programs
Government distribution (exchange stores)	□ Unique distribution □ High volume
Television marketers (infomercials, Home Shopping Network)	□ Promotion □ Close-out specialists
Superstores	□ High volume □ Large customer base

Internet, online services	□ Low cost of entry
	□ Add-on business
Professionals	□ Referrals
(physician, lawyer, CPA, etc.)	□ Expertise

Client-Centered™ Training's Business Partners	Marketing Opportunity
Acme PC Projectors	Participate in joint trade show promotion.
Lear Consulting Services	Develop a Client-Centered™ Presentation Skills workshop for their financial services clients.
Seattle Personnel Finders	Develop a disk-based telemarketing skills program.
Business Software Corp.	Include a coupon for a 20% training discount with each software upgrade package.
Alumni Association	Offer members a 20% discount on custom training programs.

Step 7: Evaluate your distribution strategy.

One of the most important decisions that your business must make is whether it should hire one or more resellers to help it market its products, or hire its own "direct" sales force. There are advantages and disadvantages to both strategies.

The more customers that are exposed to your marketing story, the more products you are likely to sell. So, many companies hire resellers to help them communicate their marketing story to customers that they could not otherwise reach. But hiring resellers is not a panacea for success. When a company relies on another company to resell its products, it loses some control over the selling situation. And, depending on how good a job its resellers do, it may build market share or it may develop a bad reputation in its market.

"If they can't get the job done, we'll hire other resellers that can."

One of my more memorable clients hired me to help it evaluate its reseller strategy. When I first met with my client and asked its president how his resellers were performing, he replied that most of his resellers were doing OK, except for his resellers in Texas. He claimed that these resellers were "not qualified to sell his company's product," and that he wanted me to help him figure out how to recruit more "professional" business partners.

I told the president that I could not help him unless I contacted his resellers in Texas to find out why they were having problems, and to learn what if anything could be done to help them become successful. He reluctantly gave me the contact information that I needed, and I picked up the phone.

The feedback from the resellers was very disturbing. All five of the resellers that I contacted in Dallas claimed that my client had misrepresented his company's products, that several of their customers were suing them, and that my client would soon hear from *their* lawyers.

My first thought after completing these interviews was that it was a good day to be a trial lawyer in Texas. My second thought was that we needed to find out as soon as possible who or what caused this great mess.

My client's product was very advanced—but it was also unstable. The software worked well in a demonstration situation, or when just a nominal amount of data was entered into the system. But over the course of four or five months, as new data was entered, the software ran slower and slower and eventually began to cause hardware problems.

If all of my client's resellers were having problems, it would have been pretty safe to assume that their problems were caused by my client's software. But resellers that I contacted in other areas of the country told me that they had many customers using my client's software that were not having any problems at all.

At this point, I felt like Sherlock Holmes! After about a dozen interviews with my client's technical support people and its resellers, I realized that two related issues were to blame.

First, I learned that the resellers in Texas did not go through my client's in-house reseller-training program. They attended a special training program that was held for them in Austin. The program in Austin did not teach the resellers how to configure my client's software properly, or the importance of educating their customers about archiving data to ensure that working files didn't become too large.

The second problem was that my client had no process in place to manage its reseller relationships—it just received orders and delivered products. So my client didn't learn about the severity of its reseller's problems until their anger and frustration had motivated them to take legal action. And that made it extremely difficult to establish a dialog with them about how to resolve their customer's problems.

Fortunately, this assignment had a happy ending. I convinced the president to take a trip with me to Dallas to meet with his resellers and to provide the technical support that was needed to resolve his customers' problems. Then, I contacted every customer that was having a problem and informed them that my client was aware of their concerns, was absolutely committed to solving their problems, and that they would receive additional on-site training for free. And lastly, to ensure that the reseller channel was managed properly, I convinced my client to hire an experienced reseller channel manager who had a Client-Centered™ approach to selling.

My client and its resellers turned around every problem account, with the exception of two customers that had already replaced their systems with competitive products. My client agreed to refund the purchase price of the software for these customers and saved thousands of dollars in legal fees. And my client salvaged its relationships with its newly retrained resellers by agreeing to credit their accounts for a portion of the money that they lost on the hardware that their customers had returned, and which they had to resell at a discounted price.

DISTRIBUTION CHANNEL BENEFITS

Distribution channels can help your company reach more customers with your marketing story and can help your company increase its sales revenues (its top line) and its profits (its bottom line). But developing a distribution channel requires the same attention, focus, and commitment that it takes to build a successful direct sales force.

Distribution Channel Benefits

□ Resellers can provide the "feet on the street" that your company needs to present its marketing story to a much larger number of potential customers than it can through its own sales force.

□ Resellers that offer competitive options may be viewed as more credible sources of purchasing information than a supplier that has a greater vested interest in promoting their own products.

- □ Resellers are usually in a better legal position to negotiate prices with their customers because they can more easily define different classes of customers.
- □ Resellers can help their suppliers manage their inventory.
- □ Resellers can help their suppliers finance their sales and manage their cash flow.
- □ Resellers can provide marketing information about competitive products and strategies, and can serve as a conduit for information about technological developments and industry trends.
- □ Resellers can repackage their suppliers' products to make them more appealing to customers.
- □ Resellers can assemble and integrate products from different suppliers to develop custom products and deliver complete "turnkey" solutions.
- □ Resellers can supply the knowledge and experience that is needed to understand their customers' needs and concerns.
- □ Resellers can specify, install, implement, and support their suppliers' products.
- □ Resellers can provide service at their customers' place of business.

DEVELOPING A COHERENT DISTRIBUTION STRATEGY

Your company can rely on three distribution strategies to help it reach new customers: intensive distribution, selective distribution, and exclusive distribution.

Intensive distribution refers to opening as many suppliers as possible to try and saturate the marketplace. If for example, your company was selling a new type of AC power surge protector, it might be in its best interests to have its product displayed in every computer store, listed in every mail-order catalog, and stocked on every distributor's shelves.

Selective distribution refers to restricting product distribution so most prospective customers can only obtain your product through one source. For example, your company might offer its products through two types of resellers or channels that target different makets, such as retail computer stores and Value Added Resellers (VARs).

Exclusive distribution refers to authorizing only one reseller to distribute your product in each market. Exclusive territories are usually set up regionally. For example, your company might work with four regional distributors. One distributor might cover your northern territory, another one your eastern territory, and so on.

Your company can use the "Distribution Strategy" worksheet to help it evaluate whether its current strategy will enable it to achieve its marketing objectives.

Distribution Strategy	Client-Centered™ Training Market Focus
Describe the geographic region(s)—including countries, states, regions, or cities—where your products are sold.	We market our products throughout North America.
Do you plan to expand distribution of your products?	We plan to expand into Europe and Asia next year, and South America in about 18 months.
Describe your company's relationships with its marketing partners. (See "Marketing Partner" table.)	☐ We work with several independent sales representatives, CPA firms, and business management consultants. They earn commissions by helping us market our training programs to their clients. ☐ A local mail order company is helping us introduce our new Sales Seminar In a Box. ☐ We work with a distributor that sells our sales training video courseware. ☐ We are working on a promotion with a cable television marketing company to produce an infomercial for our Sales Seminar in a Box. ☐ We are also working with two major Internet portal sites to help us market our services on the Internet.
Have you identified any customers, resellers, or other developers that would be willing to partner with your company to specify needs, develop prototypes, or provide product testing or prerelease marketing services?	Yes. We want to partner with or acquire a media company as soon as possible. We are also interested in partnering with a video production company to develop a series of training videos for sales management.

You can use the "Competitors' Distribution Model" worksheet to evaluate how your company's competitors are distributing their products, and why or why not your company is using the same distribution strategy.

Client-Centered™ Training Competitors' Distribution Model	
Do you use the same distribution channels as your competitors?	Basically, yes. We sell training services directly to major corporations through our East and West Coast sales offices.
	We do not understand distribution channels in Europe and Asia, so we will be working with our marketing partners.
If not, why have you chosen the distribution channels you are currently using? Advantages Disadvantages	N/A
Is so, have you considered using alternative distribution channels to increase sales of your products?	Yes, we are considering working with several regional CPA firms that can introduce us to their technology-driven clients.
	We are also considering partnering with industry-specific consulting firms in areas where we do not have direct sales representatives.

MULTIPLE DISTRIBUTION CHANNELS

Many companies employ multiple distribution channels to reach customers in different market segments. For example, if your company sells PCs, it might want to promote its products in retail computer stores that cater to home-based businesses and in mail order catalogs that reach PC buyers in larger companies.

The decision about how to best distribute your products depends on three key factors:

Your Customer—You will not be able to sell your products unless your distribution channel enables you to communicate your marketing story to your customers. Your customers may be located in major metropolitan areas, or they may be distributed over an entire geographic region. They may expect to meet with a salesperson in their office, or prefer shopping with a mail order catalog.

Your Product—Some products are complicated and can be sold only by salespeople with extensive training; other products can be sold in a blister pack on a rack display in a grocery store. Some marketing stories can be summarized on a business card, while others require a six-page glossary. In any case, your distribution channel must be capable of communicating all of the information that your customer needs to make an informed purchase decision.

Your Market—Your distribution channel must be able to reach and meet the needs of the market that you are selling into. The market for your product may be a small market segment within a vertical industry, or it may consist of all businesses in some geographic region.

In addition to considering these key factors, there are several points that you should consider before selecting a distribution strategy:

1. Most resellers want the opportunity to sell products to the widest range of prospective customers. If their territory is limited, they may feel that it is unprofitable for them to represent your products.
2. Resellers do not like to compete with other resellers that are supplying the same products to customers in their market. If competition causes price erosion, it may become unprofitable for them to represent your products. And if your resellers lose sales, they may change their supplier.
3. Well-established distribution channels within your market may obviate the value of other distribution channels. In this case, the only way to build market share may be to buy into these distribution channels. For example, if you are selling a software application, you may need to invest thousands of dollars in market development funds paid directly to a retail superstore to induce it to display your products on its shelves.
4. Although it may appear that the easiest way for your company to grow sales is to use an intensive distribution strategy, this is not always the case. For most companies, a selective distribution channel provides the win-win relationship that is needed to recruit and motivate capable, loyal resellers.

CHANNEL CONFLICT

Every company walks a fine line between overdistributing its products and losing opportunities to competitors because it is not able reach every customer with its marketing story. But the primary cause of supplier–reseller conflict is overdistribution. And the only solution to this problem is to balance your company's desire to reach every customer with your marketing story with the reality that your relationship with your resellers must remain profitable or they will find a new business partner.

Many start-up companies employ an intensive distribution strategy to build market awareness and to generate enough cash flow to grow their business. And it is hard for cash-strapped companies to turn down *any* new business opportunities. However, as companies grow, they usually implement a selective distribution strategy to maintain their competitiveness against companies that are using their own selective distribution strategy to recruit resellers.

RESELLER COMPENSATION

Your company should compensate its resellers fairly for their efforts. Most companies offer their resellers discounts based on sales volume. But some resellers, such as manufacturers' representatives that field a direct sales force, have higher selling expenses than other types of resellers, such as mail order companies, and may require higher reseller margins.

In any case, your reseller channel must be compensated for the work that it does to sell your product. And this markup or "margin" should be commensurate with the amount of work that your resellers are doing to move business forward.

If you feel that your company can get the same job done for less money than you are paying your distribution channel, it's time to "fire" your resellers and hire your own sales force to sell direct to your customers.

Fifth Law of Total Market Domination

The success of a distribution channel hinges on the ability and willingness of both partners—the supplier and its reseller—to invest the money and other resources that are necessary to achieve success.

A supplier and its resellers or distribution partners are codependent on one another to provide all of the products, sales information, and enthusiasm that are necessary to meet their customers' needs and move business forward. Suppliers, for example, depend on their resellers to meet with their customers and communicate their marketing story in a clear, concise, compelling way; deliver customer training; and service their products in the field. And resellers depend on their suppliers to provide compelling products, promotion, incentive, and technical support.

When IBM introduced its first PC, it knew that it takes almost as much time and effort to sell, install, and support a mission-critical software application on a $5,000 microcomputer as it does on a $250,000 mini-computer. And it knew that it could not afford to use its own highly paid sales representatives and support engineers to market $5,000 PCs.

IBM addressed this challenge in three ways. First, it developed systems that could be installed and managed by its customers. Second, it authorized business partners and computer resellers to market its products. And finally, it authorized and trained nationwide third-party service organizations to handle installation, product support, and warranty repairs. This strategy enabled IBM to market PCs profitably and served as a model for virtually every other computer company that entered the PC business.

Identify which distribution channels are the most profitable for your company to develop.

In most selling situations, *every* distribution channel that provides a positive return on a company's investment is worth supporting. But companies that achieve total market domination normally invest a percentage of their marketing resources in each distribution channel that they are using that is commensurate with that channel's success. For example, if Client-Centered™ Training generates 12 percent of its business through independent consultants, it would normally invest about 12 percent of its marketing resources to support this channel.

Client-Centered™ Training's Distribution Channels	Percentage of Sales	Total Revenue
Independent consultants	12	120,000
Direct telemarketing	2	20,000
Outside sales representatives	76	760,000
National consulting companies	1	10,000
Training video distributors	8	80,000
Manufacturer's representatives	0	0
Infomercial	0	0
Internet	1	10,000

Step 8: Evaluate your resellers.

Evaluating your company's resellers can be a very difficult job. It is easy to congratulate everyone for doing a good job when sales revenues are increasing at an acceptable rate. But when sales go down or when you get customer complaints, it may be difficult to establish what the problem is and how to correct it.

One of the secrets of Microsoft's market domination is its commitment to its channel partners. Microsoft has never sold its retail products directly to its customers, or set up any house accounts. And when Microsoft has failed to meet its revenue projections—this has happened—it hasn't threatened to replace its channel partners; it has developed promotions and training events to support their efforts.

Of course, the best way to handle channel problems is to plan ahead so that you can avoid them. And the most effective way to anticipate problems with your channel partners is to stay in touch with your customers. Telephone surveys, customer questionnaires, and focus groups can provide the objective data that you need to help you evaluate how good a job your resellers are doing.

RECRUITING THE BEST RESELLERS

Most companies select resellers based on two simple criteria: their ability to close business, and their ability to provide adequate customer support. However, before recruiting a reseller, you should check out its references, do one or more site visits, and meet as many of its personnel as possible. Many resellers have the ability and desire to sell and service their supplier's products in a professional Client-Centered™ manner. But some resellers do not demonstrate any commitment to excellence.

It is also important to check out resellers' credit references. Most resellers are honest and capable, but many resellers go out of business each year, leaving their suppliers with large unpaid invoices. It is tempting to extend as much credit as possible to your resellers, but it is very risky.

Your company can use the "Selecting Resellers" worksheet to evaluate the criteria that it uses to select its resellers.

Selecting Resellers	Client-Centered™ Training's Selection Factors
How do you select sales representatives?	Personal qualities, previous experience in industry, pass Internet-hosted personality test.
How do you select resellers?	Previous experience in industry, reputation, previous level of success, geographical territory, referrals, level of commitment.
How do you select distributors?	Geographical territory, previous experience in industry, reputation, previous level of success, referrals, level of commitment.
How do you select third-party service / support / product warranty representatives?	Personal qualities, previous experience in industry, commitment to program.
Do you have a training program for your resellers?	No. We may offer one in the future.
Do you have a training program for your support personnel?	N/A

CHANGING RESELLERS

In a perfect world, all resellers would be capable, ethical, and motivated. But many resellers fail to perform up to their suppliers' expectations. And it can be very difficult to terminate a reseller that has a binding territory agreement.

Any change in your distribution strategy will impact your customers. So the better your relationship is with your former reseller, the less disruptive your transition to your new reseller will be and the less likely it will be that any of your customers will defect to other suppliers.

If you decide to terminate a reseller's contract with your company, you should understand exactly what your legal position is *before* contacting them. It is very frustrating to alienate a business partner only to learn from their lawyers that your "separation" may take months or years to be resolved.

Your next step should be to make a sincere effort to communicate the reason for your decision with the reseller that you are going to terminate. You should follow up your conversation with a written communication that references your distribution agreement and specifies the reason for your action.

The process of firing a reseller can become very emotional. So whenever possible, you should implement a win-win transition strategy to avoid a contentious separation. For example, your company might offer to pay your reseller a percentage of commissions on sales made for some period after the termination of your reseller agreement to encourage the reseller to maintain a positive, professional attitude about your company and your products.

LITIGATION

Several years ago one of my clients informed me that one of its resellers was using some of its source code—the step-by-step instructions that a computer uses to execute a specific task—without permission. I suggested that my client negotiate a nominal license fee with its reseller, but the president of my client's company took it personally that a trusted reseller had "stolen his company's code" and decided, against my advice, to find justice in the courts.

My client argued that its reseller had used thousands of lines of its code without its permission, and to help prove its point, demonstrated that its copyright notice was embedded in its reseller's source code. My client's reseller argued that it had to use my client's code to make its software work properly with my client's programs, and that removing my client's code would put it out of business.

To a casual observer this might have been an open-and-shut case—the reseller *did* use my client's code without permission—but the litigation went on for over a year and cost my client several hundred thousand dollars and many weeks of senior management's time. In the end, the reseller's lawyers convinced the court that a large, powerful company was bullying their little client. And, as I feared, my client lost the case and was forced to pay its reseller thousands of dollars in damages!

Over the years, I have been involved with several companies that have become involved in litigation with resellers. In every one of these situations, my clients would have been better off using arbitration, mediation, or intermediaries to help them work out their differences, or just writing off their loss and moving on. It is not impossible to find justice in the courts, but outcomes are rarely as "open and shut" as litigators would like their well-paying clients to believe.

Step 9: Evaluate your consultants and subcontractors.

Most companies that achieve total market domination work with a small army of outside service providers and consultants, including press relations firms, advertising agencies, direct mail companies, and telephone support call centers. These resources enable these companies to focus on their core business, leverage their internal resources, maximize their profits, train their own personnel, and achieve their strategic business objectives.

Companies that achieve total market domination audit their consultants and subcontractors periodically to confirm that they are receiving quality services at competitive rates.

Use of Consultants and Sucontractors in Different Areas of Your Business.	Objective	Effectiveness 1 (ineffective) to 5 (very effective)
Administration Tasks	We do not use outside contractors in this area.	N/A
Production Tasks	We subcontract production work to our printer, copy center, and media supplier. We also work with subcontractors on custom training programs.	4
Order Fulfillment	We contract with Air Express to handle all priority shipments. They work directly with our East and West Coast sales offices.	5
Operations Tasks	We are using a direct mail company to help us launch our new seminar program.	2

Step 10: Evaluate your company's pricing strategy.

The primary directive of a for-profit business is to increase its market position by increasing its market share and its profits. So it makes sense that the objective of your company's pricing strategy should be to increase your company's market share, increase profits, or if possible, increase both market share and profitability.

PROFIT

Many companies seek a *specific target return* on their investment. The actual targeted rate of return may vary, depending on whether the company's products are entering new markets, and where their products are in their product life cycle. Depending on the industry and the level of capital investment required, companies usually target anywhere from 8 to 20 percent after tax profits.

Profit maximization strategies are most common for start-up companies. In many high-technology companies, for example, the dynamics of the market require rapid product introduction and extensive promotion. Maximizing profits on successful ventures helps to fund research and development for future opportunities.

A third pricing strategy is to provide a *satisfactory rate of return* that is acceptable to the company's shareholders. In this strategy, excess profits are discouraged because they may encourage new competitors to come into the market, which may result in a loss of market share. Well-established companies in mature markets, such as food products and manufacturing materials, often employ this strategy.

Microsoft's MS-DOS—Penetration Pricing

Start-up companies and companies that are introducing new products often use low *penetration* pricing to help generate interest in their product and build market share.

When Microsoft introduced its MS-DOS operating system, the PC industry was transitioning from 8-bit to 16-bit microprocessor-based computer systems. Digital Research's CP/M operating system was the standard 8-bit operating system and had been updated to work on 16-bit machines. Many people were familiar with CP/M, so it had a competitive advantage over the newly introduced MS-DOS operating system.

To overcome Digital Research's advantage, Microsoft provided inexpensive software licenses to computer manufacturers that were willing to bundle MS-DOS with every machine that they produced. The primary reason Microsoft used this strategy was to build market share for its operating system as quickly as possible.

Microsoft believed that there would be little incentive for hardware manufacturers and independent software developers to use another operating system once MS-DOS was established as an industry standard. And Microsoft knew that establishing MS-DOS as the standard operating system for PCs would give it a competitive advantage to build market share for its other products.

After MS-DOS became a de facto industry standard, Microsoft could have raised its prices substantially. But Microsoft chose to raise its prices nominally, to achieve a *satisfactory rate of return,* to extend and protect its market share.

Intel—The "Skimming" Champion

High introductory prices are attractive and may yield high profits, but they often lead to increased competition. This pricing strategy is referred to as *skimming*.

Intel, the leading supplier of microprocessor chips for PCs, controls market demand for its new microprocessors by setting prices that enable it to ramp production to meet its customers' needs, protect its market share for its less powerful microprocessors, and maximize its profits.

When Intel introduces a new microprocessor, it sells it for a relatively high price to help recoup its development costs, and then gradually reduces the price of its microprocessor over the product's life cycle. This pricing strategy has enabled Intel to earn the profits it has needed to build the multibillion-dollar manufacturing facilities that it requires to meet its customers' demands for increasingly powerful microprocessors.

DETERMINING YOUR SELLING PRICE

Before you can determine the most profitable selling price for your products, you must determine two factors: first, you must determine the actual cost of producing and marketing your product; and second, you must analyze the market demand for your product.

The actual cost of a product is equal to the total of its fixed costs plus its variable costs. Fixed costs refer to administrative, sales, and production costs that do not vary as a direct function of the quantity of a product that is produced. Variable costs vary directly with production volumes. For example, raw material costs vary directly with the quantity of a product that is manufactured.

It is impossible to create a successful pricing strategy unless reliable costing information is available. However, in some situations it is very difficult to get accurate costing information. For example, it is common for prices of components to vary as much as an order of magnitude over the life of a product. And in technology companies it may be hard to assign after-sale warranty and support costs between different products. In any case, your company should invest whatever resources are necessary to determine the cost of its products and services.

Your company will not be able to maximize its profits and achieve total market domination until it knows exactly how much it costs to deliver each product and service that it supplies to its customers.

CUSTOMER DEMAND

To determine the most profitable price point for your company's product, your company must determine what its customers are willing to pay for it, based on a demand curve for that quantity of production. The demand for most products is *elastic*, so product demand increases as price goes down. But for some products, such as products used in industrial applications, demand is inelastic, because it is *derived* from customer orders. If a manufacturer does not have orders to fill, it will not purchase raw materials at any price; but if a manufacturer needs raw materials to fill its customers' orders, it will pay the market price.

There are several techniques that are commonly used to determine market demand. The most common are historical analysis, market surveys, focus groups, and test marketing.

Historical analysis is usually the fastest way to assess demand for a product. The more homogeneous and stable markets are, the more useful this type of analysis is. In high-tech markets, where products are continually changing, prices of components are usually falling, and customers' expectations are constantly increasing, historical data is usually of historical interest.

Market surveys are the most common way to evaluate market demand. The challenge, of course, is designing a questionnaire that is clear and focused and that provides the information that you need to identify and prioritize your customers' needs and concerns. Customers often distinguish between the value that a product provides and how much they are willing to pay for it. So asking a customer what a product is "worth" may result in a very different response than asking them how large a check they are willing to write to have your product delivered to their business tomorrow.

Focus groups require more preparation than questionnaires and may not reveal the same opinions that a questionnaire that is completed by a larger number of potential customers will disclose. However, focus groups provide an opportunity to dialog with potential customers about your product's features and design, about your customers' needs and concerns, and about your customers' experience with competitors' products.

Test marketing products can provide the most reliable data about market demand. However, if your test doesn't recreate your customers' purchase situation, it may tell you very little about how your product will fair in a real selling situation. For example, sales presentations by your company's VP of Marketing are, hopefully, much more compelling to potential customers than dented blister-packed products stacked on a retailer's shelf.

DEMAND-ORIENTED PRICING

In *normal competitive markets*, each company's market share is dependent on its pricing strategy. And companies with a price advantage usually gain market share at the expense of higher-cost suppliers. In *intensely competitive markets*, prices are usually determined by the going market price, and there is very little pricing flexibility. In *oligopolies*, where several major market share holders and a number of minor market share holders are producing virtually identical products, there are often legal constraints on the major players, as well as product cycle and target revenue considerations that affect pricing decisions.

Oligopolies usually offer major opportunities to use pricing to gain market share. However, in most oligopolies, a price leader sets the market price. And as long as they and their competitors can make a reasonable profit, their price will hold, because price reductions, which can precipitate price wars, rarely benefit any of the suppliers.

CUSTOMER EXPECTATIONS

Some customers correlate a high price with high quality or high status. This *prestige market* is usually a very small segment of the total market, but it may be a very profitable segment. Designer fashion clothing companies, for example, often set exorbitantly high prices to attract prestige buyers.

Prices may also be made extremely low; this is called *leader* pricing. For example, in consumer electronics markets, it is common to promote low-cost, entry-level PC products that are incomplete unless additional components such as an optional video monitor and printer are purchased.

In any case, customers expect to see a clear relationship between the price they pay for a product and the value the product delivers. If, for example, a ten-page-per-minute printer is available for $200, it is difficult to justify selling a five-page-per-minute printer for the same price.

Developing a coherent pricing strategy is usually a straightforward process, but when a marginally profitable item is included in a product line, such as a loss leader, it can be a real challenge to justify the prices of other, more profitable products.

Most companies have a policy of charging every customer of the same class the same price and offering the same discounts for the same quantity of a product that is ordered. However, some companies have a *flexible* pricing policy, which means that different customers are offered different prices, depending on their bargaining ability or their relationship with their supplier.

Large companies usually avoid flexible pricing policies because they can lead to legal problems if they prevent less-favored customers from competing effectively. But in any case, it is wise to make your prices as consistent as possible. Customers do not appreciate being "overcharged" for any reason. And pricing inconsistencies or errors can cost your company sales and customer loyalty.

PSYCHOLOGICAL PRICE BARRIERS

Customers often have psychological price barriers. For example, some customers may be unwilling to pay over $20 per month for high-speed Internet access, because this is what they pay for their cable television service. It is usually possible to overcome psychological price resistance, but the advertising bill can be formidable.

BREAKEVEN PRICING

A product's breakeven point occurs when its total costs are equal to the revenue generated at a particular sales price.

Your company can use a breakeven price analysis to help it evaluate whether it is profitable to sell its product at different target resale prices.

BEP = (Total Fixed Costs) / 1 – (Variable Costs/Unit) / (Selling Price/Unit)

If you were willing to "bet your company" on being able to sell a specific quantity of goods at your BEP plus a reasonable profit, your production managers could put your company into overdrive and your pricing problems would be of historical interest. But very few products have a perfectly horizontal demand at a forecasted sales price. Which is why breakeven pricing can help your company test its pricing strategy but is not a good technique for setting prices.

MARGINAL ANALYSIS

Your company can also use marginal costs and revenues to help it analyze how it can maximize its profits. Marginal analysis establishes a cost and revenue basis for the last unit of a product that is sold. You can use this data to help you establish the most profitable quantity of a product to produce and the best price to sell it at.

Marginal revenue is the revenue that is generated from the sale of one additional unit of a product. The demand for a product usually increases as its price goes down, so in most markets, suppliers will reduce the marginal revenue on their products over time to increase their market share. For example, Client-Centered™ Training can sell 5,000 of its video seminars at $395 each. But if it lowers the price of its video seminars to $195, it can sell 50,000 units.

Marginal cost is the cost of producing one additional unit of a product. If Client-Centered™ Training's marginal cost were close to or exceeded $195, it would be more profitable to sell 5,000 units at $395 than 50,000 units at $195. On other hand, if its marginal cost were significantly lower than $195, it would be more profitable to reduce its price and sell the larger number of units.[1]

If your company's marginal cost is greater than its marginal revenue, your company will begin to lose money on increased sales. When your company's marginal cost and its marginal revenue are exactly equal, your company will still be profitable, because your company's total profits will increase up to the point that your marginal profit is equal to zero. But to maintain profitability, your company must price its products so that the marginal cost of its output is less than its marginal revenue.

SALES AND PROFITS

Salespeople are paid to sell. They are not paid to think about cash flow, profit margins, or production issues. But it is important for them to understand the relationship between selling price, sales volume, and their company's bottom line.

Many companies provide their sales force with a simple chart that illustrates the relationship between profit margins and profitability. For example, you might illustrate how profitable it is for your company to produce and sell 10 units of a product with a $10 markup on each sale, compared to producing and selling 100 units of the product with a $1 markup on each sale.

Step 11: Identify the most serious risk factors to your marketing plan.
Business is inherently risky. It is management's job to manage those risks in a way that optimizes the return on its shareholders' investment.

Your company can use the "Marketing Plan Risk Factors" worksheet to identify any potential obstacles to achieving its marketing objectives.

---

[1] Production costs usually go down as greater quantities of a product are manufactured. But at some point, the price of producing the next product will increase. This is because as production increases, it becomes necessary to increase production facilities. For example, as Client-Centered™ Training increases its production level, it may need to invest in retooling equipment, leasing larger warehouse space, subcontracting work, or adding additional personnel, which will increase its fixed production costs while its variable costs may already be at their lowest values. This is one reason why rapid growth often strains a company's financial reserves.

Marketing Plan Risk Factors	1 (not prepared) to 5 (very prepared)
Inability to raise funds to support business operations	4
Lose credit line	3
New hardware and systems software	3
Enabling technologies such as electronic messaging	2
New competitors	3
Loss of key customers	2
Price wars	4
Decline in market demand	3
Distribution channel conflicts	5
Increased production costs	4
Increased support costs	4
Supplier delays	2
Increase in cost of raw materials	3
Loss of key suppliers	3
New or stronger competitors	4
Product delays	4
Increased personnel costs	4
Loss of key personnel	1
Employee burnout	2
Loss of key distributors	3
Loss of key resellers	4
Quality assurance problems	4
Government regulations	4
Corporate theft	1
Fire, earthquake, and other natural disaster	1
Product Support problems (liability, etc.)	2
Internal attack on information systems	1
External attack on information systems	1
Delayed or unsuccessful research and development	2
Impact of emerging technology on business model	2

WHY COMPANIES STOP PLANNING

Taking the time to develop detailed marketing plans and to track your sales and marketing efforts is a proven recipe for success. But it can be difficult to find the right balance between becoming overwhelmed by supporting a complex planning process, with too many meetings and reports, and abandoning planning functions, losing control of your company's resources, and missing profitable business opportunities.

A simple way to determine whether your company is spending enough time on planning activities is to test your managers' ability to describe how your customers and your markets have changed over the last six months.

- Can you articulate your company's short- and longer-term business objectives?
- How has your market changed in the last six months?
- How has your business changed in the last six months?
- Have your business objectives changed to reflect changes in your business?
- Is your company's value equation in balance?
- Are you aware of how, when, and why your marketing resources are being allocated to specific products, marketing activities, or personnel?
- Is your company evaluating any new businesses opportunities?

The Bottom Line: Does your marketing plan provide the focus that your sales team needs to leverage its selling efforts?

Management by objectives, using key results to track performance, and implementing rewards tied to achieving specific goals is the process that most successful companies have used to achieve total market domination.

It takes careful planning to build a world-class sales organization. But taking the time to develop a logical marketing plan and a comprehensive sales kit will help ensure that all of your selling resources are leveraged to their maximum capability.

In the next chapter, you will learn how to develop effective marketing programs to identify prospective customers for your company's products.

CHAPTER 5

DO YOU HAVE EFFECTIVE PROGRAMS IN PLACE TO IDENTIFY PROSPECTIVE CUSTOMERS?

If you have nothing to say, sing it!

—DAVID OGILVY

The greater the demand is for your company's products, the less effort your company will need to make to find new customers. But if your company has just started to do business, or if its products are new or rely on new technologies, your company may need to invest a substantial amount of its marketing resources to identify prospective customers and to qualify their needs and concerns.

In the past, a company's primary marketing tools were media advertising, direct mail advertising, telephone selling, trade shows, and face-to-face selling. Today, other marketing tools, such as demonstration centers, catalog selling, and the Internet, can be used to help your company achieve total market domination.

Step 1: Evaluate the prospecting methods that your company is using to generate leads.

In most selling situations, your company will need to employ both *direct* prospecting methods, such as advertising, direct mail, telemarketing, cold calls, and trade shows, and *indirect* prospecting methods, such as referrals, barter arrangements, seminars, and networking with business contacts, to identify qualified prospects.

Every company strives to use the most effective prospecting method to identify qualified prospects for their products. But the best way to identify new customers depends on a constellation of factors:

- Number of prospects in your territory
- Geographical distribution of prospects
- Type of products or services being marketed
- Your company's market position and strategy
- Marketing budget
- Number and capabilities of sales and support personnel
- Outside marketing resources
- Competitors' marketing strategies
- Joint marketing opportunities

CHOOSING A WINNING STRATEGY

When you are deciding between investing your time and marketing resources in two different prospecting activities, such as direct mail and telemarketing, there are four questions that you should try to answer about each prospecting opportunity:

1. Will the prospecting activity enable me to communicate with my targeted marketing opportunities?
2. How much will the prospecting activity cost in terms of time and money?
3. What is my best estimate of the number of leads that the prospecting activity will generate?
4. Based on prior experience, what is the likelihood of closing the leads that are generated?

KNOW YOUR CUSTOMER

The more information that you have about your customers' purchase process, the easier it will be for you to select prospecting tools that will enable you to communicate your marketing story as efficiently and inexpensively as possible.

For example, Client-Centered™ Training's customers are high-level sales and marketing personnel. Since it is very difficult to reach these people on the telephone, it is necessary to use direct mail and trade shows to communicate Client-Centered™ Training's marketing story and qualify their interest.

Similarly, since Client-Centered™ Training's products are targeted at such a broad range of technology-driven businesses, it is more cost-effective for the company to advertise in general business magazines than in industry-specific trade magazines, which charge a premium for advertising space.

Client-Centered™ Training's Marketing Activities	Expense (High, Moderate, Low)	Impact 1 (ineffective) to 5 (very effective)
Telemarketing	Moderate	3
Direct mail (in-house)	Low	1
Direct mail service	Low	2
Direct fax	Very Low	2
Seminars	High	5
Referral program	No Cost	4
Press relations	Moderate	2
Joint marketing activities	Varies	-
Print advertising	High	2
Radio advertising	N/A	-
Television advertising	N/A	-
Internet advertising	Low	1
Trade show	High	4
Other promotions		

Your company can construct a simple decision table to help it evaluate the pros and cons of each prospecting activity that it is considering using.

Results of Direct Mail Promotion	Results of Telemarketing Promotion
Can use SIC codes, contact names, and titles to target best prospects.	Can use SIC codes to target best prospects.
Costs $10,000 to create and distribute mailers.	Cost is equal to opportunity cost of sales representative's selling time.
Requires 10,000 mailers to generate 100 leads.	Requires 200 hours of telemarketing time to generate 50 leads.
100 direct mail leads generate 10 sales.	50 telemarketing leads generate 10 sales.

Then, your company can use its decision table to help it select the prospecting activity that has the best chance of generating the number of qualified prospects that it will need to meet its sales objectives at the lowest cost per lead.

QUALITY LEADS

The cost of generating a lead must be weighed against the quality of the leads generated with each prospecting activity. For example, a telemarketing lead is often much better qualified than a lead generated from an advertisement in a magazine.

The most objective way to evaluate the effectiveness of different prospecting activities is to track the number of leads that each activity generates, and then to track how many of those leads result in new business for your company.

In the following worksheet, the *cost per lead* is equal to the amount of money spent generating leads divided by the number of leads generated; and the *quality of leads* is equal to the number of sales divided by the number of leads, expressed as a percentage. *Return on investment* is equal to the revenue generated by the marketing activity divided by the cost of the marketing activity, expressed as a multiple of its investment.

Client-Centered™ Training invested [1430 leads × $29.80 per lead =] $42,614 on direct mail and generated [51 sales × $10,000 average revenue for each sale =] $510,000 in sales revenues. So Client-Centered™ Training's ROI is equal to [$510,000 / $42,614

=] $11.97 in new sales for each dollar that it invested in direct mail promotions.

Note in the worksheet that Client-Centered™ Training has lost money on its investment in Internet advertising. Client-Centered™ Training considers this a long-term "strategic" investment and expects to break even on this promotion within the next eighteen months.

Evaluate your competitors' distribution strategy.

Client-Centered™ Training's Marketing Activities	Number of Leads Generated	Cost per Lead	Number of Sales Generated	Quality of Leads	ROI for Marketing Activity
Direct mail	1,430	$29.80	51	4%	$11.97
Telemarketing	365	$36.05	110	30%	$83.60
Cold calls	-	-	-	-	
Tip / referral club	-	-	-	-	
Trade show	65	$16.15	15	23%	$142.86
Industry directories	318	$51.19	85	27%	$52.22
Yellow pages	48	$80.84	29	60%	$74.74
Print advertising	519	$54.80	35	7%	$12.31
Radio advertising	-	-	-	-	
Television advertising	-	-	-	-	
Internet advertising	390	$148.46	4	16%	$0.69
Seminar programs	-	-	-	-	
Press tour	23	$1,819.00	2	33%	$0.48

Investigating where the most successful companies in your market are spending their marketing resources can help your company identify profitable marketing activities and avoid strategies that have not yet proven themselves in your market.

Client-Centered™ Training Competitors' Marketing Budget as a % of Sales	State College	Regional Training Firm	Independent Consulting Firm	Client-Centered™ Training
Direct mail	90	50	25	15
Telemarketing	-	20	30	35
Outside sales	-	15	15	30
Retail	-	-	-	-
Distributor	-	-	-	-
Manufacturer's representative	-	10	-	-
Infomercial	-	-	-	-
Internet	10	5	30	20

Client-Centered™ Training Competitors' Marketing Budget as a % of sales	% of Marketing Budget for Seminar Companies	% of Marketing Budget for C-C™T Seminar Sales	% of Marketing Budget for Consulting Companies	% of Marketing Budget for C-C™T's Consulting Services
Direct mail	30	10	14	12
Telemarketing	6	3	2	3
Outside sales	30	80	59	75
Retail	2	-	-	-
Distributor	-	-	-	-
Manufacturer's representative	30	-	20	-
Infomercial	1	-	-	-
Internet	1	7	5	10

THE PROSPECTING FUNNEL

If the number of prospects for your product is very small, your company can spend more time qualifying each prospect than if it has a very large number of prospects to work with. For example, if your company has a very large number of prospects, it will need to qualify its prospects using a technique, such as telemarketing, that enables its salespeople to prioritize its prospects' interests quickly and inexpensively. But if your company has very few prospects to work with, it may make sense for its sales representatives to make one-on-one sales calls.

Example of a Prospecting "Funnel" Using Direct Mail and Telemarketing	Number of "Qualified" Prospects
Total number of prospects in territory	Unknown
Initial contact—Direct mail	100,000
Initial response (5% of recipients request additional information)	5,000
Second contact—Direct mail—send detailed product information	5,000
Third contact—Telemarketing qualification by sales assistant (300 leads did not provide telephone number or asked not to be called)	4,700
Fourth contact—Sales call—Detailed needs assessment	3,000
Fifth contact—Product Demonstration/send video	2,500
Sixth contact—Proposal—90% of prospects that see a demonstration are sent proposals	2,250
Sales—70% of proposals lead to a sale	1,575

LOW-RISK PROSPECTING

Prospecting techniques that have proved to be cost-effective usually continue to be a cost-effective way to generate new leads until one or more key market factors changes and impacts your customers' purchase process. This is why magazine subscription brokers have used their "You may have won a million dollars!" direct mail campaigns to sell magazine subscriptions for the last twenty years. The formula continues to work because many people like to enter sweepstakes, wish they could get something for free, and are just as anxious to renew their subscription to TV Guide as they were two or three decades ago.

SALES FORMULAS AND REAL WORLD RESULTS

One of the most common mistakes that companies make is assuming that they can take a sales formula, apply it to their business, and achieve a predictable outcome.

Sales formulas can provide insight into how a market will respond to a marketing appeal, but every assumption about your customers' needs and concerns must be validated and verified. Depending on your selling situation, ten qualified prospects may lead to one sale, to ten sales, or to no sales at all.

The most reliable sales formula that you can use is one based on your own market research and sales experience.

PRIORITIZE YOUR LEADS

Qualification means taking action!

Most companies believe that their salespeople are working with every available sales lead that they have. But according to Inquiry Systems and Analysis, although 60 percent of prospects make a purchase decision within one year, over 40 percent of prospects receive information past the time of their need or purchase decision, and over 50 percent of leads are *never* followed up.

Priority of Lead	Client-Centered™ Training's Qualification Factors

"C"	▫ Customer has completed a contact form
	   ▫ Trade show lead
	   ▫ Advertising response
	   ▫ Direct mail response
	▫ Customer has spoken with a salesperson
	▫ Need has been established
	▫ Customer will make a purchase decision within the next twelve months

"B"	▫ Customer has seen a demonstration ▫ Money, purchase authority, and time frame have been qualified ▫ Customer has received a needs assessment and verbal recommendation ▫ Customer will make a purchase decision within the next 60 days
"A"	▫ Customer has received a written proposal ▫ Production and training schedules have been verified and confirmed ▫ Customer has had a teleconference with assigned consultant or seminar leader ▫ Salesperson has asked customer for their business ▫ Account has been reviewed by the sales manager

Taking the time to qualify your prospects will help your company increase its revenues by enabling your sales team to focus its efforts on your company's best prospects.

Most companies categorize prospects on the basis of how long their sales team thinks it will take to close their business. For example, your company may prioritize the prospects that your salespeople are working with into three categories: "A" (hottest/best qualified/close within one week), "B" (interested/needs work/close within one or two months), and "C" (potential sale within some time frame, such as six months or one year).

Step 2: Evaluate your advertising and corporate communications plan.

There are two promotional strategies that your company can use to market its products.[1] A *push strategy* assumes that there is demand for your company's products, and emphasizes personal selling to move your company's products through its distribution channels to its customers. For example, your company might sell its products to distributors, who sell your products to resellers, who sell your products to customers.

A *pull strategy* uses advertising and other promotions to *create demand* for your company's products. In this strategy, your promotion compels customers to seek out resellers to purchase your products. In this situation, resellers must ask their distributors to supply your products, and distributors must ask your company to provide products to supply their channel.

It is usually less costly to market products using a push strategy, but if demand for your company's products is weak, your company may not be able to convince resellers to invest their resources to promote your company's products.

Microsoft, like most companies, uses a *combination* of push and pull strategies to create demand for its products and support its channel partners. This strategy has enabled Microsoft to maintain its leadership position and has discouraged new competitors from entering its markets.

---

[1] "Marketing" is a general term that refers to the totality of a company's effort to sell its products. Promotion usually refers to emphasizing the visibility of a single product or service.

Determining how much of your company's marketing budget to invest in creating demand for your products is a perennial challenge. Dun and Bradstreet and many industry trade magazines publish advertising marketing budget data for companies in different markets. But depending on your company's marketing strategy, and where your products are in their life cycle, it may be necessary for you to invest more or less than your industry's average marketing budget to achieve its business objectives.

ADVERTISING SUCCESS

Opinion Research Corporation found that people who know a company well are five times more likely to have a positive opinion about it. A positive opinion means a preference, and buyer preference translates into sales. This is why companies invest billions of dollars each year to promote their products and their corporate image.

The key to creating effective advertising is to communicate the most compelling elements of your marketing story. And the "acid test" that you can use to evaluate your advertising is to ask whether it is clear, concise, and compelling, and whether it answers "who, what, where, when, and why" a customer should do business with your company.

Most companies leverage their advertising budget by advertising a product or product line until it has achieved a substantial level of customer acceptance. When a company's product is known to deliver a high level of customer satisfaction, a quality *brand* has been established. At this point, a company can invest in image advertising to promote all of its products and services.

THE PET ROCK

The success of the "pet rock" taught me an important lesson: a marketing story does not need to be complex or even to make very much sense to sell. As David Ogilvy, the advertising guru and author of the wonderful book *Ogilvy on Advertising,* says, "When you have nothing to say, sing it!"

ADVERTISING MISTAKES

Advertising that communicates clearly "telegraphs" its message to your customers.

The five most common advertising mistakes that my clients have made are:

1. Lack of focus—presenting a confusing message
2. Telling an interesting story but failing to communicate the compelling reasons to do business with that company
3. Attempting to be artistic or clever and obscuring the compelling reasons to do business with that company
4. Attempting to communicate too much information
5. Not tracking results

ADVERTISING RESULTS

The key to *evolving* a successful advertising strategy is to track the results of your advertising on a regular basis.

The easiest way to evaluate the payback on your advertising is to track the number of sales leads generated by your advertising campaign, and the amount of sales revenue that is generated from those leads. And the easiest way to evaluate whether your advertising is influencing your customers' perception of your company's quality is with questionnaires and focus groups that measure changes in your customers' brand preference.

Using these techniques will enable your company to evaluate whether or not its promotions are *compelling*, and whether increasing its advertising budget will help it build market share.

Advertising	Client-Centered™ Training's Advertising Results
Does your advertisement communicate your marketing story in a clear, concise, compelling way?	Our Internet Web site does a good job of telling our story, but our marketing brochure lacks focus and is out of date.
Does your advertisement communicate a compelling reason to do business with your company?	Our brochure provides five compelling reasons to select our company as a training partner.
Does your advertisement generate interest in your products?	Our past relationship with Microsoft helps generate interest in our approach. And our use of new computer and communication technologies is of great interest to our customers.
Does your advertisement provide the information that a customer needs to make an informed purchase decision?	We provide detailed information about our programs, pricing, and after-training support.
Does your advertisement create a preference for your products?	We compare our training to traditional selling methodologies and believe we create a clear preference in our customers' minds.
Does your advertisement explain how to contact your organization?	We include mail, voice, fax, e-mail, and Internet contact information.
Does your advertisement use space (visual media) and time (multimedia) effectively?	Our brochure provides a good executive summary of our capabilities, but it needs to be redesigned to explain how our programs differ from our competitors' programs and to promote our Web site. Our Web site includes RealVideo clips of presentations that demonstrate our enthusiasm and our competence.
How can you improve your advertising?	We plan to include RealVideo clips of customer testimonials on our Web site. We also plan to launch a newsletter called "Today's Marketing Technology" early next year. We are designing interactive pages that our clients can use to help them assess their training requirements.

Step 3: Review your advertising budget.

Investing in marketing programs is like investing in the stock market.

□ Don't invest without a plan.
□ Approach new opportunities with caution.
□ Don't invest all of your money in one "great" idea.
□ Balance your investments between known winners and higher-risk, higher-return opportunities.
□ Evaluate your investments periodically to determine whether you are getting an acceptable return on your investment.
□ If you don't play, you can't win.

The "Advertising Budget" table illustrates a simple way to compare your company's advertising budget to its competitors' advertising budgets. Your company can use this information to help it allocate its marketing resources.

Figure 5-1
1997 Advertising Spending by Resellers

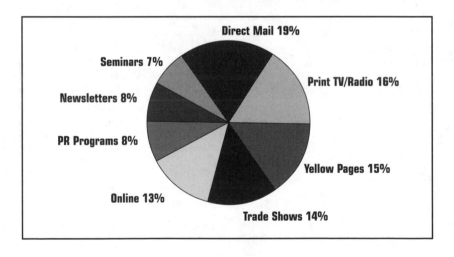

Client-Centered™ Training's Advertising Budget	Client-Centered™ Training's Advertising Expense	Percentage of Advertising Budget	Percentage of Competitors' Advertising Budgets
Direct mail	$20,000	20%	19%
Print advertising	25,000	25	16
Radio advertising	-	-	-
Television advertising	-	-	-
Yellow pages	3,000	3	15
Trade shows	25,000	25	14
Online advertising	-	-	13
Press relations	15,000	15	8
Newsletters	-	-	8
Seminar programs	12,000	12	8
Other	-	-	-

Step 4: Evaluate your corporate communications.

The old adage that "any publicity is good publicity" is balderdash when it comes to business press. Bad publicity can seriously impair your company's ability to meet its business objectives.

In most industries, a small group of editors, industry analysts, and gurus are extremely influential in helping purchasers evaluate new products and suppliers. A derogatory product review or comment about your company from one of these pundits can be the kiss of death to its revenue forecast.

Many years ago, I did product reviews for *PC Week*. Companies that were having products reviewed often asked, "How can our company work more effectively with your magazine?" Of course what I was really being asked was, "What can our company do to *influence* our editorial coverage?"

To save time, I wrote up a simple seven-step strategy for the care and feeding of editors, analysts, and industry gurus.

1. *The most reliable route to high-impact press coverage is an open, honest relationship with editors that are covering your market.*

    Your first objective should be to develop a friendly working relationship with the editors and analysts that cover your market. If you alienate these individuals, you may get your story but end up wishing it had never been written. If you don't trust the editor that you are working with to provide fair coverage of your company or your products, focus your PR effort on another publication.

2. *Be sure that your story ideas are of obvious interest to the readership of the magazine that you are approaching.*

Try to present several different story ideas, preferably in a succinct note or e-mail message, to help the freelancer or contributing editor that you are contacting sell your story idea to their senior editor.

3. *If your product is being evaluated, make sure that it is sent out in good condition and in a timely manner.*

If you are in the computer business, make sure that your hardware is burned in and checked out before it is sent out for evaluation. If you are in the software business, make sure that your software works properly. And always supply operating instructions that are simple enough for mere mortals to comprehend.

At least *twenty percent* of the products that were sent to me for evaluation did not work properly. And the people that sent me these products were usually unaware that their product had any defects—which meant that they had not tested their product before sending it out for review!

4. *Follow up to make sure that your products are working correctly.*

Assign a technically qualified person with good communication skills to answer questions about your product and to resolve any problems that the individual who is reviewing your product may encounter. When you consider the expense of purchasing advertising space, and the value of a positive review, the expense of assigning a support person to this task is nominal.

If a prerelease version of your product is being evaluated, be sure to send a final release version of your product to your reviewer as soon as possible. If you get lucky, your reviewer may have enough time to update his or her evaluation before the publication's deadline.

5. *If a reviewer makes a mistake, discuss the problem with him or her before writing a letter to his or her editor.*

Most reviewers take a great deal of pride in their work and feel accountable for any errors that they make. A revised product review or a product "update" from the editor that reviewed your product is infinitely more valuable than having an irate letter to the editor published.

6. *Always thank editors and freelancers that work with you for their time.*
    Your paths may cross again. If your thanks are sincere, they will be appreciated. Don't take diligent work for granted!

7. *If everything goes well, celebrate!*
    It is a major marketing coup to get a good review in the best of circumstance.

MANAGING PRESS RELATIONS

Wagner-Edstrom, which handles Microsoft's press relations, understands how to influence its client's press coverage and has done an amazing job of helping Microsoft develop a quality image. I have learned three things working with Microsoft's PR machine:

1. Be as consistent as possible in how and what you communicate to the press.
2. Limit access of press contacts to individuals in your company who can articulate your marketing story clearly, concisely, and in a compelling way.
3. (The politician's secret.) Regardless of what question is asked, respond with an answer that you would like to see in print.

Press Relations	Responsible Manager at Client-Centered™ Training
Who is responsible for managing press relations?	Corporate Communications Manager
Who is your company spokesperson?	VP of Marketing
Who is responsible for generating press announcements?	Director of Marketing
Who is responsible for tracking press about your company?	Corporate Communications Manager
Who is responsible for coordinating speaking opportunities?	Corporate Communications Manager

Who is responsible for coordinating government relations?	Director of Marketing
Who is responsible for creating corporate communications materials?	Director of Marketing
Who is responsible for investor relations?	N/A

NAMING YOUR COMPANY AND YOUR PRODUCTS

The name of your company and of your company's product is used in virtually every customer communication. If these names are meaningful and memorable, they will leverage every communication in which they are used.

For example, if you name your company Seattle Computer Repair, your customers will know exactly where your company is located and what kind of service your company provides. But if you name your company Acme Enterprises, you will need to explain the type of products that you sell or services that you provide every time you tell someone the name of your business. And you will waste the opportunity to use your company's name to help you move business forward.

It is not always possible to think of or to use a meaningful name for your business. But the cost of promoting your company is directly related to the length of the communication that is needed to communicate its marketing story. Which is why so many companies that achieve total market domination employ company and product names that are meaningful and memorable to help them leverage their company's marketing resources.

Is "Microsoft" a good name for a software company? Do fleas bite?

Step 5: Evaluate the effectiveness of trade shows, newsletters, user groups, and electronic bulletin boards.

TRADE SHOWS

Prospects at trade shows are usually well qualified and prepared to hear your marketing story. Nevertheless, effective trade show participation requires careful planning and attention to detail to attract attendees to your booth and qualify their interest in your company's products.[2]

Your company may choose to participate in a trade show to:

- □ *Generate Sales Leads*—Most companies attend trade shows to develop new sales leads and secure new customers. Trade show attendees are prequalified—they would not be at a trade show if they did not have some interest in the products and services that were being showcased. And trade show leads are usually easier to close than leads from direct mail or advertising programs because they are better qualified.
- □ *Reach Decision-Makers*—Trade shows may provide the only opportunity to reach product specifiers and executive decision-makers who do not want to be contacted directly by your sales representatives. Direct one-on-one contact with decision-makers can create new sales opportunities and provides a forum for market feedback.
- □ *Expand into New Markets*—Trade shows can be a cost-effective way to make the contacts you need to expand your business into new markets. By exhibiting at trade shows in new geographic markets, you can establish distribution and sales before making a commitment to open new offices or hire additional personnel.
- □ *Enhance Reseller Relationships*—Trade shows provide an opportunity to meet with your distributors and resellers. Suppliers often share their trade show booth with their resellers, or turn over the sales leads that they have collected to their resellers for after-show follow-up.
- □ *Recruit Distributors and Resellers*—Trade shows are a great place to meet resellers that are seeking new business partners.
- □ *Recruit Personnel*—Companies at trade shows can meet prospective employees and can proactively recruit competitor's personnel.

---

[2] A Dun and Bradstreet study found that trade show attendees receive over 2,800 messages at a 200-booth trade show; that 60 percent of booths are forgotten within 27 hours; and that less than 2 percent of trade show leads result in sales.

- □ *Increase Brand Recognition*—Exhibiting at a trade show can help you increase awareness of your company's products and brand.
- □ *Introduce New Products*—Introducing products at national or international trade shows can help you promote your products and can help ensure that all of your business partners hear about your new products at the same time.
- □ *Facilitate Product Demonstration*—Exhibiting at a trade show provides an opportunity to display and demonstrate products that are too large to be taken on sales calls.
- □ *Develop Press Relations*—Trade shows provide a great opportunity to hold press conferences and schedule meetings with key press contacts. Press conferences at trade shows can provide smaller companies with a much higher level of visibility than traditional marketing activities such as mailing out press releases.
- □ *Develop Comarketing Opportunities*—Trade shows are good places to interact with decision-makers in your industry and to meet potential comarketing partners.
- □ *Gather Competitive Intelligence*—Trade shows often feature presentations on specific areas of interest to attendees and provide opportunities for exhibitors to hear their competitors discuss their new products' features and benefits.
- □ *Conduct Market Research*—Companies can "pre-test" new products and new marketing ideas at trade shows with industry analysts, resellers, and attendees.

TRADE SHOW SALES = ENERGY + PRESENTATION + QUALIFICATION + FOLLOW UP.[3]

---

[3] *Client-Centered™ Trade Show Selling* (Client-Centered™ Press) is a step-by-step guide to successful trade show participation. It can help you pick the trade show that is best suited to your company's needs, develop and execute an effective trade show plan, and use Client-Centered™ selling techniques to attain your company's trade show marketing objectives. This publication is available on the author's Web site at www.daytonassociates.com.

NEWSLETTER

A *newsletter* is an excellent vehicle for advertising your company's products and promoting a positive corporate image. Your company can use its newsletter to:

- Keep customers and prospects on your company's mailing list informed about new products and sales programs
- Motivate and recognize special accomplishments by your sales and support personnel
- Inform your customers about product updates and technical support issues
- Share creative ways to use your products
- Document newsworthy activities that your company is involved with
- Advertise charitable and community relations activities

USER GROUPS AND ELECTRONIC BULLETIN BOARDS

User groups and *electronic bulletin boards* are excellent forums to facilitate dialog between your company and your customers. A user group can help your company disseminate information about new products and services, and help your company identify and resolve outstanding support issues. A user group can also help your company create demand for its products by providing a networking opportunity for professional colleagues to share ideas and information.

Step 6: Evaluate your marketing department.

Your company can use the "Marketing Department Evaluation" worksheet to help it identify its marketing department's strengths and weaknesses.

Marketing Department Evaluation	Client-Centered™ Training's Marketing Department
Do you have clear objectives for every marketing program your company is funding?	Yes. Our VP of Marketing approves a Marketing Activity Worksheet before any new project is funded.
Do you have a process in place to track the effectiveness of each marketing program?	Yes. Our Director of Marketing is responsible for monitoring the outcome of each marketing project.
How do you measure the success of your marketing programs? For example: □ Number of leads generated □ Number of products sold □ Number of new customers □ Sales revenue generated □ Change in percent of sales □ Customer retention □ Other	We monitor our telemarketing program and our advertising promotion by the number of leads generated. We monitor our trade show investment by looking at the number of leads collected and the number of sales made to new customers as a direct result of trade show participation.
Do you use key results to monitor your marketing programs?	Our manager's incentive compensation is tied to specific marketing objectives such as improving profitability and winning a specific number of new customers during a sales period.
Does the name of your company help communicate what business your company is in?	Our name—Client-Centered™ Training—helps us communicate the business we are in and helps us position our company.
What is the name of your product or product line?	Client-Centered™ Sales Seminar Total Market Domination Critical Mass: The Impact of Emerging Technologies
Does this name(s) help your customer understand the value that your company or your product provides?	Our name communicates the focus we have on the customer in the selling process. The title of our presentation indicates the importance of emerging technologies for our clients' competitiveness.
Do you have brochures and other sales support materials that describe your organization's mission and strategic objectives?	Not current ones. But we are writing a white paper on the effectiveness of Client-Centered™ Training techniques.

Do you have brochures and other sales support materials that describe your organization's products and services?	Yes. We have brochures on our training programs and on our consulting services.
Do you have brochures and other sales support materials that describe your sales program?	Not specifically. Our sales representatives receive monthly bulletins that cover sales policies, upcoming events, and other sales information.
Do you have a Reseller Kit that includes all of the information that your sales representatives and/or resellers need to promote and sell your products?	No, but we plan to create one for our European distributor.
Do you have a Service Kit that includes all of the information that third-party service organizations need to service and support your products?	N/A
Do you provide marketing aids such as portable trade show booths, sales presentations, and promotional videos to your resellers?	Yes. We have a video presentation that includes commendations from customers and a brief explanation of how we develop custom training programs. We also have a portable 10' × 10' trade show booth that we loan to our marketing partners.
Do you have an advertising plan?	No. We periodically place space advertisements in industry trade publications. Our PR agency will be developing a plan for us next quarter.
Are your corporate communications handled by an outside agency?	We work with the Seattle Press Relations Company.
Do you have regular meetings with outside service organizations that support your:	☐ Marketing: No ☐ Advertising: Yes ☐ Press relations: Yes ☐ Corporate communications: Yes ☐ Fulfillment house: No ☐ Stockholder relations: N/A ☐ Other:
Who is responsible for your company's product packaging?	Our Vice President of Sales and Marketing and our Director of Marketing

Who is responsible for maintaining your corporate identity?	Our Director of Marketing
What components, such as your company's logo, do you consider to be important to maintaining your corporate identity?	Client-Centered™ Training, Client-Centered(Selling, corporate logo, tag line: "Today's Marketing Technology," and our style guide for our training materials.
Do you believe that your corporate identity and the image it presents to your market are consistent with your company's business objectives?	Yes.
Who is responsible for managing your identity?	Vice President of Sales and Marketing
Do you have a formal licensing program to support and maintain your corporate identity?	Not yet. We may offer a Client-Centered™ Training franchise next year for consultants who are interested in presenting our seminars.

The selling process takes place at every level of product distribution. So it is important to put promotional programs in place at every level of your company's distribution channel.

Sixth Law of Total Market Domination

Before you can influence your customers' purchase process, you must establish your credibility.

Social scientists have determined that there are four ways to establish credibility:

1. *Similarity*—You should appear to have the same values and background as your customers.
2. *Propriety*—You should wear proper attire and maintain a positive, professional attitude.
3. *Intent*—You should appear sincere, honest, and willing to help.

4. *Competence*—You should appear knowledgable and display effective communication skills.

Customers will rarely tell you if you have offended them. But they will demonstrate their "outrage" by selecting your competitors' products.

Marketing communications should avoid controversial issues such as politics and religion and any ideas or images that may be construed as inappropriate, obscene, or divisive.

INNOVATIVE MARKETING

Most companies base their promotional ideas on traditional marketing promotions, which "tell them what you are selling, how much it costs, and where to get it," and on matching or besting their competitors' claims. However, in some cases, it is necessary to use innovative marketing promotions that enable your company to deliver a strong message, which addresses a specific customer concern or a specific market segment.

Innovative marketing tactics are riskier to employ than traditional marketing strategies because they rely on promotions that may appeal only to a small segment of a market. However, innovative marketing techniques such as comarketing relationships and imaginative advertising campaigns, which rely on creativity, visibility, and memorability to create a preference for your company's products, are often the only way for smaller companies to introduce new products cost-effectively.

It is a mistake, however, to think that innovative marketing techniques are just for small companies. Microsoft, Nordstrom, and other companies that have achieved total market domination employ innovative marketing techniques such as free product promotions and tie-ins with their business partners all the time.

Examples of Innovative Marketing Techniques	Client-Centered™ Training's Use of Innovative Marketing Techniques
Distribute free copies of "limited" product to build interest in full product	Display first 3 lessons of our online sales training program on our Internet site—then encourage users to purchase and download the next 12 lessons
Bundle a product with a complementary product	Bundle our Client-Centered™ Presentation Skills training program with Acme's PC Projector (summer promotion)
Promote comarketing relationship and promotion	Include a 25% discount coupon for a Client-Centered™ Trade Show Selling seminar with every purchase of an Acme PC Projector
Special promotion	Stand outside of trade show and hand out coupons for a 25% discount on our Client-Centered™ Trade Show Selling seminar
Reciprocal promotion	Display Acme's PC Projector at our trade show booth in Dallas and display our DVD-based Client-Centered™ Presentation Skills program in their booth at the New Orleans show

PERSONAL NETWORKING

One of the hallmarks of companies that have achieved total market domination is the ability of their senior executives to network with their personal business contacts. Bill Gates, for example, often meets with the CEOs of other Fortune 100 companies. These meetings are an ideal opportunity to test new ideas and forge new business relationships.

AIRPLANE MARKETING

I probably should keep this under wraps, but I have met several of my best clients flying the friendly skies. Air travel, especially in cramped coach seats, isn't very much fun, so a spirited conversation with a kindred spirit is usually a welcome relief. And living in Seattle, I often sit next to sales and marketing executives from technology-driven companies who are interested in talking shop. Putting down my trade magazine for a few minutes to network with my seatmates has enabled me to generate over $100,000 in new business over the last two years.

The Bottom Line: Do you have effective programs in place to identify prospective customers?

Most companies that achieve total market domination use both *direct* prospecting methods, such as advertising, direct mail, telemarketing, cold calls, and trade shows, and *indirect* prospecting methods, such as referrals, barter arrangements, seminars, and networking with business contacts, to identify qualified prospects for their companies' products. And they use a *combination* of push and pull strategies to create demand for their products and support their channel partners.

To *evolve* a successful prospecting plan, your company must track the number of sales leads generated by your advertising campaign, and the amount of sales revenue that is generated from those leads.

Most companies base their promotional ideas on traditional marketing promotions, but companies that achieve total market domination often rely on innovative marketing promotions that enable them to deliver a strong message, which addresses a specific customer concern or a specific market segment.

In the next chapter, you will learn how to use territory and account plans to help you achieve total market domination.

CHAPTER 6

DO YOU HAVE EFFECTIVE PROGRAMS IN PLACE TO QUALIFY PROSPECTIVE CUSTOMERS?

Market inertia can develop as a successful company lets itself get out of touch with its customers, sales force, or distributors. . . . The main cause of market inertia is management's value rigidity, which leads managers to prize things the way they have been done over the way they must now be done.

—THOMAS V. BONOMA

I recently had dinner in San Francisco's Chinatown with my best friend from graduate school. My friend left a budding career as a molecular biologist to become a forensic psychiatrist and a renowned expert on "imposters." Impostors go through life convinced that they are someone else and make whatever assumptions about reality that they feel are necessary to support their delusion. As I listened to my friend describe the symptoms of this disorder, I realized that he might just as well have been talking about some of my clients!

Many of my clients are convinced that they can understand their market without doing market research, and that they can know what prospective customers are thinking about their products without asking them. Some of my clients have maintained this delusion for their entire professional career. But most of my clients eventually realize that they are locked in a separate reality, and that they must develop a Client-Centered™ approach to selling to help them qualify prospective customers' needs and concerns, move business forward, and achieve their sales objectives.

Step 1: Adopt a Client-Centered™ selling methodology.

Companies that achieve total market domination understand the value of adopting a Client-Centered™ selling methodology, which makes it easier for their sales team to communicate effectively and help their customers move through their purchase process.

Client-Centered™ selling is based on an intuitive, five-step selling process that begins with *prospecting* for new customers, using direct and indirect prospecting techniques. After a prospect is identified, its need, budget, buying authority, and time frame for making a purchase decision must be *qualified*. If a prospect is qualified, your company can *present* its marketing story to help your customer move its purchase process forward. It is important to *verify* that your prospective customer understands how and why your product is appropriate for its needs, and that it does not have any unanswered concerns, before you *ask for its business*.

It is important to *verify* that your prospective customer understands your communication at each step of the selling process, that your customer understands your proposed solution, and that your customer does not have any outstanding concerns that will postpone its purchase decision.

If you ask your customer for its business before you have addressed all of its purchase concerns, it may feel that you are more interested in making a sale than in helping it solve its problems. But if you make an honest effort to address your customer's purchase concerns, and you verify that you have supplied the information that your customer needs to make an informed purchase decision, your customer should be prepared for you to ask it for its business.

Client-Centered™ Selling Process[1]	Objectives
Prospecting (initial contact)	□ Attract prospect to company □ Display high personal energy □ Build confidence and trust □ Qualify reason for interest

---

[1] The Client Centered™ selling process described in the author's *Selling Microsoft: Sales Secrets from Inside the World's Most Successful Company* (Adams Media) can help your company develop a world class sales force. Information on *Selling Microsoft* is available on the author's Web site at www.daytonassociates.com

Qualification	□ Qualify need
	□ Qualify money
	□ Qualify authority
	□ Qualify time
	□ Complete contact form
Presentation	□ Arouse interest
	□ Provide new information
	□ Create preference
	□ Propose solution
Verification	□ Verify communication
	□ Develop follow-up action plan
	□ Verify solution
Ask for Business	□ Close sale
	□ Support customer's buying decision
	□ Value added selling

The ability to mentally put yourself in your customers' position is the most important step on the path to Client-Centered™ selling.

Step 2: Evaluate your sales team's qualification process.

After you identify potential customers for your products, you will need to *qualify* their need for your products and their level of interest in moving toward a purchase decision. The earlier in the selling process that you qualify your customers, the less time you will waste with unqualified prospects, and the more time you will be able to spend helping well-qualified prospects move through their purchase process.

The most direct way to qualify your customers' interest, is to ask them four basic questions:

1. Do you *need* our product?
2. Do you have *money* budgeted to purchase our product?
3. Do you have the *authority* to purchase our product?
4. When (*time*) do you plan on making a buying decision?

Although at first it seems easy enough to get straightforward answers to these questions, it is often very difficult to do so. For example, your prospective customers may suspect that they need your company's products, but they may not feel that they are informed enough to make a purchase decision, or they may be unsure about whether their personnel will be able to use them. In fact, most prospective customers cannot answer these "simple" questions until they begin to move through their purchase process.

Take responsibility for establishing your customers' need, money, authority, and time.

If you look around your office, you can see many items that are essential to run your business, such as your letterhead and your telephone. And you can identify many other items, such as fancy desk accessories, that were discretionary purchases. It is important to understand that at some point, you were convinced that you *needed* these items. In this sense, need is subjective, and salespeople can influence their customers' perception of need for their products.

Most companies create budgets to help them control their expenses. And the amount of each expense is based, to some extent, on the value that the company expects to gain from its expenditure. If a salesperson can demonstrate that their product provides a greater value than a company believed it would provide when it created its budget, the company may be willing to budget more money for its purchase.

Purchase authority to many salespeople means "decision-maker." But in many selling situations, many individuals influence a purchase decision. And in some selling situations, a salesperson may never meet the decision-maker behind his or her customer's purchase process. In these selling situations, the salesperson must work with customer contacts who act as gatekeepers and influencers to win the sale. Nonetheless, in every selling situation, it is important to identify the decision-maker's needs and concerns, so that the appropriate elements of the company's marketing story can be communicated and can influence his or her purchase decision.

Customers purchase products when they believe that the advantages of making a purchase decision outweigh the risks of delaying a purchase decision. If a selling process is not moving forward, it is usually because the salesperson has not helped his or her customer understand the value of his or her product. The greater the value that a customer believes a product has, the more urgency it will feel to make a purchase decision.

Seventh Law of Total Market Domination

*Virtually every problem selling situation can be
traced back to incorrect assumptions about a
customer's needs and concerns and a failure to verify
communications during the qualification process.*

The primary way that your company can influence
its customers' purchase process is by helping its customers understand the *value* of its products.

Typical Customer Objections	Possible Reason for Objection
We need to think about it.	I am not convinced your solution will work for us.
We need to discuss it.	I do not have enough information to make a buying decision.
We like our current supplier.	I don't see the advantage of doing business with you.
Your product is too expensive.	I am not convinced your product is worth the price.
We don't need it now.	You have not made me want your product.
You need to discuss this with someone else (purchasing, engineering, etc.).	You have not captured my interest.
We want to see other products.	I am not convinced this is the best solution.
My boss wouldn't authorize it.	I don't want to sell this for you.
I don't see how it could work.	I am afraid of change.

QUALIFICATION QUESTIONNAIRE

Qualifying your company's prospects with a qualification questionnaire or contact form will help your salespeople save time, and will
help them remember to ask all of the questions that they need to ask,
to qualify their customers' *need, money, authority,* and *time,* and to
update their sales contact database.

You can use the sample "Customer Qualification" form to help you design a form for your own business.

Sample Customer Qualification Form

Contact Information

Company: Acme Corporation

Contact: Linda Parks

Address: 123 Main, Bellevue, WA

Telephone: 555-5678

Qualification Questions

Do you have an outside sales force? Yes

How many salespeople do you have in the field? 42

Do you have inside sales representatives? Yes

How many inside salespeople do you have in each office? 3 in the East and 4 in the West

Do you have access to a high-speed digital Internet connection? Yes—our salespeople all have Internet mail accounts.

Do you have any sales support representatives? We have 28.

Do you use or plan to implement videoconferencing? Not at this time.

Do you support RealVideo? N/A

Do you use or plan to implement an Internet server? Yes, we have one for distributing product information to our customers. See www.acme.com.

Qualification Priority

No interest—no need / no money / Referred to: Heidi Chan

No interest—competitive system installed / satisfaction level: _____

Low interest—call back in ___ months / Send information: _____

Interested—invite to seminar on: _____

Very interested—schedule meeting on: February 5th

CUSTOMER CONTACT FORM

It is almost impossible to remember all of the qualification information that is communicated by prospects at seminars, trade shows, and other large meetings. The easiest way to manage this information is to record it on some type of contact form.

According to the Trade Show Marketing Association, using a simple qualification form increased Honeywell Corporation's trade show leads by over 50 percent.

Sample Trade Show Qualification Form

Priority of Lead: A/B/C/No Interest

Source of Lead: Seattle Trade Show

Date: December 11, 200X

Salesperson: Terry Smith   **Sales Assistant:**

Customer Contact: Kerry Jones

Title: Vice President of Sales   **Decision Maker:** Y N

Company: Good Way Industries

Address: 456 Northern Road

Phone: 555-7890   **Fax:** 555-7891

E-mail: Kerry@server.com

Contact Profile:

Customer/ Retail/ Distributor/ Manufacturer/ Professional

Government/Education/Nonprofit Organization

Product Interest: 2-day Client-Centered™ Sales Seminar

Time to Purchase: Next 60 Days

Need / Interest: Northwest Sales Department

Budget: $25,000

Action Required: Send sample video

Follow Up

- □ Send sample seminar agenda and presenter's video
- □ Schedule Sales Call: January 21st
- □ Best Time to Call: Wednesday or Thursday afternoon

Action Items

- ☑ Review account with trainer to discuss special requirements.
- ☑ Reserve a presentation room for the 21st.
- ☑ Confirm with client 5 days before meeting

In some selling situations, such as trade shows, companies provide a nominal gift or incentive to encourage prospective customers to take the time to complete a qualification form. However, in most selling situations, customers are eager to provide the information that a sales representative needs to help them solve their problems.

CUSTOMER REQUIREMENT ANALYSIS

The most effective way to prepare a customer requirement analysis is to ask lots of questions, to make as few assumptions as possible about your customers' needs and concerns, and to verify that you have not overlooked any factors that may affect your customers' business.

Using this Client-Centered™ approach will help your salespeople communicate concern, stay in sync with their customers' purchase process, and ensure that they understand the totality of their customers' problem before recommending a specific product or solution.

If your customer requirement analysis is detailed, your salespeople should review it with their customer before making any recommendations or proposing any solutions.

Step 3: Evaluate your product demonstrations.

The key to effective product demonstrations is to plan and practice the demonstration *before* meeting with your customers.

Before demonstrating your product to your customers, your sales representatives should be prepared to:

- □ Use every product feature
- □ Explain how every product feature works
- □ Map every product feature to one or more customer benefits
- □ Recover from common error conditions

Sample Demonstration Planner

Presenter / Salesperson: Terry Smith

Customer: Acme Corporation

Date: 9/23/97 **Time:** 9:45 AM

Location: Boardroom—234 Main St., Redmond, WA

Participants: Linda Harris, Tom Brown, and Peter Singer

Decision-Maker: Linda Harris

Objective for Demonstration: Demonstrate AX-600 Internet Server

Special Interests: Acme wants to see how they can implement a Commercial Internet Server for their Catalog Sales Division. Acme is also interested in seeing our database connectivity options.

Products/Equipment for Demonstration: Bring notebook PC with remote access software and Internet browser.

Equipment Checklist: Verify that our Web site is fully functional before performing demonstration.

Final Checkout/Run Through: Use the same procedure we used at Craft Publishing last week.

Support Materials and Personnel: Linda Baker will create a sample database of Acme Corporation's catalog items.

Special Preparations: None

Fall Back/Disaster Recovery: If our server goes down we can sign on to one of our customer's commercial Web servers. If our notebook PC isn't functional we can use one of Acme's PCs.

Solution/Benefits to Demonstrate: Prove advantage of Training Wizards to enable configuration. Show how easy it is to build HTML pages from Acme's existing product files. Show relative performance with 33.6 K modem and ISDN connection.

Follow-Up Action Plan: Ask for commitment to purchase our Server software. Schedule implementation planning meeting. Obtain permission to copy Acme's catalog database. Identify contact personnel.

If your salespeople take the time to record and analyze what happened during and after their product demonstrations, they will be able to improve their presentation techniques and rectify any mistakes that they have made. The "Demonstration Follow-Up" form is a good tool for helping your sales force refine its presentation techniques.

Sample Demonstration Follow-Up

Customer: Acme Corporation

Date: 9/23/97

Presenter/Salesman: Terry Smith

Demonstration Objectives: Acme wanted to see how they could implement a Commercial Internet Server for their Catalog Sales Division. Acme was also interested in seeing our database connectivity options.

Were Objectives Achieved? The demonstration went very well. Acme was excited about our database Wizard feature.

Outstanding or Unresolved Concerns: Acme is concerned that our server will not scale to support their database. Acme's database is about twice as large as Chrome Corporation (our largest installation).

Problems During the Demonstration: Our original connection was very slow, however everything worked well.

Follow-Up Action: Ask Chrome Corporation if we can use them as a reference. If necessary, agree to implement system subject to performance requirements.

Customer Commitment:

Expect Commitment in 10 ___ × / 30 ___ / 60 ___ days

Purchase Agreement Signed: September 18, 1999

What Can Be Done to Improve Next Demonstration? I would like to have at least one modem line dedicated to demonstrations to ensure maximum performance.

Step 4: Evaluate your sales proposals.

Sales proposals usually include a summary of your customers' needs or requirements; information about products and services that are being recommended; information about installation, implementation, and after-sale support; an analysis of why a specific solution is being recommended; and information on pricing, cost justification, customer training, and product delivery.

Companies that achieve total market domination usually create comprehensive sales proposals because they know that failing to include information that their customers need to make an informed purchase decision will delay their customers' purchase process. And when a customer's purchase decision is delayed, there is more opportunity for competitors to win that customer's business.

Most sales proposals are drafted in one of three styles:

- "We want to solve your problem."
- "We have the best product/service for your business."

□ "We can solve your problem as well as our competitors for less money."

Many companies use "boilerplate" proposal templates to help their sales team generate comprehensive proposals as quickly and easily as possible. But in any case, your company's proposals should include all of the information that your customers need to make informed purchase decisions.

The "Sales Proposal Format" can help your company develop an effective proposal format for its sales force.

Sample Sales Proposal Format

Executive Summary

Scope of Work (need)

Proposed Solution
- □ Summary of work and/or requirements planning to date

Explain Solution

Financial Benefits and Cost Justification
- □ Other benefits
- □ Potential risks

Product Specifications
- □ Detail features
- □ Specify benefits
- □ Product reviews / comparisons

Company Information
- □ Qualifications
- □ References

Terms of Sale
- □ Price
- □ Delivery
- □ Default penalties
- □ Additional requirements and/or supplies
- □ Third party work
- □ Deadlines for acceptance
- □ Guarantees and warranties
- □ Financial references

Follow-Up Action Plan
- □ Installation, implementation, and support issues
- □ Customer resource and training requirements

Purchase Agreement or Work Order

Step 5: Evaluate whether your company is prepared to sell to major accounts.

Major or "strategic" customers often account for a disproportionate amount of a company's profits, because the cost of marketing to a small number of major accounts is normally much less than the cost of marketing to a larger number of accounts that purchase the same amount of product.

This is why most companies that achieve total market domination put so much emphasis on developing compelling major-account marketing strategies that enable them to win this profitable business.

Major-Account Resources Evaluation	Client-Centered™ Training's Capabilities
Do you have sufficient cash reserves or cash flow from other business activities to finance a long selling cycle?	Yes—our selling cycle is typically three to six months.
Do you have the cash reserves or the credit line you need to finance large purchases?	No. We will need to finance a new high-speed color laser copier to create training materials in-house.
Can you increase production or stock products fast enough to satisfy the needs of major accounts?	Yes. Our turnaround time for training materials is 3 to 18 days. It may take longer for video reproduction, but never more than four weeks.
Can you provide a broad enough range of support services to service major accounts?	Yes. We provide all of the sales and marketing training services our customers need to support their business.
Can you provide competitive prices, volume discounts, financing, and other terms of sale to satisfy major accounts?	Our products are priced about 10 to 15% higher than our competitors', but we offer a superior product.
Do your sales personnel have enough time to meet with multiple sales contacts within a major-account's organization?	Our normal sales cycle includes meetings with both sales and marketing management, and with one or more other senior managers from other departments.
If not, do you plan to hire additional major-account sales and support personnel?	We believe we have the best sales personnel in the industry.
Do you have a reliable source of referrals or marketing partners that can introduce you into major accounts?	We solicit referrals from past customers and industry consultants. We also promote our business on the Internet

	and through both direct mail and telemarketing.
Do you have an efficient way to qualify major accounts?	We use a standard contact form to qualify prospective customers.
Do you have high-quality sales brochures and other presentation materials?	We have a very basic sales brochure. But we rely on our Internet Web site to disseminate corporate information to prospective customers. All of our customers have access to the Internet and to electronic mail.
Has your market research convinced you that marketing your products and services into major accounts is the best use of your selling time?	Absolutely. Major accounts provide more add-on business and have led to a greater number of referral opportunities than our smaller clients.
Does your company respond to customers' requests for business reciprocity?	Our policy is to do business with our customers whenever possible. In a few situations, we have exchanged our company's services for our customers' products.
Is your company prepared to support your customers' Supplier Performance Evaluation and Review (SPEAR) process?	We meet with our customers after every training seminar to verify that we have met our customers' needs and that our account manager understands what our company needs to do (follow-up, review sessions, etc.) to meet our customers' objectives.
Can your company support your customers' JIT inventory management process?	N/A
Can your company's order-processing system interface with your customers' purchasing system.	N/A
Does your company's information system support EDI?	N/A
Have you developed a business/marketing plan for your major-account business?	Not really. We need to provide the same information (tell the same story) to all of our prospective customers regardless of their size. This is probably not the best use of our sales and marketing resources. But it makes us feel like we are making our very best effort. And it is a formula that has worked well for us. We plan to put a customer council together next year that will help us understand our major customers' requirements and concerns.

Selling to major accounts can help your company achieve its marketing objectives if your company has the pre- and postsales resources that are necessary to provide the level of support that major accounts demand. The "Major-Account Resources Evaluation" worksheet can help your company evaluate its ability to compete for, win, and support major-account selling opportunities.

SUPPLY STRATEGIES

The widespread adoption of supplier performance evaluation and review (SPEAR) and just in time (JIT) inventory management has had a profound impact on industrial marketing. Sales representatives in these industries should be prepared to discuss supply strategies, statistical process control, and quality assurance with almost every buyer.

VENDOR ANALYSIS

Vendor analysis helps companies facilitate vendor selection by providing a quantitative assessment of supplier variables in relation to a specific product. For example, your customer might evaluate its suppliers on the basis of price, reliability of delivery (availability and on-time shipment), and product reliability (defect rate). Your customer might weight each of these factors to enable them to do a quantitative assessment of the service level (value) that each supplier delivers. Depending on an individual customer's concerns and priorities, the supplier with the lowest-cost product might or might not win a specific customer's business.[2]

In the "Purchase Factors" worksheet, Client-Centered™ Training has assigned different weightings to three of its key purchase factors: price, delivery time, and print quality. Three suppliers were evaluated on each one of these purchase factors. And supplier C, which did *not* offer the most aggressive pricing, won this business because of its low defect rate and fast delivery time.

---

[2] Enterprise Requirements Planning systems are often configured to track vendor service and to automate the vendor evaluation and selection process.

Purchase Factors for Printing Services	Supplier A	Supplier B	Supplier C
Price Weight = 50%	$100 = 8 40 points	$90 = 10 50 points	$95 = 9 45 points
Delivery Time Weight = 25%	95% = 9.5 23.8 points	70% = 7 17.5 points	85% = 8.5 21.125 points
Print Quality Weight = 25%	1% defect = 9 22.50 points	2% defect = 8 20 points	1% defect = 9 22.50 points
Service Level	86.3 points	87.5 points	88.63 points

Your company's sales representatives should be prepared to *qualify* each customer's vendor analysis strategy and to map your company's marketing story to each customer's specific needs and concerns.

Step 6: Evaluate whether team selling is an effective strategy for your company.

Team selling is often the best way for technology-driven companies to deliver the combination of marketing and technical skills that are needed to solve customers' problems and move business forward in the most cost effective way.

Potential Advantages of Team Selling	Client-Centered™ Training's Approach to Team Selling
Leverage corporate resources	We enlist our training manager to help our sales team close strategic accounts.
Higher customer service level	By teaming a program development manager with our account manager on each new account, we provide a greater degree of program customization.
Win more competitive sales	Our sales manager and our VP of Marketing help our sales representatives close strategic accounts.
Generate more revenue per customer	Our training manager contacts each account after their training seminar to solicit customer feedback and to suggest additional programs that may help the client's sales force work more effectively.

Generate higher revenue per sales call	Our account representatives are trained to explore how our training products and consulting services can help our customers improve many different areas of their business.
Shorter sales cycle, fewer sales calls	Our account representatives make between 3 and 4 sales calls before asking for their customers' business. We believe that this is the right amount of presales qualification in our selling situation.

Depending on the type of products and services that you are representing, and on your customers' technical background, it may be necessary to have one or more support personnel involved in the selling process. For example, at most technology-driven companies, sales support personnel are responsible for various selling activities, including technical presentations, customer support, contract support, and customer training.

Selling Activity	Sales Support Resource at Client-Centered™ Training
Prospecting	Big Ticket Telemarketing Company Sales assistants
Performing needs analysis	Sales assistants
Working on product configuration	Training Program Manager
Custom application development	Director of Product Development
Technical presentations	Director of Marketing
Product demonstrations	Sales assistants
Pricing analysis	Sales Manager
Contract and negotiation support	VP of Marketing, Attorney
Tracking orders and delivery	Administrative assistant
Customer support	Trainer
Customer training	Trainer
Scheduling resources	Administrative assistant

SALES PLANNING

After your company has created its sales plan, it can create territory, account, and sales call plans to help it achieve its business objectives.

Step 7: Evaluate your Territory Plans.

A territory plan is a subset of a sales plan. It defines the selling activities that will occur in a specific territory, and specifies how and when those activities will achieve specific sales objectives that have been defined in the company's sales plan.

Your company can use the "Territory Plan" worksheet to help it develop a prospecting plan and a marketing budget for each territory or different type of account that it is selling to.

Territory Plan for Client-Centered™ Training's Southern Region		
Territory or Type of Account **Revenue Contribution** **Account Manager**	**Prospecting Plan**	**Marketing Budget**
Wholesale Distributors $4,880,000 Bob Johnson	□ Direct mail and trade show marketing □ Web site □ Feature "Sales Secrets" seminar	□ Exhibit at Wholesale Distributors Convention—no charge for member's table □ $35,000 direct mail budget
Manufacturers $3,860,000 Paula Smith	□ Direct mail and industry forums □ Feature "IT Audit" seminar	□ $50,000 direct mail budget
Retailers $2,755,000 Linda Evans	□ Direct mail □ Feature "Trade Show Selling Program"	□ 5-city promotional tour in August □ $28,000 telemarketing budget □ $18,000 direct mail budget
Government Agencies $1,750,000 John Hague	□ Referrals from existing clients □ Focus on consulting and keynotes	□ $11,000 for annual government training conference
Service Companies $1,640,000 Donald Ellison	□ Direct mail and regional advertising □ Focus on "Selling Microsoft" seminar	□ $60,000 direct mail budget □ $18,000 sales seminar budget
Education $235,000 Mark Fine	□ Referrals from existing clients □ Multimedia "Client-Centered™ Selling" courseware	□ $15,000 Client-Centered™ Selling scholarship budget

Step 8: Evaluate your Account Plans.

An account plan defines your company's objectives for an account and describes how and when specific sales activities will occur. A key element of an account plan is an account analysis, which describes the history of the account and its current relationship with your company.

Account plans are a valuable tool to help your company's sales force achieve its objectives. But a 1997 study by PERFORMAX found that only 20 percent of sales professionals developed account plans for their top accounts!

Your company can tailor this "Account Analysis" form to meet your account manager's requirements.

Account Analysis Form

Account / Customer Name: Acme Corporation

Contact Information: Tom Brown

Date: 9/18/97

Sales Representative: Terry Smith

Prior Sales Representative: Linda Gray

Sales Manager: Don Richard

Customer Contacts:

Initiator: Sam Shadwick

Buyer: Sally Smith

Users: Peter Thomas, Judy Sellers

Technical Manager: Richard Jones

Other Advocate: Melinda Robertson

Gatekeeper: Marsha Johnson

Manager: Sue Norman

Decision-Maker: Ann Tanner

Outside Consultant: Peter Borrow

President / Principle: Bob Backer

Account History:

Type of Business: Component Manufacturer

Account Priority: A

Installed / Competitive Products: Acme purchased Big Time Sales video sales training program three years ago. They no longer use the program.

Special Deals: N/A

Buying Practices / Cycles: FY begins in January. All budgets must be approved by December 1

What? Purchase Department approves all Purchase Orders

When? POs are approved monthly

How Much? POs over $50,000 require executive-level review

How Often?

Past Problems: N/A

Reference Account: Yes No

If not a good reference, describe problem: N/A

Situation Analysis

Objectives for Account: Sell Client-Centered™ Consulting Services and 2-day Train the Trainer program

Account Potential / Percent of Quota: $25,000–$100,000

Product: 2-Day Train the Trainer program, consulting services

Percent of Business: 100%

Competition

Good Time Sales Seminars

High Profit Training, Inc.

Outstanding Sales Opportunities

☐ Client-Centered™ Consulting Services 2-day

☐ Train the Trainer Program

☐ Client-Centered™ Customer Support program for Acme's Telemarketing Department

Special Issues / Other Notes

☐ Customer will not commit until they preview the course.

☐ Be prepared to demonstrate online training and to discuss custom program development.

☐ In the past, Acme has outsourced all training programs.

Last Management Review

Date: July 15, 1995

By: The Boss

Taking the time to identify and describe all of the individuals who will influence your customers' purchase decision will enable you to better position key elements of your company's marketing story to each customer contact.

Customer (Sales Matrix) Contacts	Typical Job Title	Involvement in Sales Process
Initiator	President General Manager Line Manager	Recognizes need for product or service Often "champions" implementation
Decision-Maker	President VP of Operations Technical Manager	Approves purchase
Influencer	Technical Support Outside Consultant Mgr. Info. Systems CPA	Influence buying decision
Purchaser	Purchasing Manager Administrative Manager	Administers Purchasing Procedure
Gatekeeper	Administrative Asst. Corporate Purchasing Administrator	Controls contact with Influencer and Decision-Maker
Users	Personnel who use products or services Support personnel	Needs must be satisfied

Taking the time to construct a "Customer Contact" table will help your sales representatives get a top-down view of the "people" side of complex selling situations.

Customer Contact and Title	Role in Process	Primary Objective	Business Concerns	Personal Concerns
Bob Smith, VP Sales	Decision-Maker	Provide best sales training available to his team	Expertise of presenter, time needed to complete training, follow-up programs	Doesn't like VP Marketing—wants credit for sales success
Ana Main, VP Marketing	Technical Support	Enable her marketing people to understand their sales team's "point of view"	Time to complete program, concerned that her marketing managers may be unreceptive to new ideas	Worried about working overtime Loves golf
Loren Peters, Senior VP Sales and Marketing	Decision-Maker	Wants to have best sales team in his industry	Concerned about time away from customers	Wants all trainers to report to him
Tom Baker, Controller	Handle Contract	Will do whatever the VP of Sales wants	Ability to reproduce training materials	

Step 9: Evaluate your Account Review process.

It is important to review your company's strategic accounts periodically. In many companies, a sales manager facilitates the review process, and each salesperson describes his or her customer's account history and any outstanding service or support issues. The salesperson also describes the objectives for each one of his or her accounts, including new contract and revenue potential.

The account review process is a great way for salespeople to communicate the status of their accounts and for management to get a top-down picture of its entire team's sales activities. However, account reviews are not a good forum for sales coaching or for brainstorming about how to handle difficult selling situations.

To meet those needs, it is best to use a less formal meeting format that has a more tactical emphasis. In the Client-Centered™ sales process, we call these meetings account focus groups.

A sales manager usually facilitates their sales team's account focus groups; however, they can also be coordinated by a senior salesperson. The primary advantage of the account focus group format is the synergism that arises from working together in a relaxed setting, and from the account focus group's ability to look at each selling situation objectively.

If, for example, a salesperson is having difficulty communicating with one of his or her customers' technical managers, outside consultants, purchasing managers, lawyers, or decision-makers, he or she would have an opportunity to solicit feedback from the group on how to work more effectively with that individual. Similarly, if a salesperson is having difficulty overcoming a competitive challenge, the group could brainstorm about how the salesperson could demonstrate the value of his or her company's solution.

Account focus meetings are not always successful, but most of the time the group is able to help salespeople address their problems. And, perhaps most importantly, salespeople learn that they can rely on the experience and moral support of their managers and their peers when they need it.

Companies that achieve total market domination use sales meetings, strategic account reviews, and account focus groups to help identify and implement best Client-Centered™ sales practices throughout their sales organization.

THE VALUE OF TIME

An average sales representative spends from one-third to one-half of his or her time working directly with customers. So, if a sales representative is paid $50,000 per year, or $26.15 per hour, his or her compensation for selling to customers is actually equal to approximately $78.45 per hour.[3]

---

[3] *Selling Microsoft* includes a chapter on time management that describes a *time audit* process, which your sales representatives can use to help them identify time wasters and manage their time.

The Yearly Salary table illustrates why it is so important to maximize the amount of time that your company's sales force spends working directly with customers.

$ Yearly Salary[4]	$ Per Working Hour	$ Per Hour Selling
30,000	15.69	47.07
40,000	20.92	62.76
50,000	26.15	78.45
60,000	31.38	94.14
70,000	36.61	109.83
80,000	41.84	125.52
100,000	52.30	156.90

Determine how much time your salespeople spend working directly with customers.

Companies that achieve total market domination enable their sales force to spend as much time as possible working directly with their customers.

Example:

365 days per year

– 104 weekend days

– 9 holidays

– 6 sick days

– 7 vacation days

= **239 Working days per year**

24 days to attend meetings

+ 5 days to attend trade shows and seminars

+ 24 days to do paperwork

+ 60 days spent traveling and waiting

= **113 Overhead days per year**

Annual Days for "Direct" Client Selling =

239 Working days

– 113 Overhead days

= **126 Selling days**

---

[4] The "Yearly Salary" table assumes that a sales representative will work 239 days per year for 8 hours a day, which is equal to 1,912 hours of work per year. These figures do not include any costs for overhead.

Assume average # of sales calls per day =
5 sales calls per day

Number of sales calls per year =
126 Selling days × 5 Calls per day
= **630 Calls**

Assume average number of customers = 100
Annual Average Sales Coverage =
630 / 100
= **6.3 sales calls / per customer / per year**

Determine how much sales revenue is necessary to cover the direct cost of a sales representative.

Companies that achieve total market domination understand the opportunity cost of making sales calls, and leverage their sales representatives' time with lower-cost sales support personnel and sales automation systems.

Example:

Assume Annual Cost of Salesperson = $36,000 [annual compensation including salary, commission, and bonus]
+ $7,000 [benefits, including health insurance, FICA, UI, and pension]
+ $4,000 [training and travel expense]
+ $3,000 [automobile allowance]
= **$50,000**

Average cost of sales call = $50,000 / 630 sales calls per year
= **$79.37**

Assume that the average gross margin per sale = 28%.
Average sales volume to cover the cost of a sales call =
$79.37 / 28%
= **$283.46**

Average annual sales volume to cover direct sales costs of salesperson = $50,000 / 28%
= **$178,571**

These figures do not include any costs for overhead.
Overhead is usually equal to 65 to 145 % of the Labor Rate.

Step 10: Evaluate your Sales Call Plans.

In most cases, a salesperson's primary objective is getting a purchase commitment; however, in many cases, the primary objective is solving a technical problem, delivering marketing materials, soliciting referrals, exploring new business opportunities, or resolving some other issue.

Regardless of their reasons for making a sales call, salespeople have a much greater chance of meeting their objectives if they know exactly what they want to communicate and what they expect to accomplish, before leaving their office.

"Flight-Plan" for a Typical Sales Call

- ☐ Schedule appointment with customer
- ☐ Define objectives for sales call
- ☐ Prepare agenda/copy customer
- ☐ Pre–sales call meeting with support personnel
- ☐ Customer meeting
- ☐ Initial greeting (establish trust)
- ☐ Power statement (arouse interest)
- ☐ Initial benefit statement (demonstrate value of relationship)
- ☐ Review agenda with customer
- ☐ Qualify: need, money, authority, and time
- ☐ Identify and analyze client needs and goals
- ☐ Summarize client's problem
- ☐ *Verify communication*
- ☐ Present company, products, resources, and prior experience
- ☐ Discuss competition
- ☐ Propose solution
- ☐ *Verify communication*
- ☐ Overcome concerns and objections
- ☐ *Verify communication*
- ☐ Close sale
- ☐ *Verify terms/expectations*
- ☐ Value added selling opportunities
- ☐ *Verify customer satisfaction*
- ☐ Ask customer for referrals

Your company can use the sample Sales Call Plan as a template to create its own sales call plans.

Sample Sales Call Plan

Customer: Acme Corporation

Meeting Location: Acme's offices

Date/Time: September 18, 1997

Primary Objective: Introduce our new Internet-based Client-Centered™ Customer Service training module to support customer's Telemarketing Department

Secondary Objective: Meet Acme's new Telemarketing Manager

Special Action Items: Be prepared to demo our system online

Special Materials/Equipment: Bring notebook PC and 18" flat-screen monitor / bring hardcopy of our introductory lesson

Other Issues: Ralph Emerson loves donuts. Linda Hay is not deaf, but she is hearing impaired—speak up!

REVIEW YOUR SALES REPRESENTATIVES' SALES CALL REPORTS

In some selling situations, such as when a sales team is working with a major account, it is necessary to complete detailed sales call reports. For example, at Microsoft, our account managers completed sales call reports that specified what company they visited, who they saw, what was discussed, what actions were taken, and a list of follow-up action items that needed to be addressed before their next customer meeting.

However, in other selling situations, it may be sufficient to summarize what happened on sales calls over a period of a week or a month. This type of sales call report might contain, for example, the number of sales calls made, the number of demonstrations given, and the revenue generated from products sold, during the report period.

In any case, the process of completing a sales call report provides an opportunity to review the sales call, plan a strategy for the next customer contact, and communicate what happened on the call to the responsible manager.

Companies that achieve total market domination use their sales representatives' sales call reports to help them evaluate their sales representatives' performance and determine whether any additional marketing resources need to be targeted on specific selling opportunities.

Sales Call Summary Report for Week of August 10–14 Sales Representative: Bill Reynolds Territory: Manufacturing and Wholesale Distribution				
Company **Date** **Time** **Contact**	**Products and Issues Discussed**	**Requirement Analysis** **Special Problems**	**Follow-Up Action Items**	**Customer Commitment Delivery Scheduled**
Company A 5/10/96 11:00–12:00 Bill Jones	2-day Sales Seminar	Focus on qualification and closing skills	Send sample video Send copy of magazine review	Expect commitment within 15 days
Company B 5/10/96 2:30–5:30 Vela Richard	Marketing Evaluation Seminar	Expects seminar to be presented in two 3-hour blocks	Have VP of Sales contact Acme Co. for a referral	Expect signed agreement by Friday
Company C 5/11/96 9:00–1:00 Mr. Fisher	Custom Training Service	Needs a half-day program on developing budgets	Discuss schedule with our training manager	Evaluation process will take 60 days
Company D 5/11/96 2:00–6:00 Theresa Lee	"Total Market Domination" keynote	Heard keynote at Construction Industry Management Association conference	Refer customer to Web site for topics	Evaluation process will take at least 90 days

The Bottom Line: Do you have effective programs in place to qualify prospective customers?

Client-Centered™ Selling *is* selling "downhill." When your company implements a Client-Centered™ approach to selling, it will be able to qualify prospective customers effectively and will be able to leverage its marketing resources to build market momentum.

Salespeople have a much greater chance of meeting their objectives if they know exactly what they want to communicate and what they expect to accomplish, before leaving their office. This is why companies that achieve total market domination employ territory, account, and sales call plans to help them manage their selling process.

Companies that achieve total market domination often focus their marketing resources on major accounts and use team selling to deliver the combination of marketing and technical skills that are needed to move business forward cost-effectively. Implementing team selling and targeting major accounts can help your company achieve its marketing objectives if it has the resources to provide the pre- and postsales support that major accounts demand.

In the next chapter, you will learn how to recruit, motivate, and evaluate a world-class sales force that can influence your customers' purchase process by helping your customers understand the *value* of your company's products.

CHAPTER 7

IS YOUR SALES FORCE PREPARED TO REPRESENT YOUR COMPANY IN A PROFESSIONAL, CLIENT-CENTERED™ WAY?

Selling is communication.

—ANONYMOUS

Earlier this year I consulted with a multinational services company that asked me to help it work on a request for proposal that it had received from Microsoft. My client was interested in learning about Microsoft's culture and wanted to use this selling opportunity to help it identify best practices for its sales organization.

My client set up a special team to handle Microsoft's proposal and brought in two division-level presidents to provide perspective and oversight at our planning meeting. As in most companies, a few of the managers that I met with were defensive about exploring new selling techniques. But most of my client's managers, including both of its presidents, were enthusiastic about changing any facet of their selling process that would give their company a competitive advantage.

We spent a day together discussing how Microsoft works with its business partners, and thinking "out of the box" about how my client could leverage new technologies to help it re-engineer its selling process.

My client relies on its senior account managers to coordinate small teams of sales and product support people to move business forward. And senior managers are often brought into selling situations to overcome specific customer concerns and to develop high-level business relationships. This strategy, which has enabled my client to become the leader in its industry, is the same approach that Microsoft uses to manage its strategic selling opportunities.

After making a brief presentation on Microsoft's organization and culture, we explored various strategies that could improve my client's chance of winning Microsoft's business.

Microsoft, like most technology-driven companies, believes that its competitiveness is contingent on using new technologies to enable it to manage its costs and provide greater value to its customers. And Microsoft likes to partner with companies that share this philosophy.

I suggested that my client communicate how it was using new computer and communication technologies, such as smart cards, electronic messaging and its corporate Web site, to help it manage customer services, such as order entry, and control internal processes, such as inventory management.

We also explored a number of ways that my client could use its Web site to help it win Microsoft's business. For example, we discussed setting up a password-protected directory on its Web site to publish a vendor transition plan, which it had developed in response to Microsoft's RFP. Publishing on the Internet is a cost-effective way to communicate large volumes of information, and I felt this strategy would position my client as an early technology adopter.

My client asked me for specific suggestions about how it could make its "corporate overview" PowerPoint presentation, which it planned to present to Microsoft's vendor selection team, more effective.

Testimonials from high-profile customers can be extremely compelling. So I suggested that my client ask its regional sales managers to hire local video production companies to tape a few of its customers' testimonials to present with its PowerPoint presentation. I also suggested that my client publish its video testimonials on its corporate Web site.

Later in the day, we explored Microsoft's motivation for changing its current supplier. Qualifying this concern turned out to be my client's greatest challenge. Microsoft was obviously dissatisfied with its current supplier, but until my client understood

Microsoft's motivation for changing suppliers, it would not be able to map specific elements of its marketing story to Microsoft's purchase concerns.

For example, if Microsoft was primarily concerned about its current supplier's service level, cost might not be a major purchase factor. On the other hand, if Microsoft was concerned about reducing its costs for the services that its current supplier provided, proposing a lower-cost solution might be the only path for my client to win Microsoft's business.

Customers sometimes conceal their purchase concerns because they feel that disclosing their problems will put them at a disadvantage when they are ready to negotiate business terms with a new supplier. But my client could not hope to deliver a winning proposal until it qualified this concern. So I suggested that my client's VP of Sales participate in the next meeting with Microsoft to communicate the importance of Microsoft's business to my client, and if necessary, to help his team qualify Microsoft's motivation for seeking a new business partner.

Companies that achieve total market domination often rely on a team selling approach to help them leverage all of their selling resources when they compete for major accounts.

Step 1: Identify the key players in your sales and marketing organization.

The only way to develop a world-class company is to assemble a world-class sales team that has the vision, skills, motivation, energy, and courage to create and market innovative products. Learning how to identify top performers and how to motivate them to make their best effort is the key to building a successful sales organization and a successful business.

When Bill Gates was asked to describe the main precepts of how Microsoft manages its people, he replied, "We started using the very best practices, which was just hiring great people and having small teams."[1]

[1] Michael A. Cusumano and Richard W. Selby, *Microsoft Secrets,* (Free Press, 1995).

Client-Centered™ Training's Key Employees	Position	Salary	Shares, Options % Ownership
Doug Dayton	President	120,000	68
Terry Smith	Administration	68,000	5
Robert Nelson	Sales	142,000	8
Paula Chong	Development	92,000	4
Scott Crane	Operations	81,000	3
Sheila Perez	Consultants	63,000	2
Ron Howard	Western Sales Manager	117,000	-
Paula Richardson	Eastern Sales Manager	124,000	-
Sabrina Petra	Pre-Sales Support Manager	78,000	-
Other	Board of Directors	-	10

Eighth Law of Total Market Domination

Diversity drives creativity in an organization, and diversity can be the catalyst that enables a company to address new markets and new business opportunities.

One of the first observations that I made as a consultant was that my client's businesses reflected the values and priorities of its senior managers. This makes sense, because managers tend to hire people whom they are comfortable working with, and that translates into hiring people who share their beliefs and values. Unfortunately, this natural tendency to hire people who make us feel comfortable can lead to hiring people who are less experienced, talented, or motivated than ourselves. And in some cases it can cause us to overlook people because they are of the opposite sex, or they are a minority or a foreign national.

Most companies realize that hiring weak personnel is an obvious prescription for disaster, but it takes a tremendous amount of personal and professional confidence to hire people who hold different opinions and who are strong enough to influence their company's decision-making process.

Do your managers have the courage to hire people who are competent, confident, and brazen enough to argue them out of their mistaken notions? Or are your managers hiring people who are more interested in getting along than in engineering success?

Step 2: Describe your corporate culture.

Companies that achieve total market domination are able to attract the very best employees by providing a quality work environment.

Your company can use the "Corporate Culture" worksheet to help your company evaluate whether it provides a quality work environment for its employees.

Corporate Culture

Describe your corporate culture:

For example: chain of command, union shop, and small work teams.

We believe in as little "top-down" management as possible. We empower our employees to take the initiative and make decisions. We recruit experienced professionals and expect them to be proactive about doing whatever is necessary to achieve their objectives. We expect our employees to take pride in their work.

Subcontractors do a great deal of our development work; we rely heavily on electronic mail to support our telecommuters.

We don't wear suits, except on customer calls, and we try to maintain an informal "collegial" atmosphere.

How do your employees perceive your company?

An employee survey indicated that our employees are "extremely" satisfied with their working conditions, that they feel our compensation plans are equal to or above average for their jobs, and that 90 percent of our employees feel "very good" or "excellent" about working with their immediate manager.

Several of our employees have indicated that they would like our company to be more supportive of childcare.

It can be helpful to have your company's sales representatives and their managers complete the Sales/Marketing Department Evaluation worksheet to identify any differences between their perceptions of their department.

Client-Centered™ Training's Sales/ Marketing Department Evaluation	1 (don't agree) to 5 (strongly agree)
Successful	3
Stable	4
Conservative	3
Formal	1
Organized	4
Autocratic	1
Aggressive	4
Creative	4
Opportunistic	3
Service oriented	5
Highly automated	2
Efficient	2
Bureaucratic	1
Other	-

Step 3: Review your company's personnel policies.

It is important to maintain an open channel of communication between your sales team and upper management, and to support your sales team with periodic performance and compensation reviews, competitive employee benefits, and recognition. If you don't treat your sales team well, you may wind up competing against them—when they leave your company to work for one of its competitors.

Evaluate Personnel Policies	Client-Centered™ Training's Personnel Policies
Number of employees	38 (including contractors)
How many employees have left your company in the last year?	2

Do you periodically review your employees' performance?	Yes
What do you cover in employee reviews?	Objectives, key results, overall performance, and compensation
Do you keep signed employee reviews and/or evaluations on file?	Yes
Do you feel your company is a fair, good, or great place to work?	Great
Do you publish an Employee/Company Policy Manual?	We have an employee manual that was created using a PC-based HR program. We plan to have our lawyer review and update our Employee Policy manual next year.

Reminder: As you complete each worksheet, take time to identify any attitudes, practices, or procedures that may impact your ability to align your sales and marketing systems with your company's primary business objectives.

Step 4: Review your organization chart to identify teams that may be restructured or automated to improve productivity.

An organization chart can help you visualize reporting relationships and can help you evaluate how and where information systems can be implemented in your company to support its selling process.

Figure 7.1
Client-Centered™ Training Organization Chart

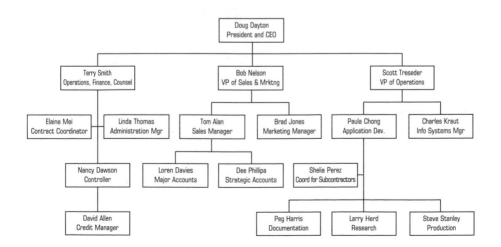

When you review your organization chart, try to detach yourself from the individuals who are involved, and focus on the responsibilities that have been assigned and the tasks that each position is responsible for.

For example, at Client-Centered™ Training, Elaine Mei reports to Terry Smith. But Elaine works with outside contractors that are developing new products. So it makes more sense for Elaine to report to Paula Chong.

Map your sales representatives' skills to specific business opportunities.

Matching salespeople with specific skills and interests to different types of selling situations can help you leverage your sales team's performance. Most companies assign their salespeople to specific accounts on the basis of geographical territories; however it is often more effective to assign accounts on the basis of other factors. Some salespeople, for example, work best with existing accounts, while other salespeople excel at demand creation and closing new business.

You can use the "Account/Territory" table to help you map individual sales representative's strengths and interests (assignment factors) to specific selling opportunities in your company.

Account / Territory	Assignment Factor
Geographical Region	□ Country (language skills, previous experience) □ State/City (travel) □ Zip or area code (inside or outside selling)
Major Accounts	□ Purchase volume (compensation program) □ Multiple locations (overnight travel) □ Centralized purchasing (one-on-one relationship skills)
Strategic Accounts	□ Joint marketing (delegation skills) □ Joint product development (project management skills) □ Perception of supplier (previous experience with supplier)
Product Focus	□ Specific product family (product knowledge)

	□ Specific technology (technical skills)
	□ Specific purchaser within customer's company (compatibility, personal selling skills)
Type of Contact	□ Telemarketing (telephone selling skills)
	□ Urban/Rural (personal selling style)
	□ Personal relationship (conflict of interest)
	□ Formal procurement (previous corporate or military experience)

THE COST OF REPLACING A SALES REPRESENTATIVE

The cost to your company to replace a sales representative can be staggering. In many cases, sales representatives leave unexpectedly, without providing any opportunity to transition ongoing sales opportunities. And your company may spend weeks or months searching for a top performer to handle its open territory.

Personnel agencies or "headhunters" typically charge $12,000 to $25,000 to help their clients recruit a senior-level sales representative. But this fee is just the tip of the iceberg. Your company can also lose from 50 to 100 percent of its open territory's annual sales quota!

You can estimate the opportunity cost of replacing your sales representative by estimating the percent of quota that your new sales representative will generate during their first few quarters on the job. In most selling situations, new sales representatives do not generate any business during their first quarter and between 10 and 50 percent of their sales quota during their next two quarters.

For example, if your new sales representative makes no sales during their first quarter, sells 40 percent of quota their second quarter, 60 percent of quota their third quarter, and 100 percent of quota their fourth quarter, your company's shortfall will be equal to 50 percent of the open territory's yearly quota. If the open territory has a sales quota of $1 million, and your company earns a gross profit of 50 percent on its sales, replacing your sales representative will cost your company $250,000 in lost profits.

There is no way to avoid all of the costs of replacing a sales representative, but investing in a sales automation system can enable your company to *reduce* these costs by managing the information that a new sales representative needs to move active selling opportunities forward. You will read more about sales automation in the next chapter.

Excessive employee turnover is a warning signal.

Excessive employee turnover is an important warning signal. If your company is experiencing excessive turnover, you will need to determine exactly why this is happening.

- Do your employees feel that your company is a good place to work?
- Do your employees feel that their compensation plan is fair?
- Do your employees enjoy working with their managers?
- Are your employees concerned about the viability of your business?
- Do your employees feel that your company provides a good career path?
- Why did each employee who left your company over the last year do so?
- Has a recent change, such as reorganizing sales territories or hiring a new manager, caused bad will?

Step 5: Identify how and where your sales managers are spending their time.

Sales managers have four sales management duties: training, coaching, motivating and evaluating.

TRAINING—HELP SALESPEOPLE IMPROVE SELLING SKILLS

Sales managers must provide their sales team with all of the information that it needs to represent its company's products or services in a professional Client-Centered™ way. Not every sales manager is a great teacher. Nevertheless, your sales manager must ensure that every sales representative on his or her team has the knowledge that is required to succeed on the job.

COACHING—HELP SALESPEOPLE OVERCOME PROBLEMS

Coaching means monitoring each sales representative to improve their Client-Centered™ selling skills. Many managers rely on weekly sales reports and monthly or quarterly commitment calendars to help them track the performance of their staff. These tools are invaluable with less experienced or geographically dispersed field representatives.

MOTIVATING—PROVIDE INCENTIVES FOR REACHING SALES GOALS

Sales motivation means ensuring that each sales representative is professionally and personally committed to making their best selling effort for themselves and their company. The key to motivation is to maintain a positive, supportive attitude toward your staff. If you follow the Golden Rule, and remain straight, honest, and fair, your staff will reward you with loyalty and their best selling efforts. Compensation plans that do not motivate performance, unrealistic or unreachable quotas, and other negative sales incentives should be banished!

Each year IBM sends each Marketing Representative who exceeds his or her sales quota on a special sales trip. IBM's 100 Percent Club is not very exclusive. Senior management reassigns quotas to ensure that the vast majority of its sales representatives make quota each year. The reason IBM's managers play games with quotas is simple; they would rather have 80 percent (or more) of their sales staff feel like winners, than have the majority of their sales force feel that they were less than "Club" members. "Winners" generate positive energy. And positive energy leads to greater selling enthusiasm and more selling success.

IBM has created a special "Eagle" club to recognize the top one percent or so of its sales representatives. This achievement is exclusive enough so that most of IBM's salespeople don't feel too bad if they fail to achieve this honor. And of course, for IBM's elite "Eagles," this honor is the ultimate recognition.

IBM has engineered a wonderful formula for sales motivation. And they haven't changed it for decades, because it keeps working.

EVALUATING—DEFINE GOALS AND MEASURE RESULTS

One of a sales manager's most challenging jobs is evaluating the performance of his or her staff. Many sales managers are reluctant to provide feedback to their sales representatives. But if a sales manager does not give his or her sales representatives feedback, they will not know how to improve their selling skills.

EVAN'S STUDY

In the early 1970s Rodney E. Evans conducted a study, which has been updated several times over the years, on how sales managers spend their time. Evans found that most companies can improve the productivity of their sales team by freeing up their sales managers' time to enable them to focus their effort on improving their sales teams' performance and meeting with strategic customers.

Figure 7-2.
How Sales Managers Spend Their Time

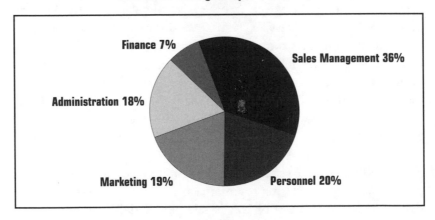

Sales Manager's Tasks	Client-Centered™ Training Sales Manager's Time	Sales Manager's Objectives
Sales Management	Two days each week	Spend three days each week working in the field with our sales team.
Marketing	Two days each week	Work with an outside marketing consultant to free up time to work with sales team.
Administration	Two hours each day	Create a spreadsheet template for our sales team's weekly sales reports to make it easier to generate a monthly sales forecast.
Personnel	Three hours per week	Work with HR department to create a more efficient salary review process.
Finance/Reports	Three days each month	Reduce reporting time to two days per month.

Companies that achieve total market domination empower their sales managers to work closely with their sales team and to spend as much time as possible with customers.

Step 6: Define your sales manager's objectives and key results.

Every sales representative and every manager in your company should complete an objectives worksheet. This worksheet can be a formal document that sets parameters for revenue performance and other objectives that are used to determine its employee's compensation.

The sample "Objectives" worksheet reflects the objectives for Client-Centered™ Training's Sales Manager.

Your company can use this worksheet to evaluate whether the objectives of its senior sales and marketing managers are in sync.

Objectives	Client-Centered™ Training's Sales Manager
Profit	Increase profit margins by 3%
	Increase profits on sales by 20%
Markets	Review territories in Southeast region
	Begin search for representative in Asia
Products or Services	Launch Client-Centered™ Trade Show Selling seminar
	Complete production of new Client-Centered™ Selling training guide
Production	Coordinate sales forecast with production department to help reduce production delays on seminar study guides
Sales/Distribution	Finalize contract with multimedia production firm
	Review telemarketing scripts
Training/Support	Invite all representatives to Client-Centered™ Time Management Seminar
	Have all sales personnel trained on new contact management program
Research and Development	Send new product requests and service/product concerns to Research and Development Manager
Financial (IPO etc.)	Enforce credit-checking policy
	Require management sign-off on all seminar orders taken without 50% prepayment
New Businesses Other	Evaluate sales potential of Dayton Associates training materials
	Submit findings at Managers' meeting

Step 7: Adopt a specific selling methodology.

Sales managers can improve their effectiveness by mastering a selling technology, such as Client-Centered™ Selling, and then introducing it to their sales force. Building on a common framework of selling skills makes it easier for a sales team to communicate more effectively and to work together to resolve problems and move business forward.

The Client-Centered™ Selling process is described in detail in *Selling Microsoft: Sales Secrets from Inside the World's Most Successful Company.*

The ability to mentally put yourself in your customers' position is the most important step on the path to Client-Centered™ Selling.

Step 8: Evaluate your sales training programs.

Developing your company's sales personnel's selling skills is the key to maximizing its sales team's selling efforts.

Sales Training	Client-Centered™ Training In-house Sales Training
Who is responsible for training your sales force?	Our VP of Sales is responsible for managing our sales force. Our VP of Sales approves all training programs.
Has your company adopted any formal training methodology?	Yes, we have adopted Client-Centered™ Selling.
Do you use an outside training company for any of your programs?	Yes, we have a contract with Dayton Associates to deliver Client-Centered™ training programs.
Do you have regularly scheduled sales training programs?	We schedule sales training programs on a quarterly basis. At each program, we attempt to focus on a specific selling skill, such as qualification skills or time management.
How do you train new sales personnel?	We bring them up to speed on Client-Centered™ selling skills, and then partner them with a senior salesperson who acts as a mentor for their first six months on the job.
Do you provide product training?	Yes, our product managers meet periodically with our sales team to introduce new products and review product features and benefits. We encourage our salespeople to sit in on all of our courses as soon as possible to become familiar with their content.
Do you provide training on competitive products and industry trends?	Our product managers develop and distribute comparative product reports for our sales team. Our sales representatives have prepaid subscriptions to industry reports and periodicals that provide up-to-date information about our industry. We have hired industry analysts to make presentations to our sales group on competitive products and emerging market trends.
Do you provide training on internal policies and procedures?	Our VP of Human Resources schedules a monthly meeting to review general company policies for all new hires. We also publish a comprehensive employee handbook. Our VP of Operations delivers a one-hour presentation each quarter to review internal policies that relate to production, support, scheduling, and other areas of operations.

Do you provide computer-training classes?	Our IS Manager schedules classes on Microsoft Windows, Microsoft Office, and our Sales Force Automation system each month.
	Review classes and one-on-one help is available on an as-needed basis.
Do you solicit input from your sales team before implementing new training programs?	All new hires receive a PC Workbook that explains lead tracking, order entry, scheduling and other essential computer tasks.
	We haven't in the past, but we plan on distributing a questionnaire to our sales force next month to determine what new programs to bring in-house.

Step 9: Evaluate the systems that you have in place for goal setting, motivation, and personnel appraisals.

Your company's planning and reporting systems provide the "infrastructure" for effective decision making.

The "Personnel Issues" worksheet can help your company evaluate the systems that it has implemented to support and evaluate its selling process and to help it retain its top performers.

Personnel Issues	Status
Do you set goals for your employees?	Yes—on a quarterly basis.
Frequency of one-on-one meetings	Managers meet with direct reports every week.
Frequency of departmental meetings	We meet every two weeks.
Frequency of company meetings	We meet once every four to six months.
Do you have appropriate nondisclosure, confidentiality, and noncompete agreements on file?	No, but legal is working on this.
Do you have key manager insurance policies in place?	Only for our CEO.
Do you have written job descriptions?	Yes.
Do you have adequate incentives in place for key personnel? Are these reviewed periodically?	We are having a consultant review our compensation plan for hourly employees.
Are your employee benefits competitive within your market segment?	Yes—we provide full medical coverage for employee's family.

Do you maintain a personnel handbook that details company policies and employee benefits?	Yes, but it needs to be revised.
Is your company unionized?	No.
Do you encourage employee participation through newsletters, staff meetings, after-hours social activities, or other activities?	We have a corporate newsletter, but it is targeted at customers. We have a TGIF party once a month at a local restaurant.
Do you have company meetings and outings to help increase employee goodwill?	We have a company softball tournament each summer. We tried basketball but we had too many injuries!
Do you have an employee suggestion box? Do you provide incentives for suggestions that lead to reducing costs, improving products, or new marketing opportunities?	We don't have a suggestion box—but everyone has the President's e-mail address. We occasionally award bonuses for work that is above and beyond the call of duty.
Would you rate employee morale as poor, good, or excellent?	Morale is very good.
Are any personnel in your company "irreplaceable"? List irreplaceable personnel	We are a small company—losing any of our senior managers would be a setback.
Do you have a succession plan for these personnel?	We have department managers in Sales, Finance, and Development who could be promoted. Our Operations Department is weak.
Do you have a Board of Directors? If so, how often does it meet? Include resumes for your Directors	Yes—it meets biannually. To be attached.
What additional expertise would be helpful on your board?	We would like an IT expert on our board to help us evaluate emerging technologies and to help us focus our IT strategy.
Does your company currently employ any Human Resources consultants or advisors?	We have retained outside counsel to review our employment policies. We also work with a company that puts together incentive programs to help us motivate our sales team.

Step 10. Evaluate your sales recruiting process.

There are over 9 million salespeople in the United States and about 35 million more salespeople in the industrialized world. Finding the right salesperson to represent your company's products requires careful planning and thoughtful execution.

The first step in the recruiting process is to define a job requirements checklist that reflects your "ideal" candidate's previous work experience, educational background, technical skills, personality type, and management potential.

Jobs Requirements Checklist
Educational Background
☐ High School
☐ College/Graduate School
☐ Technical/Trade School
☐ Professional Certification/Training
☐ Sales Training
Work Experience
☐ Sales Experience
☐ Sales Support Experience
☐ Outside Sales
☐ Commission Sales
☐ Remote Territory Sales
☐ Route Sales
☐ Major Account Sales
☐ International Sales
☐ Joint-Marketing Sales
Specific Industry Experience
☐ Direct Competitive Sales Experience
☐ Knowledge of Customer Base
☐ Knowledge of Territory
☐ Existing Customer Relationships
Product Knowledge/Presentation Skills
☐ Verbal Skills
☐ Writing Ability
☐ Telemarketing Skills

□ Cold Call Skills

□ Foreign Languages Skills (Oral/Written)

□ General Product Knowledge

□ Technical Skills

□ Analytic Skills

□ Organizational Skills

□ Office Skills

□ Computer Skills

Management Skills

□ Sales Management Experience

□ Product Marketing Experience

□ Other Management Experience

□ Previous P&L Responsibility

Personal Traits

□ Honesty

□ Loyalty

□ Work Ethic

□ Persistence

□ Confidence

□ Intelligence

□ Creativity

□ Problem-Solving Abilities

□ Empathy/Listening Skills

□ Professional Appearance

Other Qualifications

□ Desire to Travel

□ Conversational Skills

□ Relevant Hobbies (Example: Golf)

□ Other

After you have completed your job requirements checklist, you can create a success factor matrix, which will help you determine whether different job candidates are well suited to your specific selling situation.

Success Factor Matrix	Candidate's Profile
Company Size/Culture	□ Likes informal environment
	□ Enjoys support and structure of large company
Products	□ Likes simple product story
	□ Challenged by complex technical information
Customer Mix	□ Enjoys "personal" side of selling smaller companies
	□ Enjoys complexities of major account selling
Sales Cycle	□ Needs frequent sales
	□ Enjoys landing large orders
Compensation	□ Security oriented
	□ Motivated by commission
Potential for Advancement	□ Wants management experience
	□ Career salesperson
Level of Supervision	□ Needs supervision
	□ Likes to work alone
Personal Needs	□ People oriented
	□ Task oriented

After your have completed your success factor matrix, you can develop a job description for your open position, which you can use to help you recruit and screen potential job candidates.

Sample Job Description: Major Account Sales Manager

Position Overview

Client-Centered™ Training provides a unique opportunity for a sales manager who enjoys selling professional education products to technology-driven companies.

The Major Accounts Sales Manager's primary responsibility is to develop and manage our company's strategic customer relationships.

The Major Accounts Sales Manager's responsibilities include:

□ Track and report lead generation and sales activity

□ Develop new strategies for reaching and penetrating major accounts

□ Develop sales programs to meet individual customer needs

□ Coordinate account reviews with strategic customers

□ Participate in marketing and product development activities to provide information on customer requirements and cost targets

The position reports to the Vice President of Sales and Marketing. Compensation depends on previous experience.

Application Requirements

Experience and a record of advancement in professional education sales or a similar environment; a proven ability to interact with and influence senior-level business executives; a proven ability to lead and motivate a team of professional salespeople; and a fundamental understanding and appreciation of professional sales training.

The Company

Client-Centered™ Training provides sales seminars and consulting services based on the Client-Centered™ Selling process developed by Doug Dayton.

During the previous six years, Client-Centered™ Training's annual growth rate has exceeded 20 percent. The company has been in business for twelve years, is profitable, and has no debt.

The most attractive aspect of Client-Centered™ Training is its culture. The company's leaders are positive, progressive, and forward looking; the environment is creative; and the company's information technology systems are sophisticated and well maintained.

There are no venture capital investors waiting to clean house if the quarterly numbers slip. The company is working toward a long-term vision of bringing the Client-Centered™ approach to selling to leading technology-oriented companies throughout North America.

Responsibilities

☐ Planning—Develop and define a major account sales plan. Develop new customers and product concepts.

☐ Account Development—Define and pursue opportunities for new training opportunities with current customers.

☐ Documentation—Implement and administer a comprehensive customer- and lead-management database. Maintain records of all mailings, meetings, presentations, and proposals.

☐ Seminar Development—Work with program designers to develop objectives, schedules, and milestones for prototype projects. Define a "seminar review" process.

☐ Policies and Procedures—Communicate delivery expectations internally. Simplify tasks and approval process to accelerate the sales cycle.

☐ Leadership—Improve Client-Centered™ Training's industry profile and reputation for innovation and service. Serve as a role model for professional conduct at all times. Communicate persuasively and positively.

☐ Management Style—Client-Centered™ Training is a team-based company. This implies a coaching rather than a directive leadership style. Flexibility and adaptability are important attributes. Successful candidates must be willing to "roll up their sleeves" to help the company achieve its objectives.

☐ Personal Qualities—Client-Centered™ Training demands a high energy level and a commitment to hard work. We are looking for an honest, sincere, motivated individual who is a team player and a good listener. Along with these qualities, we are looking for an individual who is motivated by results, has a positive attitude toward customers, and is absolutely committed to being successful in this position.

Performance Indicators (Objectives)

☐ Revenue Generation—Meet quarterly revenue objectives.

☐ Profits—Maintain an average gross margin of 50 percent or greater on all projects.

☐ Customer Meetings—Meet with all active customers on a quarterly basis. Schedule at least two President/CEO meetings each month.

☐ Trade Shows—Attend five major trade shows each year. Schedule at least two regional sales presentations each quarter.

☐ Mailings—Maintain written communication with current customers and active leads. No less than one mailing every three months to all active leads.

☐ Management Priorities—Schedule at least 50 percent of time in field to work with sales team.

☐ Proposals—Develop a minimum of ten written proposals per quarter.

☐ Recruit and Train Sales Personnel—Recruit and train personnel to support the growth of the major account sales team.

☐ Systems—All systems must be routinely backed up and upgraded in a timely fashion. All meetings and customer communications must be documented. All customer and prospect databases must be maintained and secured.

☐ Service—Return customers' phone calls within four hours. Prepare customer mailings on the day requested. Accept "personal responsibility" for profits and customer satisfaction while providing an exceptional level of customer service.

☐ Personal Growth—Develop and implement a plan to ensure professional skills development, awareness of advances in computers and communications, and proficiency in a foreign language (optional).

APTITUDE, EXPERIENCE, AND MOTIVATION

To determine whether a job candidate has the requisite skills to communicate your company's marketing story effectively and to stay in sync with your customer's purchase process, you must test his or her communication skills, problem solving skills, and product and industry knowledge.

The best way to evaluate these capabilities is to observe a candidate making sales calls. Unfortunately, it is rarely possible to do this during the hiring process. In most situations the only practical way to evaluate a candidate's selling skills is to observe them "selling" themselves during their interview. This is why it is important to structure sales interview questions in a way that enables each candidate to demonstrate his or her selling skills.

SALES QUALIFICATION QUESTIONS

You can use these sales qualification questions to help you evaluate an individual's sales potential.

Sales Qualification Questions	
Describe your last three sales jobs.	IBM—worked as a sales representative in the General Systems Division—sold systems to distributors and manufacturers.
	Microsoft—managed sales and contract support group in Microsoft's OEM Division—sold software to PC manufacturers.
	Corporate Training Associates—provided sales and marketing consulting services to technology-driven companies—executive-level training sales.
What did you do during a typical day on your last sales job?	Met with senior-level sales and marketing personnel. Performed sales audits and provided marketing consulting services.
Describe the products that you used to sell.	Sold sales audits, sales training seminars, and marketing consulting services.
Describe your sales cycle.	Existing clients normally referred prospective customers to his company.
	First step: Had an initial meeting with client to discuss its requirements and to sell a one- to two-day "strategic planning" session.
	Second step: At the strategic planning session, worked with client to identify specific issues that needed to be addressed and to develop an "action plan." Then, depending on a client's specific requirements, he would schedule additional consulting or training services.
Describe your customer base.	About 80% of clients were technology-driven companies in the computer industry. Other customers were product or component suppliers (manufacturers and resellers) and government agencies.
How many customers did you service?	Worked with three to five clients at a time. Customer base included over fifty clients, but most of these were inactive. Customer base is company confidential to Corporate Training Associates. Seems honest about maintaining this confidentiality.

What percentage of your time did you spend cold calling?	Less than 5%. Attended business conferences and trade shows and presented talks to business groups.
What percentage of your time did you spend telemarketing?	None.
Were you involved with team selling?	Yes. Often brought a product development specialist, a senior sales manager, CEO, or in rare instances, a support engineer on sales calls.
Did you work with a technical support team?	Yes. Product development specialists worked with customers to develop custom programs, and technical support engineers worked with customers on sales force automation projects.
Who did you report to?	VP Sales and Marketing.
Did you have any direct reports?	Yes—an inside sales assistant.
What was the dollar value of an average sale?	$40,000.
What was your annual sales quota at your last job?	$650,000.
What percentage of your salary was directly tied to commissions or to quota attainment?	60%
How much money did you make on your last job?	$135,000, including commission and bonus.
Role-play a customer meeting based on products you represented in your last job. *(This is often the most revealing component of the interview process.)*	Candidate displayed a deep understanding of Client-Centered™ presentation and communication skills. Candidate was a good listener, verified all communications, summarized concerns before making a recommendation, and asked for my business with a simple closing question.
What did you like about your last job?	Liked the people at Corporate Training Associates very much. Manager was very supportive, and the company delivered exactly what it promised to its customers. Represented a quality product.
Why do you think that working here will be a better opportunity for you?	Client-Centered™ Training has a broader product line than Corporate Training Associates. The company is larger and has the resources to use new technologies, such as the Internet, throughout the company.
	Is confident that he will be able to make more money and that he will have an opportunity to manage a sales team within two years as our company expands.

If you ask each candidate that you interview the same questions, your hiring process will be more objective, and it will make it easier for you to evaluate and compare different candidates that you screen over a period of time. And if you are interviewing several candidates, you can save time by creating a form to record your impressions and by writing down your comments right after your interview, while they are fresh in your mind.

MICROSOFT'S HIRING PROCESS

Companies that achieve total market domination hire world-class sales and marketing professionals, and Microsoft is no exception.

Bill Gates has been quoted as saying that he looks for four qualities in Microsoft employees, "ambition, IQ, technical expertise and business judgement, with IQ being the most important." The average employee at Microsoft is about thirty years old. About half of Microsoft's professional hircs come directly from one of the approximately fifty universities that are visited by Microsoft's recruiters each year. Microsoft's recruiters manage the hiring process, but department-level managers usually make hiring decisions for their teams.

Prospective employees who are invited to an interview usually meet with three to six Microsoft employees. Prospective employees are screened carefully, and about 10 percent of the candidates that are interviewed are invited back for a second interview. Of these, about 10 to 15 percent are offered a position with Microsoft. In total, Microsoft hires about 2 to 3 percent of the people that it interviews.

If your company wants to achieve total market domination, it must be prepared to invest whatever time and money is necessary to recruit top performers. If your company hires great salespeople, these "superstars" will attract other great salespeople to work with your company. But if your company is impatient and settles for marginal performers, it will be difficult for your company to build the success that attracts world-class personnel.

PSYCHOLOGICAL TESTING

Many companies use psychological tests to evaluate different job candidate's character and motivation, and to attempt to predict whether a candidate has the personality needed to be successful in a specific selling position. These tests are far from perfect, but the companies that sell these tests can provide compelling statistics that confirm that using them to screen job candidates results in fewer hiring mistakes and greater employee retention.

When you consider the opportunity cost of hiring the wrong individual, it is easy to justify the time and expense of almost any process that can give you more insight into the qualities and motivations of the person that you are evaluating. Nevertheless, most hiring managers eschew psychological testing and rely on their "gut" instinct about each candidate that they evaluate.

BACKGROUND CHECKS

Employees with credit problems, drug dependencies, or a history of criminal behavior can impact your company's productivity and put your company at risk of expensive legal action. To avoid these problems, many companies hire personnel firms, credit bureaus, detective agencies, and drug screening services to run background checks on their job candidates.

It is reasonable to give each job candidate the benefit of any doubt—but it is naive to believe that every job candidate will be honest or will reveal personal issues which may impact their job performance. At some point, your company must decide how much latitude it is willing to give job candidates who are less than truthful about who they are, what they have done in the past, or how they will perform if you offer them a job.

Your company should consult with its attorney to ensure that it is in compliance with all federal and state employment laws.

Personal Character Questions	
What were your most important achievements in your last job?	Convinced Acme Business Systems to implement an action plan to move it into a new market. Learned how to use an automated sales management system to organize and manage his customer database.
Why were they important to you?	The first because it was the largest sale his company has ever made. And the second because it enabled him to feel for the first time that he could keep track of every selling opportunity in his sales territory.
What was your greatest business challenge?	Greatest challenge is working with difficult people. However, he said that if he can think of just one thing that he likes about them, or respects them for doing, then he can usually get along with them pretty well.
What did you learn from it?	He learned that by making a sincere effort to appreciate his customers' qualities, that he could almost always build a productive dialogue with them and influence their purchase process.
What was the most difficult problem you encountered?	The most difficult problem that he encountered was not having access to new technologies, such as multimedia training facilities. Many of his larger customers expected this level of support.
How did you handle it?	Developed a joint-marketing relationship with our company to provide advanced sales training materials. That is how he was first introduced to our sales team. We have made sales calls together several times. (Two of our sales representatives said that he did an excellent job on their sales calls.)
Who was the most difficult person to work with at your last job?	He thinks that the CEO of Corporate Training Associates is an egomaniac.
How did you overcome this problem?	When he brought his CEO on sales calls, he encouraged him to tell his company's story. The CEO loved describing how he started his company with $200, and his customers loved hearing the story. It was a "win-win" for everyone.
What was the most important course or project that you completed in school?	An acting course that he took in high school.
Why was it important to you?	It got him over his fear of public speaking. And it gave him an opportunity to try on different "personalities." He feels that being able to flex his

	selling style helps him get along with almost everyone.
Why do you think someone with your experience should be chosen for a job that requires (fill in your own job requirement) experience?	Said he has the experience, the motivation, and talent to succeed. . . .
What are you looking for in a new job opportunity?	Wants to work with a company that has the financial backing and the development resources to provide state-of-the-art sales training products. Wants an opportunity to become a sales manager within the next two to three years.
Convince me that you have what it takes to do this job!	See notes on the sales call that we role-played. He said that he wanted to work for Dayton Associates at least four times during our interview. He has had experience and success in our business, and he is a positive, energetic individual.

Step 11: Evaluate your sales compensation plan.

Your company can use financial incentives to attract qualified salespeople, retain top performers, and motivate its sales force to achieve its marketing objectives.

Type of Compensation	Value to Employee	Effect
Recognition	Intrinsic rewards	Performance-based compensation
Contests	Focused effort	Performance-based compensation
Over Target/Quota Incentive Pay	Outstanding pay	Performance-based compensation
Target/Quota Incentive Pay	At risk pay	Performance-based compensation
Salary	Non-sales-related pay	Fixed compensation
Profit Sharing	Non-sales-related pay	Fixed compensation
Employee Benefits	Security needs	Fixed compensation
Sales Expenses	Reimburse employee	No impact if paid promptly

According to a study by Dartnell, 5 percent of companies offer straight salary, 5 percent of companies offer straight commission, and 90 percent of companies develop a Total Target Compensation plan or TTC, based on a combination or "pay mix" of base salary and incentive payments, such as commissions and bonuses.

Incentives are any form of variable compensation, including commissions, bonuses, and nonmonetary compensation. *Commission* is a percent share or monetary amount paid based on sales revenue performance, unit sales, or the amount of profit generated. And *bonus* is a percent of base pay or cash payments that are paid for achieving specific goals. A *combination plan* comprises a base salary plus a commission or a bonus or both a commission and a bonus.

Total Target Compensation is based on achieving specific objectives. For example, if a company sells $1 million, its sales force may earn 18 percent of sales; however, if the company sells $2 million, its sales force may earn more or less than 18 percent of sales, depending on the compensation plan that is adopted.

DETERMINE TOTAL TARGET COMPENSATION

Many sales managers believe that the only way to motivate their salespeople is to tie financial incentives to specific sales objectives. But being totally results oriented can demoralize a sales force and can erode customer satisfaction. Salespeople *are* motivated by financial incentives, but leadership, loyalty, recognition, praise, and every positive communication that they receive during their workday will help them build the positive attitude and self-esteem that they need to be top performers.[2]

In any case, sales compensation plans can help you improve sales performance if you take the time to design a plan that reflects the expectations that you have for your sales team and that meets your sales team's expectations for security and earning potential.

---

[2] According to a 1997 study by Watson Wyatt, 30 to 50 percent of sales professionals do not feel that they will achieve their sales goals. And only 65 percent of surveyed sales representatives feel that their senior sales management does a capable job.

To determine the TTC that your company is prepared to pay your salespeople, you will need to determine:

1. How much do sales people in your industry earn?
2. How do your competitors compensate their salespeople?
3. Do you plan to implement any sales plan qualifiers, such as house accounts, commission caps, or performance thresholds for bonuses?
4. Are there any factors, such as discount travel for family members, that make working for your company especially attractive?
5. Will your TTC for your sales force cause problems with employees in other areas of your business?
6. Is your TTC appropriate for the scope and complexity of your selling situation?
7. To determine your *pay mix* or salary and incentive split, your company must evaluate its TTC strategy, the needs of your company, your salespeople's comfort with risk, and any cultural issues that may impact employee loyalty.
8. Is your company willing to pay a premium to attract the very best salespeople?

Tailor your compensation plan to meet your business objectives.

The greater the influence of the salesperson in the selling process, the greater the impact will be of increasing the percentage of incentive payments to base salary. So, for example, if your company is selling commodities into a mature market, it may provide a TTC = 70% base salary + 30% variable compensation. However, if your company is selling a new type of communication system, it may hire senior sales representatives and provide a TTC = 50% base salary + 50% variable incentive.

Salary and incentive splits vary by industry. Banking typically offers a 90 percent base salary and 10 percent incentive; food products offer 67 percent base salary and 33 percent incentive; manufacturing businesses offer 61 percent base salary and 39 percent incentive; and insurance companies offers 43 percent base salary and 57 percent incentive compensation.

Start-Up Market	Growth Market	Mature Market	Declining Market
Uncapped commission	Ramped commission	Base plus commission	Base plus commission plus bonus
Reps manage own accounts	Reduce pay	Lower earnings	Challenge to maintain quota
Company concerned about cost of sales	Control territories	Control selling process	Training emphasized
Hire experienced sales rep	Hire both experienced and new sales reps	Hire competitors' sales reps	Reduce number of sales reps

MICROSOFT'S GOLDEN HANDCUFFS

Many companies that achieve total market domination use stock options to help them retain their most valuable employees.

Microsoft, for example, pays its employees relatively low salaries. But Microsoft has produced more millionaires than any other company in the world by awarding generous stock options to its key personnel.

Compensation at Microsoft includes a biannual bonus of up to 15 percent, stock options, and payroll deductions for stock purchases. An employee can exercise 25 percent of his or her stock options after working for Microsoft for eighteen months, and another 12.5 percent every six months thereafter anytime within ten years, with new options granted, depending on performance, every two years. Employees can also put up to 10 percent of their salaries into stock purchases, at 85 percent of Microsoft stock's current value.

If your company is not in a position to offer its employees stock options, it can develop a profit-sharing program to help it motivate and retain its employees.

INCENTIVE COMPENSATION

The most common way to compute TTC for salespeople is to use a combination of salary and incentive pay. For example, your company might provide a base salary of $3,000 per month plus commission computed monthly or quarterly based on achieving a threshold sales volume, meeting a sales quota, or selling over quota for the period.

The "TTC Plans for Sales Representatives" table illustrates three ways to compute sales compensation: flat commission, ramped commission, and ramped commission with thresholds and caps. Thresholds can be used to motivate a sales force to make its best effort, but most companies that achieve total market domination eschew caps on sales commission because they can decrease motivation—why play if it doesn't pay!

Examples of Different TTC Plans for Sales Representatives	Percent of Sale Amount	Percent of Gross Margin	Dollars per Unit Sold
Flat Commission [3]	10%	25%	$5,000
Ramped Commission			
□ Up to 100% of quota	10%	25%	$5,000
□ Over 100% of quota	15%	35%	$7,000
Ramped Commission with Threshold and Cap			
□ To 75% of quota	0	0	0
75%–100% of quota	10%	25%	$5,000
101 to 150% of quota	15%	35%	$7,000
Over 150% of quota	0	0	0

Tailor your compensation plan to achieve your marketing objectives.

Your compensation plan should take into account your sales representatives' job functions. For example, if your company's

---

[3] Commission can vary by product. For example, your company might pay a 25 percent commission on product sales and a 10 percent commission on sales of services.

objective is to build market share by winning new accounts, rather than by selling a greater quantity of products into its existing accounts, it may need to hire aggressive salespeople who are motivated by a compensation mix that includes a greater percentage of commission pay.

Example of TTC For Two Different Types of Sales Positions		
TTC Factor	**Sales to Major Accounts**	**Direct Channel Sales**
Market Objective	Focus on building market share by winning new accounts	Focus on building sales volume in existing accounts
Job Functions	Selling tasks 40%	Selling tasks 70%
	Work with orders 15%	Work with orders 5%
	Service accounts 10%	Service accounts 5%
	Product support 10%	Product support 0%
	Territory management 15%	Territory management 15%
	Other 10%	Other 5%
Performance Measures	Sales to existing accounts 50%	Sales to existing accounts 20%
	Sales to new accounts 25%	Sales to new accounts 60%
	Customer satisfaction 15%	Customer satisfaction 0%
	Total sales 10%	Total sales 10%
	Profit margin 0%	Profit margin 10%
Compensation Mix (Salary/Incentives)	Base salary 75%	Base salary 50%
	Incentives:	Incentives:
	Commission 20%	Commission 35%
	Bonus 5%	Bonus 10%
	Contest	Contest 5%

COMPENSATING INDIVIDUALS
WHO WORK ON A SALES TEAM

Because of the complexity of developing a compensation plan for a sales team, many companies use a pay mix that comprises 100 percent base salary plus a performance bonus based on a percentage of the sales team's base salaries. For example, a sales team that has sold 100 percent of quota at a 20 percent contribution margin might receive a bonus equal to 5 percent of each team member's base salary. While another team that has sold 120 percent of its sales quota at a 25 percent contribution margin might receive a bonus equal to 10 percent of each team member's base salary.

However, while most employees are willing to support their group's effort, self-interest may cause conflicts with the group's objectives. And while most salespeople are comfortable with a collective evaluation of their group's performance, top performers may not feel that they are being compensated for their extra effort.

To address these issues, most companies that achieve total market domination employ a compensation mix that depends on individual members' job function. For example, the incentive compensation as a percent of TTC may be 30 percent for account managers, 20 percent for product specialists, 10 percent for postsales support, and 5 percent for administrative personnel.

Job Function on Sales Team	Performance Factors	Incentive Pay As a Percent of TTC
Account Manager	Sales volume and profitability	30%
Product Specialist	Number of new accounts	20%
	Customer retention	
Postsales Support	Customer satisfaction	10%
Administrative Support	Order processing and delivery	5%

Compensating Top Performers

Top performers are often responsible for bringing in a significant percentage of a company's business. So companies that achieve total market domination put a great deal of consideration into developing compensation plans that ensure that they are able to retain all or almost all of their top performers.

The key to compensating most top performers is to tie their TTC to their own sales performance and to offer a high percentage of incentive compensation with no salary caps and with bonuses for reaching specific sales targets.

However, no matter what compensation strategy your company implements, and no matter how generous your TTC plan is, one or more of your top performers will inevitably leave your company to work for a competitor.

Companies that achieve total market domination know that the only way to prevent this inevitable turnover is to offer their top performers "golden handcuffs," in the form of stock options and generous profit-sharing programs, to retain their loyalty.

CUSTOMER SATISFACTION AND RETENTION

Maintaining a high level of customer satisfaction can help your company build market share, but it does not always improve customer retention. For example, if a competitor markets a new product that is less expensive than the one that your company sells, it may win over some of your customers, regardless of your customers' satisfaction with your company's products or service.

Many companies that achieve totoal market domination design their compensation plans to encourage their sales, marketing, and support personnel to maintain a high level of customer service. However, most companies structure their compensation mix so that a much larger amount of incentive compensation is earned by generating new business than by servicing existing accounts.

COMMUNICATE CLEARLY AND PUT IT IN WRITING

Your compensation plan should communicate how every aspect of your sales personnel's performance, including sales volume, territory growth, product mix, new account development, and customer satisfaction, will help your salespeople achieve their financial goals.

Your compensation plan should also be clear, concise, and compelling. If your compensation plan is clear, your salespeople will be able to use it to focus their selling activities on achieving your company's objectives. If your plan is concise, it will be easy for your company to manage and administer. And if your plan is compelling, it will motivate your salespeople to make their best effort to achieve your company's objectives.

Your company's compensation plan is a legal agreement between your company and its sales personnel. It should be communicated in writing and presented verbally with an opportunity for your salespeople to ask questions about any points that they do not understand.

If your salespeople do not understand their compensation plan, it will not motivate them to stay focused on the accounts and the products that are strategic to your company's success, and it will not motivate them to make their best effort to reach your company's sales objectives.

Compensation Evaluation	Compensation Plan
Is your TTC appropriate for your market?	Yes, we offer a base salary of 50% and 50% commission at 100% of quota. Our average sales representative earned $111,000 last year.
	Our inside sales representatives are on a 75% base salary and can earn commissions and bonuses based on performance. Our average inside sales rep earned $44,000 last year.
How much are salespeople in your industry being paid?	TTC for sales reps in our industry is about $78,000 per year. We do not have any data on inside sales representatives' compensation.
How do your competitors compensate their salespeople?	A few of our competitors offer straight commission—usually 25 to 35% of the selling price of their products. Others offer a 40 to 60% base salary and commission.
Do you plan to implement any sales plan qualifiers such as house accounts, commission caps, or performance thresholds for bonuses?	No—we believe that it is counterproductive to use caps, qualifiers, or performance thresholds. We want our sales force to get rich!
Are there any factors, such as free airline travel for family members, that make working for your company especially attractive?	We try to be objective about the value of our workplace to our employees—it is appropriate for the business we are in and the clients we serve.
	We have a great company reimbursement policy to encourage our employees to take courses and finish degrees at our local university.

Is your TTC appropriate for your budget?	Our cost of sales—about 21% of revenues—is in line with our business plan, and our industry's average.
Is your TTC for your sales force reasonable compared to compensation for your other employees?	We are in a relatively low-paying business. Some of our training personnel have expressed interest in moving into sales to increase their compensation—but most of the people in development love their work and are satisfied with their compensation.
Is your TTC appropriate for the scope and complexity of your selling situation?	Our sales force calls on high-level executives in large corporations. They must not only be effective at closing new business; they must quite literally demonstrate the Client-Centered™ Selling skills that we teach! We hire the very best people that we can find.
Does your pay mix or salary and incentive split reflect the needs of your firm, your salespeople's comfort with risk, and any cultural issues that may impact employee loyalty?	We review our compensation program each year with our sales force. So far, the feedback has been very positive. Less than 10% of our salespeople are under quota each year. And these reps either improve or are asked to find another job. Our sales philosophy is simple—we want every salesperson on our team to feel and act with the confidence of a peak performer.
Is your company willing to pay a premium to attract the very best salespeople?	Our average salespeople earn 25% more than the industry average and have an easier job—because they represent the best product on the market.

Step 12: Evaluate your sales personnel.

Most salespeople are evaluated on two simple criteria: do they make quota, and do they make trouble. If they make a great deal of trouble, they better excel at bringing in new business. Unfortunately, this "binary" evaluation process does little to help a sales manager improve his or her sales team's performance.

To understand sales performance, a sales manager must consider a constellation of factors, including:

- Size of territory
- Product penetration (saturation level)
- History of sales territory
- Rate of sales growth
- Number of new accounts
- Number of lost accounts
- Percentage of business for "A," "B," and "C" level accounts

- Number of sales calls, demonstrations, and proposals generated
- Spectrum of products sold
- Size of quota (attainment factors)
- Date of last sale
- Performance against other salespeople
- Customer relations

Each one of these factors can signal a potential problem, which if rectified can help weak salespeople meet their revenue objectives.

Typical Selling Problems	Possible Cause or Solution
Size of territory	Salesperson cannot deal with so many prospects.
Product penetration	May have to focus on selling secondary product line.
History of sales territory	May have problem accounts that have "poisoned" the territory.
Rate of sales growth	If growth is slow and steady, it may be time for a new marketing campaign, or products may need to be updated or replaced.
Number of new accounts	No new accounts usually indicates strong competition, or that more time should be spent prospecting.
Number of lost accounts	Many lost accounts usually means customer service is low or products are obsolete.
Percentage of business from "A," "B," and "C" level accounts	If all business is from "A" level accounts, the salesperson may not have the time or energy to work smaller opportunities. You may need to reassign "B" and "C" opportunities to other salespeople.
Number of sales calls	If very few sales calls are being made, the salesperson may be burnt out, or may be uncomfortable making cold calls.
Number of proposals	If very few proposals are being written, it may be time to put together a proposal "template," or a boilerplate proposal that can be used by all of your salespeople.
Spectrum of products sold	If your salespeople are only selling a few of your company's products, you will need to evaluate whether market acceptance, lack of product knowledge, your sales compensation program, or other factors are responsible.
Size of quota (attainment factors)	If your salespeople have doubts about their quota, you may need to "resell" it to them.

	If a quota is very low, it is not motivating; if a quota is too high, it can be de-motivating.
Date of last sale	If it has been a long time since your salesperson's last big sale, he or she may be burnt out or need a mini-marketing campaign to put life back into his or her territory.
Performance against other salespeople	If one salesperson is doing poorly, it is probably the salesperson; if the entire sales force is having problems, it is time to re-evaluate your marketing programs, product focus, and support infrastructure.
Customer relations/complaints	If a salesperson is extremely well liked, but is doing poorly, he or she may be socializing too much.
	If a salesperson is disliked, he or she probably needs to work on his or her interpersonal communication skills.
	If a salesperson is despised but is consistently at the top of the sales charts, he or she should be tolerated until you can replace him or her.
Organizational skills	If office work isn't getting done, you can change your compensation program to motivate your salespeople to complete their paperwork properly, or you can hire more support personnel so that your salespeople can stay in front of their customers.
	If a salesperson has difficulty showing up for meetings, he or she may have personal problems or be involved with substance abuse.

Performance reviews provide an opportunity for upper management to evaluate and reward employee performance. The more objective and relevant a performance review is, the more influence it will have on employee work habits.

Companies that achieve total market domination "engineer" success into their organization by linking employees' bonuses and salary adjustments to achievement of specific objectives and key results.

Performance Review Worksheet
Date: December 11, 1997
Employee: Nathan White
Supervisor: Tom Black

Job Title: Sales Manager

Job Standards:

Adopt Client-Centered™ Selling.

Show professional attitude and leadership at all times.

Motivate sales team to excel.

Specific (Quantifiable) Objectives for This Review Period:

Achieve sales quota for quarter: $850,000.

Improve profit margin to 24%

Open 15 new accounts.

Hold a two-day sales training meeting each month.

Perform monthly sales review.

General (Qualitative) Objectives for This Review Period:

Demonstrate positive attitude towards company and customers at all times.

Motivate sales team to improve performance.

Performance Rating (Rate employees in each area from 1 to 5):

1.   *Training Period*: This rating is used for employees who require additional training or experience to meet expected performance standards.

2.   *Marginal Performance*: This rating is used for employees whose performance requires some improvement to meet expected performance standards.

3.   *Average or Expected Performance*: This rating is used for employees whose performance meets expected performance standards.

4.   *Exceptional Performance*: This rating is used for employees whose performance occasionally exceeds expected performance standards.

5.   *Performance above Job Classification*: This rating is used for employees whose performance consistently exceeds expected performance standards. Employees with this rating are usually being groomed for promotion.

Quality of Work	3
Production Level	3
Technical Skills	4
Interpersonal Skills	3
Organizational Skills	3
Planning Skills	2
Personal Development	2
Training/Education	3
Leadership	4
Management Skills (Leads or Managers)	4

Major Strengths/Abilities :

Excellent leader.

Good technical skills.

Enthusiastic.

Significant Contributions/Improvements:

The customer database is in much better shape.

Improvement in These Areas Will Improve Your Overall Performance:

Planning skills are weak. May benefit from taking a course on "managing the planning process."

Need to make an effort to grow industry skills.

Additional Factors Considered in Overall Performance Rating:

Consistently put in overtime during last phase of Fall Promotion Special.

Was gone for one week of training at Microsoft's offices in Redmond, Washington.

Overall Performance Rating (1 to 5): 3

Performance Incentives/Bonus for This Review Period:

Bonus = $3,500

Cost of living raise = 2%

New base salary = $52,700 per year.

Objectives and Key Results for Next Review Period:

(Specify revisions to current objectives and key results.)

Maintain current budget levels for department.

Increase sales revenues by 15%.

Increase profit margin by 2%.

Manager's Comments:

You are doing a very good job. We appreciate the work that you do and the positive attitude that you maintain when you are on the job.

You need to work on your planning skills—this will help you interface more effectively with other departments and better manage your department's budget.

You have done an excellent job recruiting personnel—keep up the good work.

Manager's Signature/Date:

Employee's Comments:

I would like to move into product development next year. I would find it very challenging to have responsibility for creating a new training product. I realize that I need to have additional product planning experience before I will be ready for this type of assignment.

Employee's Signature/Date:

Senior Manager's Signature/Date:

EGO AND PRAISE

Most salespeople have never been given any guidance about how to deal with rejection, and they take their customers' decisions to choose competitive products personally. This is why many salespeople who appear overconfident actually suffer from a lack of confidence in their ability to influence their customers' purchase process.

Unfortunately, many managers don't understand why their salespeople have "large" egos, and they are reluctant to praise their salespeople's successes. But companies that achieve total market domination have learned that praise is a wonderful thing. It encourages salespeople to strive to achieve greater success. And the performance review process is a perfect opportunity to provide the encouragement and support that salespeople need to build real confidence.

EMPLOYEE SELF-EVALUATION

Many companies have employees submit a self-evaluation form to their manager prior to their performance review. This process gives employees an opportunity to review their achievements since their last review and makes it easier for their manager to complete their performance review.

Salespeople can be very critical of themselves, but it is important for their managers to be as objective about their job performance as possible. An employee evaluation is most valuable if it is based on events and activities that can be measured and changed.

Your employees' attitude *is* your company's attitude.
Companies that achieve total market domination maintain an open dialog between their sales team and their senior managers to ensure that potentially inflammatory issues, such as disagreements about crediting sales commissions, will not impact their employees' morale.

Being respectful of employees and maintaining an open dialog about issues that they are concerned about can help your company earn the loyalty that it needs to retain its top performers and dominate its market.

Employee's Self-Evaluation
Date: December 11, 1997
Employee: Nathan White
Supervisor: Tom Brown
Job Title: Major Account Manager
Areas of Greatest Strength or Improvement: Good people skills. Stay focused on projects until they are completed correctly.
Significant Contributions: Closed Acme Freight account; got add-on order at Blue Sky Co.; developed proposal boilerplate.
Areas That Need Improvement:
I need to do a better job of following up on new business leads.
I am still uncomfortable with our new telemarketing program.
Future Business/Career Objectives:
I would like to move into product development next year. I would find it very challenging to have responsibility for creating a new training product. I realize that I need to have additional product planning experience before I will be ready for this type of assignment.
Employee's Comments:
I think I have done a good job of managing our strategic relationships with our major accounts.
I would like an opportunity to take some additional sales management training classes to improve my professional selling skills. I have signed up for a public speaking workshop that meets on Tuesday evenings. I hope this will help me become a better communicator.
Employee's Signature/Date:
How do you feel about the Performance Review Process?
I appreciate the feedback and I look forward to my salary review.
Manager's Signature/Date:
Senior Manager's Signature/Date:

PROBLEM SOLVING

When sales are down, companies must take decisive action. Some companies engage in a careful analysis of their situation to help them determine the cause of their problems, but many companies respond in a reactive way without learning exactly why they are having trouble meeting their marketing objectives.

The truth is, the vast majority of problems related to unrealized sales performance are a function of flawed marketing programs, *not* incompetent sales people.

- *Advertising and Corporate Communications*—Advertising and promotional campaigns are usually the first line of defense against upper management's wrath when sales are down. Launching a new promotional campaign gets everyone off of the hook, at least for a while. Unfortunately, as often as not, a new advertising campaign diverts attention from what is actually causing weak sales, which is almost always a critical market factor, such as a better competitive product, which has not been identified or is not being addressed.

- *Pricing Strategy*—It is easy to blame weak sales on aggressive competitive pricing. But price is only one of the factors that customers use to make their purchasing decisions. It is a mistake to change your company's pricing strategy until you identify and evaluate at least three other potential causes of your problem.

- *Reorganize the Sales Organization*—If 10 percent of your sales force is performing under quota, it may be time to recruit new talent. But when 50 percent of your company's sales force is performing poorly, it is time to reevaluate your company's marketing strategy.

- *White Knight*—Bringing in a new sales manager to "turn around" your sales team can be an effective remedy if your sales manager is incompetent or is extremely difficult to work with. But replacing a sales manager will not improve sales if your marketing strategy is unsound or if your company is not providing the resources that your sales force needs to help it leverage its selling efforts. And your company may lose whatever sales momentum it has while your new sales manager gets up to speed on your company's products, procedures, and policies; develops new objectives; wins his or her sales team's confidence; and becomes familiar with your company's customer base.

☐ *Redesign the Sales Compensation Plan*—In some selling situations, it is possible to spur sales by increasing sales commissions and providing other sales incentives. However, this strategy will fail unless your marketing strategy is sound.

☐ *Change Product Strategy*—To ensure product demand, your company must track market trends, competitors' strategies, and your customers' ever changing product requirements. If your products are less desirable than your competitors' products, you may need to reposition your products or develop an entirely new product strategy.

☐ *Distribution Channels*—Restructuring a sales channel is like replacing a sales manager; it should only be done as a last resort, and it inevitably results in some loss of customer goodwill.

☐ *Strategic positioning*—If your company loses its focus on its primary business objectives, it may lose its competitive advantage.

The major challenge that faces sales and marketing managers is not *developing better marketing strategies—it is properly executing the marketing strategies that have already been adopted.*

Step 13: Evaluate your sales and marketing department's workload.

Most employees work best when they work a reasonable number of hours each week. When employees work overtime hours week after week, their stress levels rise and their health begins to suffer.

In the Human Resources Evaluation worksheet, a 100 percent workload means that the average employee in the department is *working* forty hours each week.

Client-Centered™ Training – Human Resource Evaluation		
Department – Workload	Limitations, Bottlenecks, or Problem Areas	Priorities
Administrative – 80%	No limitations	Market Internet site
Marketing—75%	Advertising	Review advertising agency
	Telemarketing	Recruit three Telemarketing Representatives
	Direct Mail	Hire a direct mail marketing company.
Sales—115%	International Sales	Hire two senior account managers
		Locate distribution and marketing partners for Europe, South America, and Asia
Support—90%	Telephone Support	Link telephone support with Internet server database
Financial—75%	Credit Line	Explore relationship with Big National Bank to increase credit rating
Production—65%	Packaging	Explore new packaging for "In-the-Box" Training Programs
Development—130%	Turnaround time on bids for customization of standard training programs	Hire an outside consultant to review and help us re-engineer our customization process.

Step 14: Evaluate your sales and marketing group's overall effectiveness.

Your company can use the "Sales and Marketing Effectiveness" worksheet to help it evaluate its strengths and weaknesses, and to identify specific tasks or processes that need to be revised or re-engineered to enable it to achieve total market domination.

Sales and Marketing Effectiveness	Client-Centered™ Training 1 (ineffective) to 5 (very effective)
Market share	2
Price vs. Competitors	3
Margin	4
Sales	3
Profits	4
Credit terms	4
Customer service	5
Customer training	3
Aggressiveness last year	3
Aggressiveness today	3
Reputation	4
Customer follow-up	3
Corporate image	5
Sales management	4
Financial management	4
Administration management	3
Employee satisfaction	4
Internal training	4
Day-to-day operations	3
Financial controls	4
New product development	2
New market development	2
Promotion/advertising	3

The Bottom Line: Is your sales force prepared to represent your company in a professional, Client-Centered™ way?

The best prescription for a successful business is to hire the best sales and marketing personnel that are available, to provide them with the resources that they need to be successful, and to put incentives in place that motivate them to make their best efforts.

By standardizing on a comprehensive, proven sales methodology, such as Client-Centered™ Selling, your company's sales force can leverage a common frame of reference for planning and documenting its selling activities. And when your entire sales force masters Client-Centered™ Selling, it can truly begin selling "downhill."

In the next chapter, you will learn how to use computer and communication technologies to help your company achieve total market domination.

CHAPTER 8

IS YOUR COMPANY USING COMPUTERS AND COMMUNICATION TECHNOLOGIES TO LEVERAGE ITS SALES EFFORTS?

*Virtually everything in business today is an
undifferentiated commodity except how a company
manages its information. How you manage
information determines whether you win or lose.*

—BILL GATES

New computer and communication technologies such as the Internet, network computing, and electronic commerce are redefining the selling process. And many of these new technologies provide a *window of opportunity* for your company to gain a competitive advantage over competitors that fail to adapt their business to take advantage of these powerful tools.

The key to effective sales force automation is implementing systems that can help your sales force become more effective at selling. And the key to accomplishing this is to implement systems that provide the support that your company's salespeople need to help them move business forward:

□ Provide better sales information—especially advanced information on new selling opportunities, competitive products, and support issues.

- ☐ Improve their ability to present their company's marketing story in a clear, concise, compelling way and demonstrate the value that their company can deliver to its customers.
- ☐ Provide more efficient ways to manage customer orders, sales agreements, and contracts.
- ☐ Facilitate communications with other salespeople and with decision-makers in other departments, such as marketing, service, production, and shipping.

If your company does not focus its sales automation efforts on these issues, it may implement systems that can help it administer its sales process but that diminish the ability of its sales force to sell.

In many companies, for example, sales correspondence, presentations, and reporting tasks that used to be handled by sales support personnel have been turned over to PC-equipped salespeople who do not have the training, the time, or the interest to do a good job of managing these tasks.

Is it the best use of a sales manager's time to spend weeks or months learning software applications that will enable him or her to generate fancy reports that describe the sales team's achievements? Or would this time be better spent working with the company's sales representatives and customers to build market share?

There is no "correct" answer to these questions, but companies that achieve total market domination consider the implications of automating each step of their sales process to evaluate the impact it will have on their sales force's ability to become more effective at selling.

Step 1: Document your sales infrastructure.

Before you can evaluate the benefit of implementing any new technologies, you must evaluate your current sales infrastructure, which comprises all of the policies, procedures, and administrative services that are required to support your selling activities and deliver products and services to your customers.

Your company can use the "Sales Infrastructure" table to help it document all of its sales processes.

Sales Infrastructure	Process
Contact/Lead Management	□ Prospecting activities
	□ Data collection
	□ Data (contact) input
	□ Contact forms
	□ Database access
	□ Mail response
	□ Fax response
	□ Telemarketing response
	□ Sales call follow-up
	□ Lead routing
	□ Sales forecasting
Order Entry	□ Product guide/catalog
	□ Product configurator
	□ Comparative product reference guide
	□ Order forms
	□ Order Entry system
	□ Authorization or approval
	□ Custom orders
	□ Internal order tracking
	□ Customer inquiries
Credit and Billing Procedures	□ Invoicing
	□ Credit checking
	□ Credit authorization
	□ Payment discounts
	□ Special promotions
	□ Special discounts
	□ A/R policies
	□ Collections
Customer Service Policies	□ Delivery options
	□ Installation
	□ Implementation
	□ Support
	□ Warranty
	□ Service options

	□ Return merchandise authorizations
	□ Special requests
Internal Business Procedures	□ Audit procedures
	□ Check authorization
	□ Reimbursement
Marketing Automation System	□ Competitive analysis
	□ Internet-based research
	□ Marketing materials
Sales Force Automation System	□ Training
	□ Access
	□ Security
	□ Sales tracking
	□ Sales forecasting
	□ Database Maintenance
	□ Backup and Archive
Sales Support Personnel	□ Assignments
	□ Priorities
	□ Territories

FLOWCHART YOUR SALES PROCESS

Creating a flowchart of how information and documents move through your company can help you visualize every aspect of your sales infrastructure. For example, creating a flowchart of your order entry, credit checking, and billing process can help you determine whether your company can re-engineer these processes to reduce the amount of time that your salespeople spend entering and tracking orders, handling billing errors, and helping with collections.

Figure 8-1.
Client Centered™ Training's Order Entry and Billing Process

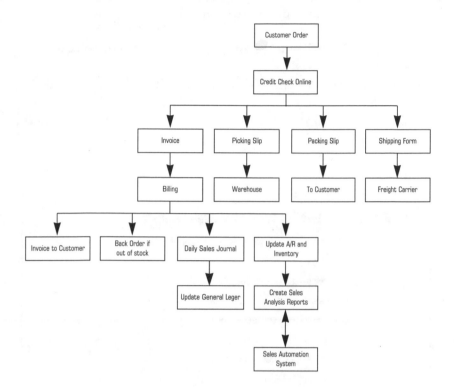

The sample order entry and billing flowchart tracks the forms that Client-Centered™ Training uses to process orders for its training materials. The customer's credit is checked when an order is entered into the system. Picking, packing, and shipping forms are generated by the system and are sent over to a printer in the warehouse. In the billing department, the billing clerk matches the original order with the picking slip from the warehouse, and an invoice is generated for the customer or a back order is reported. The order entry system automatically updates the sales journal, accounts receivable files, and inventory files. The general ledger is updated each month when the accounting period is closed, and sales analysis reports can be run at any time.

Client-Centered™ Training's sales analysis program, which is used to generate its sales reports, has been modified to share information (interface) with its sales automation system. This modification enables Client-Centered™ Training's salespeople to access up-to-date customer information, such as a customer's order history and credit limits, that they need to help them manage their accounts.

Step 2: Identify areas of your sales infrastructure that should be automated.

According to a recent study by Booze Allen, the cost of making a sales call is increasing 11.2% each year. And over the last ten years, the actual selling time that sales people spend in front of customers has declined 19.5%. There is no doubt that the cost of selling products has driven companies to leverage their marketing resources with automated systems.

Example of an Automated System That Can Facilitate the Sales Function

- □ *Lead generation*—automated telemarketing system
- □ *Lead qualification*—skills-based telephone routing
- □ *Lead tracking*—prospect database
- □ *Sales presentations*—presentation software
- □ *Sales fulfillment*—Internet e-mail
- □ *Proposing a solution*—word processor
- □ *Closing the sale*—videoconferencing
- □ *Placing the order*—order entry system
- □ *Revenue forecasting*—electronic spreadsheet
- □ *Sales training*—online training materials
- □ *Marketing materials*—desktop publishing

The "Sales Function" worksheet shows how Client-Centered™ Training can use automated systems to help it leverage its selling resources.

Sales Function	Client-Centered™ Training's Current Business Process	How Can Automated Systems Leverage Your Selling Resources?
Lead generation	Inside sales/ representatives do telemarketing	Automated/telemarketing system Use computer telephone integration system to facilitate telemarketing process

Lead qualification	Customer contact forms	Automate as much data entry as possible
Lead tracking	Use paper system to track sales leads	Use computer system to track leads and coordinate follow-up
Sales presentations	Use PowerPoint to create presentation materials	Use company's Web site to publish marketing information
Sales fulfillment	Customers interface with inside sales personnel	Customers can track their orders in our Order Entry system through the Internet
Proposing a solution	Use MS Word to create custom proposals	Use document routing and e-mail to notify managers about special customer requirements
Closing the sale	Use faxes to support negotiation process	Use e-mail and video conferencing to communicate with clients
Placing the order	Telephone in order, submit written confirmation within 24 hours of customer's verbal commitment	Enter order directly into our training scheduling application through the Internet
Revenue forecasting	Use Excel to create forecast	User Internet to publish forecast and communicate with managers
Sales training	Develop, copy, and distribute videotapes Schedule in-house seminars	Use streaming video to enable customers to view training materials on the Internet
Marketing materials	Send materials out to a service bureau	Use desktop publishing system to create marketing materials

The easiest way to determine your automation requirements is to use a "Sales Automation 'Story'" worksheet to help you analyze each step of your company's sales process. For example, you might create the following "Sales Automation 'Story'" worksheet to help you evaluate the pros and cons of using a sales automation system to help you manage your prospect database.

Sales Automation "Story"	
Activity	**Lead Tracking**
Sales Process	Lead tracking
Who is involved	Sales representative, sales manager, marketing personnel, and senior management
Inputs to the task	Contact information from sales calls, data from contact forms, e-mail messages, and fax documents.
Process/the task	Organize and store contact information; provide reporting capabilities; interface with other office systems.
Outputs from the task	Contact lists organized by zip code, SIC code, sales territory, current supplier, size of opportunity, and priority.
Where does task occur?	Each sales representative maintains his or her own lead tracking (prospect) database. We want this database to be centralized.
When does task occur?	Contacts are entered when they are qualified.
Why is the task done?	We want to build a database of information on our entire prospect list to support our marketing programs.
How can automation improve productivity, decrease expenses, or provide new business opportunities?	A prospect database can provide easier access to sales information and reduce the time spent interfacing with other personnel and with other office systems such as word processing (mail merge) and fax-back services.
Estimate of total cost of ownership	□ Total Cost of Ownership (TCO) is $150,000 for the first year of operation (see Steps 9 and 10 below) □ Increase profit $160,000 (use online MIS to help close new sales) □ Decrease expenses $130,000 (time saved managing paperwork) □ "Bottom line" savings $140,000
Expected impact of automation/change	Sales force must be equipped with notebook computers and attend training programs.

Management Approvals	
Feasibility	Operations Manager
Reasonability	VP Sales and Marketing
Cost-effectiveness	CFO
IT Department	IT Manager
Final approval	The Boss

Step 3: Evaluate your sales automation system.

According to the Gartner Group in Stamford, Connecticut, the market for sales force automation software is expected to grow from $1.4 billion in 1997 to $3.9 billion by the year 2000.

There are four key factors driving the sales automation market:

1. Global competition is forcing companies to re-engineer their selling process to reduce their cost of sales.
2. The Internet and electronic commerce have redefined customers' purchase process.
3. Sales automation enables companies to improve the effectiveness of their sales and marketing personnel.
4. Declining hardware and software costs have reduced the cost of implementing sales automation systems.

Sales automation systems can help your salespeople track prospects, maintain account histories, and generate sales reports on demand.

- Reduce the number of sales calls that must be made to close a sale—ideally down to one.
- Empower salespeople with all of the information that they need to make decisions in the field.
- Access information on customers, products, company policies and procedures, competitors, and industry trends.
- Track all customer contacts from initial contact to postsale follow-up sales activities (opportunity management system).
- Access market research from government agencies and private sources.
- Track sales leads, prospects, contacts, and customers.

- Track and analyze sales cycles.
- Record and track each customer contact.
- Maintain a history of each customer account.
- Support team selling and workgroup collaboration.
- Help salespeople configure optimal solutions for customer's needs.
- Help salespeople develop and present custom sales proposals and presentations.
- Help salespeople generate sales contracts.
- Help salespeople schedule customer orders.
- Maintain individual and organization-wide calendars.
- Facilitate workflow and electronic document routing.
- Support computer telephone integration.
- Support electronic messaging and videoconferencing.
- Track and report sales expenses.
- Record and report appointments, meetings, demonstrations, presentations, proposals, and correspondence.
- Help salespeople generate territory and account management reports.
- Help salespeople generate sales forecasts.
- Provide online sales training.

The "Sales Automation System Components" table illustrates how manual office systems can be replaced with automated systems.

Sales Automation System Components	Manual Office System	Automated System
Contact Information System	□ Index cards □ Post-it™ notes	□ Contact database access via palmtop and sub-notebook computers
Product Information System	□ Sales brochures	□ Online, multimedia product information
Competitive Information System	□ Outdated marketing report	□ Internet access to competitors' marketing information □ Intelligent agent program for analysis and reporting
Personal Information System	□ Day-Timer™	□ Computer Telephone Integration □ Wireless palmtop computers □ Synchronization between local and remote office systems

Configuration Management System	□ Photocopied price list	□ Online product configuration guide
Proposal Generator	□ Typewriter □ Word processor □ Copy machine	□ Online proposal generator, electronic messaging, document publishing, automatic routing and distribution
Account Management	□ Verbal and written reports	□ Opportunity management system
Communications	□ Telephone □ Fax □ Internal e-mail	□ Global e-mail □ Document conferencing □ Videoconferencing □ Universal in-box

SALES AUTOMATION CAPABILITIES/ FUNCTIONAL REQUIREMENTS

When you understand each step of your sales process well enough to flow chart it, you are ready to evaluate the pros and cons of implementing different sales automation solutions.

Sales Automation Capabilities	System 1	System 2
Contact Information System	Yes	Yes
Product Information System	No	No
Competitive Information System	No	No
Personal Information System	Yes	Yes
Configuration Management System	Yes	Yes
Proposal generator	No	Interface with Microsoft Office
Account management	Yes	Yes
Communications (Internet e-mail)	Yes	Yes
Maintain a prospect database	Yes	Yes

Maintain a customer database	Yes	Yes
Track sales history	Yes—product and customer	Yes—customer only
Provide sales analysis	Yes	No
Track customer contacts	Excellent reporting	Minimal reporting
Track outstanding sales orders	No	No
Track opportunities	Tracks opportunities by salesperson	Limited—can prioritize contacts
Develop sales call reports	Minimal—basic form is included	No
Data synchronization	Can synchronize server with Windows CE	Can synchronize server with 3Com Palm Pilot
Telemarketing script	No	No
Cost	$1,200 per user	$800 per user
Installation	Good	Good
Implementation	Easy	Complex
Support	Good	Excellent
Service	Yearly maintenance contract	Yearly maintenance contract

A detailed, "Sales Automation Software Evaluation" worksheet, which is based on Information Systems Marketing, Inc.'s annual *Guide to Sales, Customer Service and Marketing Automation,* is included in the Appendix at the end of this book.

SUCCESSFUL ADOPTION OF
SALES AUTOMATION SYSTEMS

Complexity and negligible payback have hampered many sales automation projects. In 1997, the Gartner Group reported that 55 percent of the sales automation projects they tracked failed to deliver a measurable return on their client's investment. And a recent Forrester report found that only 28 percent of Fortune 5000 companies are reporting highly successful sales automation efforts.

Successful implementation of sales automation systems, like other information systems, can only be achieved with careful planning and management focus. So before embarking on a sales automation project, you should confirm that you have clear objectives, reasonable expectations, and adequate resources to ensure the success of your project.

1. Do you have clearly defined objectives and key results for your sales automation project?
   - □ Most information system projects focus on decreasing expenses, but sales automation projects focus on increasing revenues.
2. Are you aware of the potential problems that your company may face before, during, and after implementing your sales automation project?
   - □ It is very difficult to define user's requirements *before* a system is developed or implemented. Revising specifications *during* the development process usually increases costs.
   - □ It is very difficult to estimate software development costs.
   - □ Custom software projects become more difficult to justify as user expectations grow.
   - □ It is often necessary to scale hardware purchases to support anticipated system usage. So companies typically purchase more hardware capacity than necessary to accommodate future growth.
   - □ Most hardware and software becomes obsolete in two to three years.
   - □ It is often impractical to maintain legacy systems because suppliers are unwilling or unable to support obsolete products.
3. Do you have reasonable expectations for implementation and payback?
   - □ Senior management often takes a short-term view of information system requirements.
   - □ Information Technology (IT) managers face an uphill battle selling infrastructure, such as upgrading network components. It is easier to justify more visible productivity tools such as notebook computers for outside sales representatives.
   - □ Many companies outsource their computing requirements to help control information system expenses.

4. Are you prepared to invest all of the resources that are necessary to ensure that your sales force and your IT personnel are prepared to install, implement, and maintain your sales automation system?
   □ Most information system projects are finite and have fixed budgets before implementation. However, most sales automation projects are multiphase, ongoing, and require periodic cost justification validated by real world results.
5. Do you understand the functions, processes, and systems that you're trying to automate, so that your implementation will fit you company's needs and help it achieve total market domination?
   Step 1. *Business Audit*—evaluate your selling processes, policies, and capabilities.
   Step 2. *Information Systems Audit*—evaluate your computer and communication systems.
   Step 3. *Evaluate New Technologies*—evaluate new products, such as customer information systems, that can help your company leverage its selling resources and provide better customer service.
   Step 4. *Action Plan*—improve your competitiveness by reengineering your selling processes and implementing a customer information system.

Your company can use the "Sales Automation Capabilities" table to help it evaluate its current sales automation capabilities.

Sales Automation Capabilities	Client-Centered™ Training's Sales Automation Capabilities
Is a sales management/contact tracking system being used to track prospects and customers?	Yes. We use Symantec's ACT!
Does the sales automation system interface (share information) with the organization's order entry and billing system?	No.
Is the Internet used to support internal e-mail?	Yes. We have e-mail boxes on our ISP's server.
Is the Internet used to support outside e-mail?	Yes. We communicate with most of our clients using the Internet.
Is the Internet used to access corporate databases?	No. But we use the Internet to research prospective clients.

Is the Internet used for order entry and tracking?	No. But we purchase many of our office supplies and research materials on the Internet.
Can customers access internal systems using Internet connection?	No. Our ISP maintains a "virtual" firewall.
Do individual salespeople have portable (notebook) computers?	All of our salespeople have notebook PCs and run Microsoft Office and a contact manager program that can be synchronized with our sales automation system.
Do salespeople use handheld computers?	No.
Do salespeople use cellular or PCS telephones?	Yes, we have standardized on Sprint's PCS system.
What office equipment do remote salespeople have in their remote office or their automobile?	Desktop PC, stand-alone fax, PC scanner, laser printer or color inkjet printer, surge protector/power strip. Telephone lines for Internet access and fax.
Do salespeople have access to videoconferencing facilities?	No. But we plan to implement videoconferencing using Microsoft's Net Meeting groupware product next year.

Ninth Law of Total Market Domination

Early technology adopters can gain a competitive advantage against companies that are unwilling or unable to adapt their marketing strategy to leverage new computer and communication technologies.

For example, the Internet has impacted businesses throughout the industrialized world. As the cost of storing, processing, and transmitting information declines, and as the availability of network bandwidth increases, it is becoming irrelevant where information is stored on the Internet or where people that rely on Internet services work.

This paradigm shift presents a *window of opportunity* for companies to re-engineer their sales infrastructure using Internet marketing, online customer support, and e-commerce to help them reduce their marketing costs, address new business opportunities, and achieve total market domination.

MANAGING CUSTOMER INFORMATION

Using computers to help your company manage its customer information provides the greatest payoff, relative to other automation opportunities, for improving the effectiveness of its sales and marketing resources.

When your company invests time qualifying prospects, it acquires valuable information. Each fact that it collects, such as a buyer's name, or the type and age of installed competitive equipment, can be used to help it market its products and services. The most efficient way to keep track of this information is with a computer database.

Using a computer database for *database marketing* enables your company to save all of the information that it has spent its marketing resources to acquire, and then "borrow" that information to help it achieve its sales objectives. When your company develops new products, introduces special promotions, or initiates a new sales campaign, your database can help it target its selling efforts to its best-qualified prospects.

The key to database marketing is that it is knowledge based—every contact is tracked to profile your customers' needs and concerns and to track their purchase history. Tracking this information enables your company to profile each one of your customers and establish a one-to-one communication that addresses their key purchase factors.

Database marketing is synergistic with other selling activities because it can serve as a lead tracking and generation system, and because it can help your company prequalify its leads. Database marketing can also help your company build customer loyalty, develop new business relationships, generate repeat business, and increase customer retention.

Step 4: Evaluate your customer information system.

Customer satisfaction is based on a customer's perception of the quality and the timeliness of the services that your company renders. Small businesses usually have all of the information about a customer that they need to provide a high level of customer service. For example, the proprietor of a corner store may know a customer's product preferences, purchase history, spending patterns, credit history, personal concerns, and his or her potential value to their business. However, salespeople in larger companies often do not have real-time access to the information that they need to provide a high level of customer service.

It is difficult to manage customer information in a large company because customer information is usually stored in many different areas of the business and in many different databases. For example, a company may store customer information in its sales force automation system, customer service and support system, financial and accounting systems, operations and production systems, and marketing systems. To manage this disparate, distributed data, companies must develop a unified customer information system.

A customer information system (CIS) is composed of customer management applications (CMA), sales force automation (SFA), and marketing information system (MIS) applications.

Customer Information System (CIS)		
Customer Management Applications (CMA)	Sales Force Automation (SFA) Applications	Marketing Information System (MIS) Applications
Internal Help Desk	Sales Force Automation	Manage sales campaigns
External Customer Support	Telemarketing	Web-based lead generation
External Customer Service	Telesales	Manage and distribute sales collateral
Quality Control	Sales Configuration	Automate product fulfillment
Field Service Management	Call Center Automation	Intelligent workflow to automate selling activities

Different software companies provide different services and use different terminology to describe how they automate customer interaction and the selling process. For example, sales automation and customer information systems are sometimes referred to as customer relationship management systems, customer interaction systems, customer asset management systems, and front office applications.

*The only practical way to distinguish between different customer infor-
mation and sales automation systems is to carefully evaluate each system's
capabilities.*

CUSTOMER INFORMATION SYSTEM BENEFITS

Customer Information Systems are strategic. They are part of the
sales infrastructure in most technology-driven businesses, and are
necessary to compete in many markets that are driven by a high-level
of customer service during the selling process.

- Manage opportunities
- Manage territories
- Manage accounts
- Manage contacts
- Qualify leads
- Automatic needs analysis
- Product configuration
- Telemarketing
- Cross-selling in call centers
- Team selling
- Scheduling orders
- Schedule sales activities
- Communicate marketing story
- Generate sales quotes and proposals
- Evaluate sales performance
- Track sales orders
- Prioritize sales orders
- Sales forecasting
- Fulfill literature requests
- Configure products
- Order products
- Track competitive information
- Evaluate marketing promotions

- Manage sales team's time
- Facilitate workflow in sales process
- Remote connectivity
- Available on portable computers
- Complete synchronization between all systems
- Knowledge search and retrieval
- Integration with decision support facilities
- Increase localization
- Conform to IT standards, such as IP, to facilitate data sharing
- Link customer directly to supply chain
- Reduce service and support costs
- Reduce COGS
- Faster delivery
- Improve customer service level

DECISION SUPPORT

Managing your customer encounter in real time is critical for customer retention. So anything your company can do to anticipate your customers' needs, and to customize and deliver your services in real time, can help your company gain a competitive advantage. The Gartner Group has coined the management term "zero-latency" to refer to this process.

Companies that achieve total market domination use their customer information system to "mine" the information that they have acquired about their market, their customers, and their competitors so that their sales team can predict customer behavior, respond quickly to changing customer expectations, and better manage their customers' purchase experience.

DEPLOYING A CUSTOMER INFORMATION SYSTEM

Depending on your company's priorities, where responsibility for systems management is in your organization, and the conflicting goals of different business units, your company may need to develop some of its CIS functionality in-house or in partnership with an IT consultant or system integrator. In any case, your CIS, like any other automated system, will be successful only if your company is prepared to re-engineer its obsolete or ineffective business processes and systems.[1]

- Most companies that implement a CIS link heterogeneous applications from multiple suppliers to create a comprehensive "best-of-breed" solution. However, some companies purchase all of their CIS components from one supplier to ensure rapid implementation and integration.
- Most companies implement a customer information system or CIS in phases, moving from their legacy accounting and

---

[1] The information technology audit process described in the author's *Information Technology Audit Handbook* (Prentice-Hall) can help your company balance its need to maintain cost-effective, mission-critical information systems, with its need to reposition itself for competitiveness and survival as emerging technologies impact its fundamental business model. Information on the *Information Technology Audit Handbook* is available on the author's Web site at www.daytonassociates.com.

customer database systems to automated customer support and service applications, to enterprise-wide sales force automation systems.

- ☐ Larger companies often implement data warehouses or data marts (application-focused data warehouses) that are scaled for enterprise deployment, to support their CIS. And most companies access and analyze their customer data using Online Analytic Processing (OLAP) tools, which enable them to answer specific questions about their customer's needs, concerns, and behaviors.

- ☐ Implementing a CIS can be an expensive and time-consuming process. Entry-level sales automation applications, which do little more than provide basic contact management, cost from $50 to $250 per user, but enterprise scale CIS can cost from $500 to $3,500 per user. However, the Total Cost of Ownership (TCO), which includes costs for all software, hardware, communications and Internet access, training, and ongoing support, may easily be five to ten times this amount.

Your company must balance its short-term objectives of containing IT costs and providing reliable IT services with its longer-term objectives of improving your company's competitiveness and building market share.

The Customer Interaction System Spectrum[2]				
Lower Costs ⇦ ⇦ ⇦ ⇦ ⇨ ⇨ ⇨ ⇨ **Increase Revenues**				
Internal Help Desk	Customer Support	Field Service Management	Telemarketing and Telesales	Sales Force Automation
Call logging and tracking, problem resolution, knowledge-bases, integration with network and systems management	Event logging and escalation, customer self-service, integration with billing, inventory and dispatch	Call tracking and scheduling, automatic call back, service routing, request tracking on the Internet	Telemarketing pools, fully integrated call centers	Lead tracking and opportunity management, sales configuration, competitive comparisons, e-commerce

[2] Source: Adapted from The Aberdeen Group

CUSTOMER INFORMATION SYSTEMS ON THE INTERNET

Implementing a CIS on the Internet can help your company link its entire supply chain together—from resellers to up-stream suppliers—and can provide instant customer feedback. But Internet-based customer information systems are still relatively new and are just beginning to be deployed and field tested by major corporations.

Many companies are concerned about deploying *any* mission-critical systems on the Internet that require reliable 24x7 access and secure connections for e-commerce. And some companies are concerned that an Internet-based CIS will open their internal business processes to competitors.

Fortunately, these problems can usually be handled by limiting access to sensitive information to password protected areas of a company's Web site and by deploying virtual private networks. Virtual private networks are extensions of company's internal private network that piggyback on the public Internet. The primary advantages of a virtual private network are that it can reduce a company's network costs by using the Internet infrastructure, and that it can provide a higher level of data security and performance.

CUSTOMER SUPPORT CALL CENTERS AND WEB-BASED CUSTOMER SERVICE

Maintaining customer support call centers costs companies about $20 to $30 for each call that is handled. Implementing Web-based customer service can reduce these costs to $2 to $3 per call. Early adopters that hope to achieve a competitive advantage over companies that are not ready or able to deploy this technology are implementing internet-based customer support centers today.

Microsoft, for example, has recently implemented Silknet Software's eService 98 system to support its 6,000-person Worldwide Product Group's sales team. eService 98 makes up-to-date multimedia support information encompassing voice, video, and Internet hyperlinks, which are stored in a knowledge base, available to answer Microsoft's field representative's questions. The system provides enhanced e-mail-telephone integration and business-process-driven workflow management capabilities, which enable field representatives' queries to be routed to a product manager who can answer their questions. And the system manages thousands of action items entered each day, using a database feature called a trigger to automatically notify system users of deadlines for action items and to escalate action items to managers if they become critical.

Step 5: Evaluate your communication systems.

Communication is the cornerstone of any sales organization. Anything that your company does to improve communication will ultimately help your sales force leverage its time and become more successful.

Communication Systems	Capabilities
Is your telephone system adequate for your business needs?	No, we want to implement VOI (voice on the Internet) capabilities to reduce telephone charges and to interface with our internal Web server.
Do you use an electronic mail system?	Yes, we have recently implemented Microsoft Mail.
Is it adequate for your business needs?	Yes.
Do you use the Internet for electronic messaging?	Yes, all of our sales representatives have e-mail accounts on our Internet server.
Do you maintain your own Web server?	Yes, at www.daytonassociates.com.
Does your system support remote access services?	Yes, we are running Windows NT, which provides RAS.
Do you plan to make any significant changes to your communication systems within the next twelve months?	Yes, we plan to implement long distance telephone services on our Internet (IP) server.

COMPUTER TELEPHONY

Computer telephony, the convergence of data and voice—computers and telephones—has moved from its origins within large corporate call centers to its current rapid growth in workgroup environments on PC-based servers and desktop PC workstations.

Companies that achieve total market domination are using Computer Telephony, or CT, to improve their customer services, enhance their employees' productivity, simplify their network, and provide operational cost efficiencies by automating complex call center functions.

In the past, a company in Quebec might, for example, employ a telephone receptionist to determine whether its customers spoke English or French, and if necessary, to route their call to a bilingual customer service representative. Today, a company can use an integrated voice response system to identify a French-speaking caller, and use skills-based routing to automatically route their call to a bilingual agent in its call center.

Computer Telephony Applications	
Feature	**Function**
Audio conferencing	Enable one or more multiparty audio connections
Audiotext	Dispenses prerecorded information to callers
Automated attendant	Automatic voice response function answers phone and performs basic receptionist tasks
Call routing	Enable automated, intelligent call switching
Electronic commerce	Supports voice, image, and data transmission over IP link
Enhanced fax services	Provided for subscribers by telephone companies for fax transmission via least-cost lines
Enhanced paging services	Adds voice, fax, and e-mail messaging to simple numeric or alphanumeric paging
Fax broadcast	Enable fax transmission to multiple fax machines
Fax-on-demand	Instant document delivery to fax line based on caller's response to prompts
Fax server	LAN-based server that receives and transmits faxes
Follow Me service	Enables subscribers to receive messages via various types of media, such as phones, PCs, pagers, fax servers, and Web TV™, regardless of geographic location
Interactive voice response	Provides transaction processing that changes or interacts with a database of information
Internet telephony (Voice Over the Internet)	IP-based telephone services that enable users to talk PC-to-PC or PC-to-phone using the Internet
Multimedia conferencing	Voice, data, and video conferencing over a telephone line or Internet connection

One-pipe products	Any offering that combines voice, data, and/or video capabilities on a single network
Personal communication services (personal mobility services)	Individual telecommunication services that enable people with phones, PCs, or pagers to communicate regardless of their physical location
Personal productivity services	Contact management, calendaring, and sales management services that tie into corporate call centers and Internet Web sites
Skills-based routing	Distributes calls to telephone support representative with the skills to respond to a specific customer concern
Telemarketing/inbound	Functions that enable a high volume of inbound calls
Telemarketing/outbound	Functions that facilitate a high volume of outbound calls
Unified messaging	Products that integrate voice, fax, e-mail, image, and video on one platform
Video conferencing	Enables one or more multiparty video conferences
Voice mail	Records, stores, plays back, and distributes voice messages
Web-based call centers	Systems that enable customers to reach businesses for information or e-commerce on the Internet

NEW WAYS TO REACH YOUR CUSTOMERS

Wireless communication, videoconferencing, document conferencing, electronic forms, and workflow computing can help your sales force improve customer service, and reduce your company's cost of sales.

Early adopters that implement these emerging technologies can reduce their customer support costs and achieve a competitive advantage over less automated companies.

Wireless Communications

Over 50 million people in the U.S. are mobile workers who are involved in occupations that require them to be away from their office for a significant period of time. Wireless communications enables these workers to stay in touch with their customers and business partners.

A study by the Business Research Group in Newton, Massachusetts, examined the applications that remote workers access, and found that 66 percent access corporate network e-mail, 47 percent access Internet e-mail, and 31 percent access public network e-mail. The study also reported that 40 percent of remote workers access corporate database files, 36 percent work with client/server applications, and 30 percent access sales and order entry applications.

Videoconferencing

Videoconferencing, which enables users to view each other as they talk over a standard telephone or computer network connection, is emerging as an important business technology—and as a powerful sales and marketing tool. However, there are two issues that are slowing implementation: universal access and limited network bandwidth. Fortunately, both of these challenges are being addressed by new technologies.

Microsoft's NetMeeting and other videoconferencing applications enable videoconferencing over the Internet, and will ultimately enable universal access. And advances in high-speed digital communications, by telephone carriers and cable and satellite communication companies, are being implemented in worldwide voice/data networks that can support high bandwidth multimedia applications such as videoconferencing and Internet access.

Many early adopters are using desktop videoconferencing to help them communicate with customers and with sales personnel who work in distant locations. These businesses justify the cost of videoconferencing with saved travel time and expenses.

Document Conferencing

Document conferencing is another tool that early adopters are using to help them communicate with their customers and business partners. Document conferencing enables PC users in different locations to look at a common image, such as an electronic spreadsheet model or a slide presentation, while they discuss it over a telephone connection.

Document conferencing systems transfer images of drawings, slides, or documents, using a "white board" metaphor, by delivering an image on their computer's monitor that is analogous to the image you would see on a white board during a meeting. This enables two PC users to view and manipulate documents and images while they discuss them over the telephone.

Figure 8-2.
How Mobile Workers Communicate
(Source: Business Research Group, 1998)

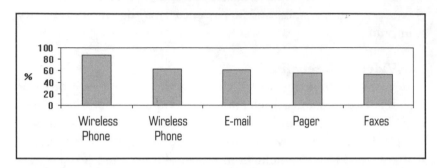

Microsoft and Intel have developed messaging and document conferencing standards that will help ensure that Internet-based meetings become commonplace over the next few years.

Electronic Forms and Workflow Computer Applications

Most salespeople hate to spend time completing paperwork because it prevents them from spending that time working with their customers.

The paper form is the most common and proven business tool, but paper-forms-based office systems can be very inefficient. Inaccurate information and incomplete forms often result in incorrect data; re-entering information that is common to multiple forms wastes time; and circulating paper forms through an organization often results in important information not being available when it is needed.

The most effective way to reduce the amount of time that your salespeople spend doing paperwork is to re-engineer your company's paper-based systems with automated electronic forms-based systems. Saving information in electronic forms that are linked to computer databases makes critical information accessible to those who need it in real time. And integrating electronic mail services with electronic forms automates the process of transferring information between users in an organization.

Many companies that have achieved total market domination have implemented workflow computer applications, such as Lotus Notes and Microsoft Exchange, to help them automate business processes that involve routing electronic forms and messages, such as entering customers' purchase orders. Capturing this information in electronic forms can help your business speed response time, improve cash flow, support communications between different work groups, and make your organization more efficient and responsive to your customers', suppliers', and employees' needs.

Electronic Data Interchange

Electronic Data Interchange (EDI) enables different computers to send data back and forth, to buy and sell products and services electronically, across telephone lines, without user intervention.

Many companies use EDI to automate their inventory tracking and ordering process. EDI systems can, for example, enable low- or out-of-stock items in an inventory system to generate electronic purchase orders automatically, and can post those orders directly into a supplier's order entry system. EDI systems can also be used to generate invoices and post accounts receivables.

EDI capabilities are required to do business with many large companies, but a simple standard for EDI has failed to emerge—many different proprietary data formats are used to transmit and receive EDI documents.

Fortunately, an emerging Internet standard can help resolve this EDI standards battle. XML, which extends the functionality of the HTML language, used to publish and display information on the Internet, makes it easy to support EDI messaging. Over the next few years, as communication standards, data security, and other implementation issues are resolved, companies will replace their proprietary EDI systems with "open" Internet-based systems that use XML.

As Internet-based EDI emerges, many smaller companies will have a window of opportunity to use this technology to reduce their operating costs and address new business opportunities.

Electronic Mail

Over 200 million people use electronic mail or "e-mail" to communicate with their coworkers, customers, and suppliers. The primary advantage of e-mail is that it is an almost instantaneous store-and-forward technology, like voice mail, so the person whom you are communicating with does not have to be available at the time you send your message.

- □ E-mail enables you to send messages almost instantaneously to other e-mail users.
- □ E-mail recipients do not have to be present when their mail is received.
- □ E-mail is not as intrusive as voice messaging.
- □ E-mail is a very inexpensive way to communicate.
- □ E-mail tends to be brief and less formal than other business correspondence.
- □ Most e-mail systems enable you to carbon copy a message to multiple recipients on a mailing list.
- □ E-mail is a convenient way to communicate with mobile and remote coworkers.
- □ E-mail gateways are available to link disparate e-mail systems together.
- □ If your company's local area network has a gateway to the Internet, your company can send e-mail to customers and suppliers around the world, using their Internet e-mail address.

Over the next few years, as emerging telecommunication and network directory service protocols become widely adopted, and low-cost, high-bandwidth Internet access becomes available, the Internet and IP-based messaging will provide the infrastructure for low-cost, universal access to a universal in-box for multimedia communications. This technology will simplify electronic communications and will have a tremendous impact on how we communicate with one another and how we transact business.

E-mail: The First "Zero-Cost" Marketing Medium

E-mail's immediacy and casual nature make it a powerful tool to build relationships with new customers, to gain insight into customers' needs and concerns, and to help companies move from mass marketing to customized, individual marketing.

Your company can, for example, use e-mail to test a marketing story for less than one cent per message, generate a trackable 10 percent response in an hour without requiring a bank of telephone operators, and enter foreign markets with virtually no added investment. And your company can give your customers a virtual store delivered to their desktop to enable them to purchase your products by simply linking its e-mail message to its commerce enabled Web site.

Spam

Many companies are sending unsolicited commercial e-mail or "spam" to millions of Internet addresses. The cost to send massive quantities of spam is negligible, but response rates are usually infinitesimal, and the annoyance can result in the spammer's e-mail server being bombarded with hundreds of thousands of irate e-mail replies.

Many companies outsource spam mailings to a junk e-mail company.[3] However, some companies are bringing this technology in-house as e-commerce server applications that can support mass e-mail campaigns become more widely available, and tools to support multimedia message presentation, personalized messaging, and automated campaign management, begin to emerge.

For example, DoubleClick, Inc., a Web-based advertising brokerage, has set up an advertising network that enables companies to target online ads to users in a specific community or geographic region. DoubleClick sorts viewership of a site by identifying the network that viewers are using to dial into the Web.

As e-mail marketing becomes more pervasive, consumer privacy and protection are becoming greater concerns. However it is likely that a combination of intelligent filtering software to block spam and voluntary adherence to the Direct Marketing Association's direct e-mail standards will thwart the most flagrant abuses of Web

---

[3] The U.S. government is attempting to curb spammers; however it very difficult to draft effective laws without limiting all commercial e-mail or violating constitutional rights.

"netiquette." With these caveats, e-mail may become the most powerful marketing medium of the twenty-first century.

Your company should explore how it can use e-mail marketing to help it achieve total market domination

Step 6: Evaluate your accounting system.

Depending on your company's sales infrastructure, it may be necessary for your salespeople to access information from your accounting systems, such as customer credit and inventory reports.

OLAP or online application processing applications, and "data mining" tools are available that make it relatively easy for sales and marketing managers to generate reports that they can use to help them manage their territory and evaluate their marketing strategies. For example, a marketing manager might customize an inventory report to track initial demand and subsequent reorders of a new product, and a sales representative might access a customer's purchase history.

You can use the "Accounting Systems" table to identify which modules of your financial system can be accessed by your sales and marketing personnel.

Accounting Systems	Automated = X	Sales Force Access
General Ledger	X	
Order Entry	X	X
Order Tracking	X	X
EDI		
Invoicing	X	
Inventory (BOM)		
Accounts Payable	X	
Accounts Receivable	X	X
Credit Reporting	X	X
Purchase Order	X	
Job Costing		
Sales Tracking/Reports		
Customer Database		
Human Resources		
Payroll	X	

Manufacturing Systems		
Production Control		
Shop Floor Control		
MRP/ERP		
CRP		
Scheduling	X	X
Time and Billing		
Data Collection Systems		
Other		

IT SOUNDS SO EASY. . .

The financial applications business led by SAP, Baan, PeopleSoft, and Oracle is growing at a rapid pace, but according to a Deloitte & Touche survey of 221 executives who have recently implemented these systems, most users are not satisfied. The study found that only 9 percent of users describe their system as "world class," and that 85 percent claimed their system "fell short of expectations." The survey also reported that 57 percent of users want better reporting tools, and 48 percent of users want better ad hoc analysis capabilities.

DECISION SUPPORT

You can use the "Decision Support Capabilities" table to help your company evaluate whether your sales force has access to the reports that it needs to support its selling activities and to provide a high level of customer service.

Decision Support Capabilities Track sales performance by:	Client-Centered™ Training's Financial System's Information Access and Reporting
Business Unit	Yes
Customer Class	Yes
Geography	Yes
Product Line	No
Product	No
Sales Group	Yes
Sales Representative	Yes
Other	—
Summarize Sales Trends	No
Overall Satisfaction with Decision Support Capabilities	Our current system is not providing the information we need to help us manage our sales team. We need reports that will tell us which sales representatives in which territories are selling specific products.

Client-Centered™ Training's system cannot generate reports on specific products, so it is very difficult for the company to determine whether product specific-factors or other market factors, such as a downturn in the economy, are impacting its sales.

Step 7: Evaluate your information systems support and service.

Many companies fail to realize the full benefit of their information systems because they have implemented overly complex or poorly performing systems, or because they have not provided the training and support that their personnel need to work with their systems efficiently.

The "Information Systems Bottleneck" table can help your company identify inefficiencies that waste resources and make it difficult for your company's sales and marketing people to do their jobs.

Information Systems Bottlenecks	Client-Centered™ Training's Primary Concerns
System Administration	Too much time spent entering data manually. Should be able to interface contact manager with e-mail and fax back systems.
System Management	We would like to implement an automated backup procedure.
Timeliness of Receiving Data	Good.
Accuracy of Data (Data Integrity)	Usually accurate—some salespeople are sloppy about entering data and completing online forms.
Data Access/Reporting Capabilities	Poor—we need a more powerful reporting tool.
Flexibility	Barely adequate.
System Response Time	Good.
System Reliability	Very good.
Security	We have not done a security audit, but we suspect we are at risk from both internal and external attack.
Systems Integration (Interoperability)	Our accounting system does not interface with our other office systems.
Extensibility (Expansion Capabilities)	We plan to replace our current system.
Rapid Application Development (RAD) Capabilities	Our current system is not programmable.
Support (Suppliers)	We have had good support from our supplier.
Service (Suppliers)	We have not had any service problems.
Service (Internal Personnel)	We need to invest more time training our sales representatives on proper use of our systems.
Is a plan in place to resolve these outstanding problems?	We plan to upgrade our system.
Can any of these problems be resolved by outside suppliers?	We plan to hire a consultant to help us develop an IT plan that will enable us to align our IT systems with our business objectives. We plan to implement a security audit early next year.

Many salespeople are uncomfortable using computers. Providing easy-to-understand documentation and fast, friendly technical support will help these salespeople overcome any concerns that they have about working with automated systems.

Your company can use the "Technical Support and Documentation" worksheet to evaluate the technical support that your company is providing to its sales and marketing personnel.

Technical Support and Documentation	Responses by Client-Centered™ Training's system manager, the sales team's PC coordinator, and several sales representatives.
Is your documentation accurate?	Yes.
Is your documentation concise?	No, we have 5 different user guides. Most of our salespeople have never read any of them.
Is your documentation easy to use?	Yes. But the documentation looks more formidable than it really is.
Is your documentation easy to maintain?	No. There is no way for us to update or customize our documentation.
How much time do users spend resolving technical problems?	Less than 1 hour per week.
What is the IT department's average response time?	30 minutes.
When was the last training class scheduled?	Last February.
Was a follow-up review class scheduled?	No.
Were personnel tested to ensure skills transfer?	No.
Do you publish a user satisfaction survey?	No, but when our salespeople complain, we pass their comments along to our DP department.
Vendor Documentation (installation, implementation, and operating instructions)	We have standard manuals for our system. They are too complicated for some of our salespeople to understand.
IT Procedures Manuals	See DP Department.
Accounting Procedures Manuals	See Finance Department.
System Administration Documentation	See DP Department.
Emergency Documentation	None.
Help Desk	We do not have a formal help desk, but we are planning to assign one person to

	answer questions for 2 hours each morning.
Vendor's Telephone Support	This is billed at $60 per half hour.
Online Training/Tutorial	There are online tutorials for Microsoft Windows and Office.
User Documentation (Procedures)	Our DP Manager has promised that she would have someone create a step-by-step user guide for our SFA system.
Video Training	We have just purchased a video training tape on Microsoft Office.
Classroom Training	We have had one training class, but only three of our salespeople could attend, and it did not seem to help very much.
Subscription Help Services	None at this time.

PATHWAYS TO CRIME

The only way to ensure the integrity of your information systems is through diligent attention to computer security procedures such as controlling access to information with secure passwords, encrypting sensitive communications, and implementing firewalls to protect corporate servers connected to public networks.

Figure 8-3.
Percent of Companies Reporting Security Problems

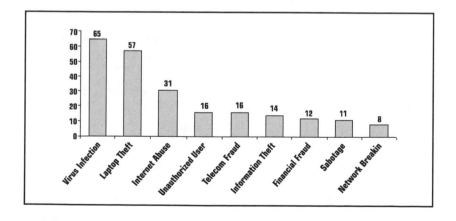

A Computer Security Institute report for the FBI surveyed companies reporting financial losses attributable to specific types of high-tech criminal activity and other factors.[4] The study revealed that outside salespeople pose a special risk to corporate security, because 57 percent of all computer crimes are ultimately linked to a stolen laptop computer. Safeway Insurance estimates that over 300,000 laptop computers were stolen in 1998—at a cost to businesses of over $1 billion, not including the value of lost data that was stored in the stolen computers.

There are several safeguards that your company can implement to help thwart laptop thieves:

- □ Use passwords to help protect system access. (Most portable computers include this feature.)
- □ Use smart cards, which act like ignition keys, to help prevent unauthorized system access.
- □ Use data encryption technology for all information transfers.
- □ Install antitheft software such as Absolute Software's CompuTrace (www.computrace.com), which can automatically trace phone calls made by a stolen computer every time its modem is used to dial out.
- □ Implement an outside security audit to help your company assess its exposure to information theft and system sabotage.

Step 8: Evaluate your use of the Internet and network computing.

The Internet is the primary driver of the digital revolution. Over 200 million people in 159 countries are using the Internet for electronic mail, market research, marketing, customer support, electronic commerce, education, research, news, entertainment, and a constellation of other applications.

According to an August 1998 study by Nielsen Media Research on Internet commerce, the number of Web purchasers has reached over 20 million people, and the number of shoppers—people checking out or comparing products and services on the Web—has reached 48 million people. The study estimated that 79 million

---

[4] Computer Security Institute report for the FBI, published in *Sales and Field Force Automation,* March 1997.

people over the age of sixteen are now Internet users in the United States and Canada, which is a gain of almost 40 percent from a previous study eleven months ago. And according to Jupiter Communications, 55 percent of U.S. households and 32 percent of European households will be online by the year 2002.

If your business is involved with international trade, it is time to explore how the Internet can bring your business closer to your customers!

Developing an Effective Internet Presence	Resource/Impact
What is your objective for creating a Web site (e.g., information, promotion, entertainment, merchandising)?	We would like to use our Web site to promote our seminars and to sell our publications.
Who is your target market?	Business managers and salespeople.
Have you completed a competitive site analysis?	Yes, we have evaluated 15 training companies' sites—we believe that our site does a good job of communicating our marketing story and establishing our professional approach to program development.
Who is responsible for creating your Web content?	Alan Johnson is coordinating the process for our Sales Manager.
Who is responsible for designing your site?	Lauren Stake.
Who is responsible for maintaining your site?	Bob Newark.
How will information be updated?	Our marketing manager is responsible for updating all sales materials. Our site manager is responsible for maintenance and links. Our sales manager is responsible for handling all customer feedback and RFIs.
Does your site require any special technology requirements (e.g., secure access, streaming media, etc.)?	Our site supports RealVideo files. We handle credit card transactions online through our bank.
What is your Internet site budget?	Our budget is $35,000 in direct costs, plus management time.
Who is responsible for approving your site architecture?	Bob Newark.
Who is responsible for final design approval?	Our VP of Sales.

Have you considered browser issues such as use of frames, Java, GIF animation, tables, style sheets, and streaming media?	We use frames for our navigation buttons, animated GIF files, and tables to format worksheets.
Are you using <meta> tags to increase your relevance to search engines?	Yes. We use <meta> tags for "sales," "training," "Client-Centered™," "Dayton Associates," and "sales seminar."
Is your Web site listed on the leading search engines?	We are listed on Yahoo!, Infoseek, AltaVista, and Excite.
Have you evaluated formats for graphics, audio, and video?	We support RealVideo files. We are testing their latest beta-release.
Have you determined which development tools/environment you will use for coding, graphics, audio, video, and animation?	We use Microsoft FrontPage and Win FTP. We are using a diagnostic tool to evaluate how our site rates on various search engines.
Do you plan to host a newsgroup or chat room on your site?	We are going to launch a newsletter next year.
What do you plan to do to market and promote your site?	We advertise our site in our books and publications. We also promote our site at our speaking engagements.
Do you have a plan in place for postproduction listing on high-visibility search engines?	We are listed on the top 20 search engines.
Will you coordinate your launch with your company's PR firm or advertising agency?	We coordinated the launch of our site with the PR that was done for our new book *Selling Microsoft*.
How will you collect feedback on your site (e.g., contact information, electronic forms, e-mail)?	We have a feedback form on our Web site that creates an electronic form that is e-mailed to our site automatically.
Do you have an infrastructure in place to handle user feedback and orders?	We respond to all customer inquiries within 48 hours. We follow-up all inquiries with a telephone call to qualify our prospect's interest.
Do you plan to use untargeted e-mail to market your site? This is also referred to as unsolicited commercial e-mail or "spam."	No. We think it would alienate many potential customers. We don't like getting Spam and believe that what goes around comes around!
Who is responsible for updating links to and from your site? (link exchange can provide free promotion)	Bob Newark.

Do you plan to sell banner advertising or other space on your site?	We are undecided. Our hit rate is fairly low. We think it makes more sense to share links with our strategic business partners.
Does your Web site communicate your marketing story in a clear, concise, compelling way?	We think so.
Are you prepared to fund the ongoing evolution of your site?	We plan to increase our budget at least 50% over the next 6 months, and will evaluate the payback from our site at that point.
Have you done any customer focus groups or retained any outside experts to get feedback on the ease of use and the effectiveness of your site?	We have had two customer focus groups and have hired an experienced Web design firm to review our site and make suggestions about improving its ease of use and navigation. The focus groups were invaluable. We learned that our site had way too many pages and that many of the images we were using took too long to download. We also learned about a minor bug in our feedback form.

MARKETING YOUR WEB SITE

Most companies rely on offline media such as television, radio, newspapers, and magazine advertising to build and promote their brands, and to create awareness of and drive traffic to their Web sites.

However, the primary vehicle for promoting Web sites is advertising on other high-traffic sites. For example, if your company is in the travel business, it might advertise on Expedia, which is a travel site on the Internet. Or if your company is a realtor, it might advertise its properties on the HomeAdvisor and the Realtor.com Web sites.

Regardless of how you attract visitors to your site, it is absolutely imperative to ensure that their experience is rewarding or they will not return.

TRACKING VISITORS

Monitoring how many hits your site has had over a period of time provides a good indication of the popularity of your site. However, to extract more meaningful data, you will need to program your site to track the specific pages that were accessed; the specific files, such as RealVideo or PowerPoint presentations, that were viewed; and your visitors' IP addresses.

Internet Site	Client-Centered™ Training's Visitor Analysis
Who is visiting your site?	Demographic information: 75% United States, 5% Canada, 10% Europe, 8% South America, 2% Asia 90% corporate visitors 10% individuals
What are they interested in and what they are looking at?	60% access information on seminars and presentations 40% access information on consulting services 25% access information about publications 30% access RealVideo clips 70% access information about our newsletter
How do visitors move through your site?	Most users jump from our home page to either our seminar page or our video-clips page
What makes a viewer take action?	We do not know exactly how or why our site is compelling visitors to request additional information—when polled, visitors say that they were "impressed" by our site, that they thought our videos were helpful in assessing our capabilities, or that they wanted pricing information. Many competitors have visited our site and requested detailed information about our services— including pricing information. We try to qualify RFIs before providing this information.
How often do viewers revisit your site?	We think that about 7% of visitors return and that less than 2% visit three or more times.
What percentage of visitors leaves contact information?	Less than 1% of visitors leave contact information.
What percentage of visitors become customers?	We have closed business with 6 clients that learned about our company on the Internet over the last 14 months.
Is your site meeting your objectives?	No. We want to provide training services on our site, and we would like to have the capability of selling our publications and tapes directly through our site.

MASS CUSTOMIZATION

Web sites can use "cookies" (downloaded script files) to enable them to store information on a visitor's computer. Cookies can track where viewers go on your site, how long they are there, how often they visit your site, and whether they are responsive to banner advertising and other promotions.

If you combine cookies with program scripts, you can create a custom entry screen for each visitor, route visitors to pages that will be of special interest to them, automatically send visitors personalized e-mail, and display special Web pages to reinforce your marketing message. For example, if a visitor is interested in sports, they can configure Microsoft Network's (MSN) home page, when viewed on their PC, to display the top sports news stories of the day. This same technology can enable your company's Web server to respond to customers' preferences and to deliver specific content, such as new product recommendations, based on your customers' previous visits to your Web site.

This ability to "mass customize" your Web site can enable your company to improve customer response and service, and drive your company's sales revenues.

INTERNET ADVERTISING

According to Jupiter Communications, the top 10 sites on the Web attract more than 50 percent of all online advertising revenues, which are expected to grow to more than $7 billion by the year 2002.

Banner advertisements can be tightly targeted and can provide excellent statistics on click through. However, depending on your product and your promotion, banner advertising may be a very expensive way for your company to generate leads.

Your company can purchase banner advertising directly through most search engines and portal sites, or through a market maker such as DoubleClick, Inc.

In most cases, you can determine the number of exposures your banner will have, the number of different banners that will be displayed, the frequency of each message, and any special criteria that may determine which type of information the person who views your banner is interested in.

PORTALS

At this point, it seems likely that a handful of popular Internet sites, such as America Online, Yahoo!, Microsoft Network, and Netscape, will become strategic "portals" to the Internet, and that these portals will have an inordinate influence over Internet users' navigation choices. However, it is not clear whether these portals will become as influential as television networks are in the broadcast industry or whether, over time, the implementation of high-bandwidth Internet connections and convergence with cable television and voice communications will obviate the importance of a users' home page.

E-COMMERCE

International Data Corporation recently announced new findings that indicate the Internet economy is about $200 billion worldwide, and that by the year 2002, it will be larger than the economies of Greece or Portugal. Companies today spend over a dollar and a half for every dollar of benefit received from the deployment of Internet technologies. However, IDC predicts that the crossover point—from investment to payback—could come as soon as the year 2000.

IDC also forecasts that the percent of users buying goods and services on the Web will grow modestly—from 26 percent in December 1997 to 40 percent in December 2002—and the actual number of Web buyers will expand from 18 million in 1997 to more than 128 million in the year 2002.

Although the United States continues to lead the world in the adoption of the Internet and the number of consumers and businesses conducting business electronically, the Internet is a worldwide phenomenon. IDC estimates that the worldwide Internet economy in Western Europe will be about a third of the U.S. Internet economy. And that in spite of Asia's current economic struggle, this region will experience the strongest growth in the number of users between 1997 and 2002.

Figure 8-4.
Worldwide Internet Commerce Revenues:
Business and Consumer Segments, 1996–2002
(Source: International Data Corporation, 1998)

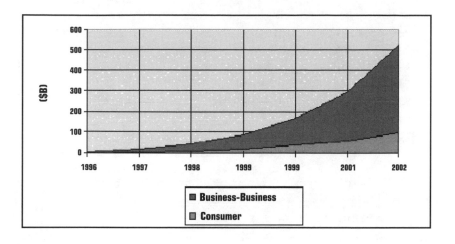

E-commerce redefines the cost of doing business.

Thousands of companies are using the Internet to sell their products and services. For example, banks are using the Internet to help them drive down the high cost of processing their customers' transactions and to market new financial services, such as insurance programs, to their customers.

Figure 8-5.
Impact of Internet Banking on Profits

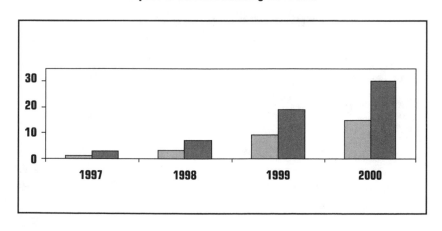

Figure 8-6.
Impact of Automation on Bank Transaction Costs

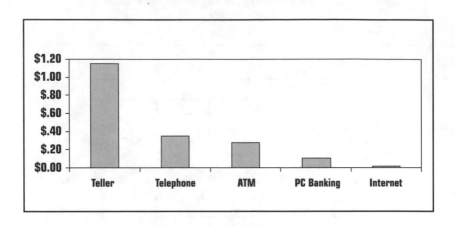

E-commerce creates new markets.

E-commerce sites that deliver a *compelling* marketing story can create new markets. For example, Ebay.com is a popular online auction site that matches buyers and sellers of different products ranging from antique jewelry to notebook computers. And Priceline.com, which brokers discount airline fares, has auctioned over 10,000 airline tickets in its first six weeks of operation. Online swap meets and discounted airfares are very compelling!

Whether your company is selling tangible products, such as automobiles, or intangible products, such as "peace of mind" from insurance, it is becoming imperative for your company to establish its own Internet-brand.

GOVERNMENT REGULATION

As the Internet becomes more pervasive, pressure is increasing for government regulation of Internet suppliers and users. New laws are being debated to collect taxes on goods and services, regulate adult content, protect intellectual property, control the use of data encryption, and ensure competition.

The U.S. government has enacted a moratorium on taxing electronic commerce for several years, but it is unclear whether state and local governments will be able to restrain themselves from taxing e-commerce as soon as they can legally do so.

THE FUTURE: INTERNET-IN-THE-SKY

Teledesic, founded by Craig McCaw, is building a global "Internet-in-the-Sky" network, which will enable broadband telecommunication access for businesses and individuals everywhere on the planet. Using a constellation of over 260 low-Earth-orbit satellites, Teledesic and its partners network will provide low-cost, worldwide, high-bandwidth Internet access, videoconferencing, and high-quality voice communication. Teledesic's network is expected to begin operation in 2003. And, if Teledesic delivers on its promise, it will virtualize many world markets and drive international commerce.

As Internet access becomes more global, companies in less developed economies will be able to access and compete in worldwide markets and achieve total "worldwide" market domination.

THE VIRTUAL OFFICE

Many salespeople maintain virtual offices by using computers and telephones to help them manage information and stay in contact with their customers and coworkers. For these salespeople, their "office" is any convenient place they agree to meet with their customers and coworkers.

If your company's salespeople meet customers outside of your office and are comfortable using portable computers, you should take the time to analyze whether or not you need to maintain a "physical" office. Your company may be ready to implement a "virtual" office of the future today!

☐ *Provide immediate access to customer, product and market information on sales calls.*

The better prepared your sales force is to represent your products, the more effective they will be on their sales calls.

Several years ago, Compaq Computers cut its sales force nearly in half, shut down three of eight regional offices, and asked its salespeople to work out of their homes. Then it equipped each salesperson with a laptop computer (a Compaq of course!) and configured the company's internal Marketing Information System (which stored over 38 gigabytes of customer, product, and market data) for remote access.

During a period when computer prices fell by over 50 percent, Compaq's "virtual" sales force managed to increase Compaq's sales by over 30 percent!

☐ *Reduce office overhead.*

Real estate salespeople often use their automobiles as mobile offices, relying on cellular telephones to stay in contact with their buyers and sellers, and portable computers with modems to access their real estate listing service.

☐ *Reduce or eliminate commuting time.*

Your company can improve the quality of life for its employees by enabling them to work out of their homes.

Companies that achieve total market domination empower their sales force with "today's marketing technology." And in many selling situations that technology is a virtual office.[5]

Step 9: Evaluate the total cost of ownership of your information systems.

The total cost of ownership of information technology systems is equal to the sum of all procurement, installation, integration, maintenance, upgrade, training, support, service, disposal, and finance costs. Many companies are surprised to learn that the cost of purchasing hardware and software accounts for less than 25 percent of the total cost of installing and implementing an automated system. For example, the total cost of ownership for implementing a PC includes the cost of:

☐ Hardware
☐ Software
☐ Custom software applications
☐ Training
☐ Installation
☐ Hardware service
☐ Software support and update fees
☐ Personnel's time
☐ Telecommunications and Internet access charges
☐ Other charges, such as off-site data storage

---

[5] *"Today's marketing technology"* is Client-Centered™ Training's tagline.

IMPLEMENTATION CONCERNS

Most companies have a constellation of concerns about adopting new technologies.

Implementation Concerns	
Competitive Advantage	Will the system help us provide better customer service?
Functionality	Will the system be able to handle data from all of our divisions?
Compatibility	Is the system compatible with our electronic messaging system?
Interoperability	Can the system share data with our accounting applications?
Risks of implementation	Will our salespeople understand how to use the new system?
Scalability	Will the system handle our growth over the next 5 years?
Viability of supplier	Will our consultant be available to customize our system next year?
Service	Does our system integrator provide 24 × 7 onsite support?
Support	Is the system guaranteed to meet our needs?
Qualified personnel	Do our salespeople need to be trained to use the system?
Training	How long will our salespeople be in training classes?
Impact on operations	Will our marketing group be able to use the system's reports to generate product forecasts?
Paperless office	Will we generate more or less paper after we automate?
Running parallel	How long will we need to run our current system in parallel with our new system?
Data integrity	Is there any possibility that our customer data files will become corrupted?
System security	What do we need to do to secure our system against hackers?
System reliability	How can we run our business if our system goes down?
Opportunity cost	What will it cost us if we put off purchasing a system for another year?
Total cost of ownership	How much will it cost us to implement this system?

Despite these concerns, companies are willing to implement new technologies when they believe that the risks of implementing the new technology are balanced by the competitive advantage that they can win by being an early technology adopter.

IT DESERVED IT!

When I worked for IBM about twenty years ago, one of our customers asked to have a customer engineer come out to repair his System 34 computer. When the customer engineer arrived, he observed what appeared to be a large bullet hole in the side of the computer.

When the customer engineer asked his customer about the hole, the customer replied that he had in fact shot his computer in the hard drive, but that it deserved it, and that IBM should fix it under warranty.

It is unfortunate that with all of the advances in computer technology over the last twenty years—literally bringing the power of a mainframe computer to a desktop PC—many of us still face this same level of frustration in dealing with the systems that I humbly refer to as "confusers."

Fortunately, network computing will, as Internet-based office automation applications become available, help drive the complexity out of most of our computing tasks.

Step 10: Develop a budget for your sales automation project.
Your company can use the "Information Systems Budget" worksheet to create a budget for its sales automation systems.

Information Systems			
Budget Worksheet	Last Year's Budget	This Year's Budget	Percent Change
Salaries, wages, other payroll expenses	$113,000		
Recruitment expenses	8,500		
Training, continuing education, travel, entertainment	4,600		
Operating supplies	850		
Services	23,000		
Equipment depreciation	29,000		
Maintenance	7,500		
Hardware rental/lease	N/A		
Software	21,000		
Networking	16,000		
Application development services	3,200		
Strategic planning/consulting	15,000		
Building/office depreciation or rent	N/A		
Utilities	N/A		
Telephone/facsimile charges	5,100		
Communication and Internet connection charges	9,700		
Taxes (other than payroll)	N/A		
Miscellaneous administrative expenses allocated to IT Dept.	18,300		
Outsource to system integrator	N/A		
Total budget amount	$274,750		

Step 11: Evaluate your system suppliers.

Your company can use the "Vendor Sales and Support" questionnaire to help it evaluate competing information system suppliers.

Vendor Sales and Support Questionnaire	Services Provided
Equipment supplied:	Pentium III notebook computers.
Do you charge separately for: □ Options/accessories □ Delivery □ Installation □ Maintenance □ Support □ Training	Options include: DC Power supply, extra memory, external storage disks, PCMCIA V.90 and ISDN modems, and 10-100 Megabit Ethernet cards.
Do you rent or lease this equipment? Describe terms: Do you provide discounts for:	No.
Quantity orders?	Yes.
Bundled deals?	No.
Promotional packages?	We bundle Microsoft Windows, Office, and Small Business Manager.
Beta or trial user sites?	We do not support any beta or trial software.
Do you cover shipping costs?	Yes.
Do you guarantee shipping times?	Yes.
Do you accept or broker trade-ins? If so, how does your trade-in program work?	No.
Do you sell reconditioned or demonstration equipment? What warranties are available on this equipment?	No.
What services are included with installation? Facility planning Other	We will replace any systems that fail within the first 30 days.
Who is responsible for installation planning?	Customer.
Machine Replacement	See above.
Machine Checkout	All systems are checked before being shipped to our customer.
Software System Generation	We will install your Sales Force Automation system at no additional charge.

Do installation charges include any necessary travel or lodging expenses?	No.
Do you perform a comprehensive system check during installation?	Yes.
Do you perform installation optimization or system diagnostics?	Yes—we run a system diagnostics test program and a virus scan.
If you do not provide warranty service, maintenance and system support?	Yes.
What coverage does your Service Agreement provide? For example, "telephone support 24 hour × 7day" or "8:00 A.M. to 5:30 A.M. PST Monday through Friday."	Manufacturer's warranty, except that we will replace any systems that fail within 30 days.
How are parts and labor covered? For example, "1 year parts, 90 days labor warranty" or "all parts except printer suppliers."	3 years parts, 1 year labor at our repair depot. (Average turnaround 48 hours.)
Cost for Service Agreement Payment Terms	Extended 3 year parts and labor warranty is $119 per system.
Period of Service Agreement	3 years as above.
Is your Service Agreement transferable?	Yes, if new owner has sales receipt and sales invoice.
Is local support available?	Yes.
What are the qualifications of supplier's service personnel?	We are a factory-authorized repair depot.
Is a minimum configuration a prerequisite for maintenance?	No.
Does installing components that have not been supplied by the vendor void warranty or Service Agreements?	Not unless they break the machine.
Do you provide telephone support?	Yes, this is limited to two support calls for each registered user.
Do you provide remote diagnostics?	No, but a diagnostics disk is included with each system.
Do you pay shipping on parts?	Yes.
Do you have a formal training program for your support personnel?	No.
When, where, and for how many hours/days is training offered?	Not applicable.
How much does your support training program cost?	Not applicable.

Step 12: Costs and benefits—competitive advantage and survival.

Over the last several years, as companies have begun to face the impact of global network computing and electronic commerce, senior managers' concerns have shifted from competitiveness to survival. And many companies have begun making enormous investments in network computing and the Internet to help ensure that they are able to maintain their market position, and to find new business opportunities.

□ How and when will emerging technologies such as the Internet and electronic commerce impact your company's business model?

□ When should your company adopt emerging technologies to gain a competitive advantage?

These questions are difficult to answer. But by taking the time to analyze your sales infrastructure and evaluate the latest sales automation systems, you can assemble the information that you need to make informed decisions about how and when to implement sales, customer service, and marketing automation tools. And by evaluating the total cost of operation for your information systems, your company can make more informed business decisions about when and where to install new applications to help it manage its sales process.

For example, if Client-Centered™ Training were considering equipping its sales team with notebook computers, it might create this simple cost/benefit analysis:

□ Total Cost of Ownership $150,000 (see Steps 9 and 10 above)

□ Increase profit $160,000 (use online MIS to close new sales)

□ Decrease expenses $130,000 (time saved managing paperwork)

□ Value to company $140,000

The Bottom Line: Is your company using computers and communication technologies to leverage its sales team's efforts?

Most businesses today are technology driven, and most competitive advantage is driven by technological innovation.

Companies that achieve total market domination are often early technology adopters that are willing to take managed risks to gain a competitive advantage over competitors that are less comfortable implementing new technologies such as network computing and the Internet.

In the next chapter, you will learn how to provide the Client-Centered™ customer support that will enable your company to achieve total market domination.

CHAPTER 9

DO YOU HAVE AN EFFECTIVE CUSTOMER SERVICE AND SUPPORT MODEL?

Quality is what your customers say it is.

—ANONYMOUS

Your customers' perceptions of the products, value, services, and support that your company provides are the building blocks of your corporate image. And these are the same elements that your customers use to select business partners to supply their needs.

Microsoft, Hertz, Nordstrom and many other companies that are striving to achieve total market domination have adopted a Client-Centered™ formula for creating a positive customer experience:

The Golden Rule + Common Sense = Quality Image.

CLIENT-CENTERED™ CUSTOMER SUPPORT

Behavioral studies have shown that people are drawn to positive experiences and strive to recreate positive experiences that they have had in the past. So it makes sense for your company to strive to make your customers' experience as positive as possible by employing a Client-Centered™ approach to marketing your company's products.

- □ Provide a quality product.
- □ Provide quality support and service after the sale.
- □ Charge competitive and reasonable prices.
- □ Keep your promises.

When you put yourself in your customers' position, it is easy to understand why customers want to align themselves with suppliers that provide great products, great value, and great service.

ONE CHANCE TO MAKE A FIRST IMPRESSION!

One of my first clients released its first notebook computer before it was adequately tested. The units offered many innovations, but the first production run of several hundred systems required three visits back to the factory to get problems fixed.

My client may have been able to save its reputation by replacing its defective units with newer units that worked properly, but it chose to have its customers repair their systems under its warranty program. A year later—with moribund sales and its reputation tarnished—my client stopped manufacturing notebook computers to "focus on its desktop systems business."

Step 1: Evaluate your service and support model.

Good customer service and support can help your company differentiate its products from those of your competitors, reinforce customer loyalty, and generate repeat business and referrals.

Your company can use the "Service Model" worksheet to help it evaluate how good a job it is doing providing customer service and support.

Companies that achieve total market domination develop Client-Centered™ customer support policies and procedures.

Service Model	
Support Policies	**Client-Centered™ Training's Support Policies**
Do you maintain a support organization?	Yes.
How many employees provide customer service/support?	10.
How do you bill their time/work?	Hourly or on support contracts.
What percent of customer support time is billable?	About 40%.

What is your billing rate for service?	$85.00–$125.00/hour.
Is this rate low, average, or high for your industry?	Average for industry.
Who determines billable hours?	Vice President of Sales.
Are support services automated?	Yes, all support personnel are on a network.
Are support requirements cyclical?	No.
Is the service organization a profit center?	Yes—but marginally.
When was the last time you evaluated the cost of providing customer service?	Last year.
Who is your service/support manager?	Production Manager.
Who does the service/support manager report to?	Vice President of Operations.
Do you have service contracts with third-party service organizations?	No.
Have you audited your Support Department in the last 12 months?	No.
Do you send out customer surveys to evaluate your customers' satisfaction with your support services?	Yes.
Date of survey:	February, 1997
Comments:	Our Clients are satisfied with our services—but they would like us to provide better payment terms.

THE PIPE GAME

I often ask my clients to visualize a set of pipelines between their company and their customers. Then I ask my clients to explore the different ways that their company can deliver whatever information or resources that its customers need to purchase, implement, and support its products through its pipelines. For example, my customer may "pipe" information about its product's benefits through a reseller "pipe" or through an advertising "pipe."

In most selling situations, customers' requirements are constant and are independent of the "pipe" that a company uses to provide information and support resources. But some "pipes" are more effective—higher bandwidth and less expensive to use—than others. For example, one of my clients recently invested in an Internet-based customer support system to decrease the investment that it must otherwise have made in its telephone support call center.

You can use the "pipe" game to help you think creatively about how your company can deliver the information and resources that its customers need to solve their problems. Thinking "out of the pipe" can help your company develop a Client-Centered™ approach to selling and supporting its products, which can put your company on the path to total market domination.

Tenth Law of Total Market Domination

It is ten times more expensive to acquire a new customer than to retain a current customer.

There are three straightforward steps to delivering the Client-Centered™ customer service that you need to retain your customers and achieve total market domination:

1. A positive, friendly, concerned attitude.
2. Consistent and reasonable customer service and support policies.
3. A company policy to treat all customers in a Client-Centered™ way.

More customers are lost through indifference than dissatisfaction. To retain customers, you must remind them periodically of the value of your business relationship.

Step 2: Perform a customer satisfaction survey.

A study done by the Technical Assistance Research Institute found that only 4 percent of dissatisfied customers ever complain. The majority of customers that do complain to a company will do business with the company again if their problem gets solved quickly, but 65 to 90 percent of dissatisfied customers never buy from the same company again.

When customers do take the time to complete customer satisfaction questionnaires, you should thank them for their effort, respond immediately to any concerns that may be expressed, and use their comments to re-engineer your internal systems and evolve your marketing story.

Many companies employ customer satisfaction questionnaires to measure their customers' satisfaction with their service and support. But the truth is, dissatisfied customers often use the time that they could spend completing satisfaction surveys to look for new suppliers! Companies that dominate their market are *proactive* about implementing internal quality control programs and employ creative techniques to help them understand their customers' experience. For example, if you own a chain of retail clothing stores, you might hire company shoppers to visit your stores. And if your company sells tools, you might use focus groups to help you understand how customers use your product, and to identify any potential problems that they may experience.

Your company can use the "Customer Satisfaction Evaluation Process" worksheet to verify that it has a process in place to evaluate its customers' level of satisfaction with its products and services.

Customer Satisfaction Evaluation Process	
When was the last time your company did a customer/user satisfaction survey?	Last August.
Did you do a direct mail or a telephone survey?	Direct mail.
If you did a direct mail survey, did you follow up on all customer concerns?	Yes.
What were the results of your user satisfaction survey?	Generally our results were very positive. See Average Ratings on Customer Satisfaction Form. (All of our major accounts responded. The survey was done by an outside research firm.)
Do you supply customer feedback cards? If you have received two or more feedback cards with the same criticism or concern, what did you do to respond to your customer's concern?	No.

Your company can use the "Customer Satisfaction" questionnaire as a template to help you develop a questionnaire for your own business.

Client-Centered™ Training's Customer Satisfaction Questionnaire	Rate on a scale of 1 (poor) to 5 (excellent)
Customer Name: Smith Electronics	
Contact Name: John Smith	
Contact Information: (425) 555-1234	
Overall satisfaction with our company	4
Are you satisfied with our company's products?	5
Are you satisfied with our company's service?	4
Are you satisfied with our company's sales representatives?	4
Are you satisfied with our company's support representative?	3
Are you satisfied with our company's telemarketing personnel	N/A
How can we improve our relationship with your company? We would like you to offer a broader range of management training programs.	
What additional products or services would you like us to offer in the future? We would like to provide Client-Centered™ training for our support staff.	
Are you satisfied with our company's policies? Yes.	
How do we compare to your company's other suppliers? We are very satisfied with your company's products and services.	

Forty-five prcent of customers switching suppliers cite customer service issues as the reason for their decision.[1]

CREDIBILITY

Most businesses prefer to do business with large, established suppliers because they believe that they will provide a higher level of

---

[1] Richard Whiteley, *"The Customer Driven Company: Moving from Talk to Action,"* Perseus Press, 1993.

customer service and product support than small, less-established suppliers will.

Regardless of the size of your company, there are many ways that your business can demonstrate its credibility and its commitment to customer service and support. For example, your company could:

- □ Promote customer testimonials
- □ Participate in product competitions
- □ Earn favorable product reviews
- □ Offer extended warranties
- □ Offer 24-hour-a-day, 7-day-a-week service
- □ Introduce customers to your repair technicians
- □ Partner with a national company to provide on-site maintenance
- □ Provide special support options for strategic customers
- □ Invest in a repair depot
- □ Hire a Quality Control manager
- □ Become ISO 9000 certified

INDUSTRY STANDARDS

Companies, such as Nordstrom and Eddie Bauer, that achieve total market domination often set their industry's standards—especially those related to customer service and customer expectations, such as product evaluation periods, warrantees, and return policies.

Step 3: Identify any production issues that may impact your business.

If a customer cannot acquire a product that they need from your company, they will be *forced* to do business with one of your competitors. Companies that achieve total market domination maintain the highest possible customer service level.

The "Production Issues" worksheet will help your company evaluate its ability to deliver its products on demand.

Production Issues	
Do you have adequate production resources?	We want to bring most of our printing in-house over the next two years.
Personnel—specify areas that are understaffed.	Our Training Guide production group is understaffed.
Equipment—describe production load limitations.	We can seat only 20 people in main training room.
Describe any capital (mission critical) equipment nearing the end of its useful life.	Our network laser printers need to be replaced within six months.
Do you have a backup plan for equipment failure?	We need additional portable computers and computer presentation equipment. We do not have an adequate disaster recovery program if our main file server crashes.
Inventory Control—describe your inventory control system.	We are running Inventory Management software on a Windows/NT server that is connected to our LAN. All of our training materials are warehoused at our East Coast and West Coast sales offices.
Do you have a backup plan to obtain products or supplies that are difficult to obtain, on allocation, or provided by a sole supplier?	Our Production Manager is working on a detailed purchasing plan.
Do you have any plans to improve your inventory control system?	We plan to begin bar coding all of our training materials next quarter.
Shipping/Warehousing—describe your shipping procedures.	All materials are shipped from our sales offices directly to our customers. We use Air Express for all expedited orders.
Do you experience any difficulties shipping product during peak periods?	No.
Do you have any plan to improve your shipping procedures?	Yes. Bar coding our inventory will help us improve turnaround time in our warehouse.

Step 4: Identify any quality control issues that may impact your business.

Companies that achieve total market domination control their customers' experience by implementing processes and procedures to help them maintain the highest possible level of product quality and customer satisfaction.

Quality is what your customers say it is!

Quality Control Issues	
How does your company ensure the quality of its products?	First, we do not let any trainer present one of our programs until he or she has gone through the program at least four times with one of our senior trainers.
	One of our managers sits in on each trainer's seminars at least once each quarter. After the seminar, our manager gives the trainer a written evaluation that details any improvements or curriculum changes that he or she thinks should be made to improve the quality of our product and the effectiveness of our trainer's presentation.
	We also solicit customer feedback with customer feedback cards, customer questionnaires, and personal phone calls from our senior managers, and then pass this feedback along to whoever is involved inside our company.
How does your quality control compare to your competitors'?	We believe that we put more effort into ensuring the quality of our product than any of our competitors do.
Are you ISO 9000 certified?	No.
Would ISO 9000 certification help you market your products?	We believe it would, but we have not researched this yet. The European distributors we have talked with have asked us our plans.
Do you have a plan in place to become ISO 9000 certified?	We are considering getting certification for our documentation group next year.
	If we decide to work toward ISO certification, we will hire an outside consultant to help us through the process.

PROMOTING A QUALITY IMAGE

Developing a quality image is an important step on the path to market leadership. Most companies promote their image through customer testimonials, reports from objective industry analysts, and through compelling explanations of exactly how and why their products deserve a "quality" reputation.

Most companies believe that they can use the quality of their products to promote a quality image. However, to use your product's quality to differentiate your products from your competitors' products, you must be able to demonstrate a significant difference in relevant purchase factors, such as performance or reliability. For example, advertising that your company warrantees its paint for seven years is not very compelling if your competitors offer a six-year warranty on their paint. In this situation, it would be more compelling to choose a much longer warranty period, say twelve years, or to match your competitors' warranty period, and differentiate your product's quality using another purchase factor, such as color retention.

Companies that achieve total market domination use their customer's key purchase factors to help them position their products as having exceptional quality. In most selling situations it is easy to map specific purchase factors to your company's products and services. However, in some selling situations, customers' key purchase factors are neither intuitive nor obvious. For example, many fast food customers are as concerned about the cleanliness of a restaurant as the taste of the food that is being served! So fast-food restaurants must maintain an exceptional level of cleanliness to achieve a quality image.

Step 5: Evaluate your company's sales order process.

If your company's sales order process is arduous, it will dissuade customers from doing business with your company. But if your company's sales order process is efficient, it can provide a competitive advantage. This is why companies that achieve total market domination *streamline their sales order process* as much as possible. Hertz, for example, allows its customers to complete a special rental agreement that enables them to go directly from their plane to a waiting rental car without completing any additional paperwork each time they rent a car.

Streamlining your company's sales process can also help its customers avoid buyer's remorse. The more complex a purchase decision is, the more likely it is that a customer will "second guess" their own purchase decision. And in some selling situations, such as retail consumer sales, it is important to complete business transactions before customers have a chance to talk themselves out of spending their money.

Many companies, such as department stores, consumer electronics superstores, and car dealerships, that achieve total market domination use automated systems to help them streamline their sales order process and approve their customer's credit "on the spot"—after verifying their customer's identity and checking their credit history through a credit bureau.

Client-Centered™ Training's Sales Order Process	
Describe your customers' purchase process:	Normally, our customers sign our standard training contract, which includes a detailed description of the program that we will present and all terms and conditions of our agreement. Our contract also details any special arrangements that have been agreed to, such as supplying extra copies of our workbooks. We ask our customers to pay a nonrefundable scheduling deposit when they sign our agreement.
What processes or procedures does your company have in place to ensure the quality of its customers' purchase experience?	One of our senior managers contacts our customers within two business days after we have received their contract to determine whether they have any questions or concerns about our services or our personnel.
Is there any way to reduce the amount of time that your customer spends in the purchase process after making a purchase decision?	We have eliminated a detailed customer questionnaire that we used to ask our customers to complete when we took their order. Now, our training manager completes this form during a preseminar planning meeting.

Strive to become a zero-latency enterprise.

The Gartner Group has coined the term "zero-latency enterprise" to describe a company's ability to respond almost instantly to business events such as transactions and customer interactions. The key to achieving this goal is to wire up a business with its partners and its customers to conduct business in *real time* and to bring information as close as possible to the people that need it.

Traders on Wall Street were the first to adopt zero-latency systems. However, as the cost of deploying Internet-based messaging and transaction processing systems declines, it becomes possible for companies in other businesses to take advantage of this strategy. For example, Delta Airlines has developed an internal system called Flight Legs, which enables it to respond more quickly to unexpected situations such as flight delays caused by bad weather. This system has enabled Delta to improve its planes' turnaround time on the ground and lets them handle more flights with the same number of planes.

One caveat is that while becoming a zero-latency enterprise is a noteworthy goal, it is not possible for every process, especially when people are involved, to become zero-latency. Nevertheless, improving the efficiency of a process by a day, an hour, or even a few minutes can provide a competitive advantage, which can help your company provide better customer service and ultimately achieve total market domination.

Step 6: Identify any order fulfillment issues that may impact your business.

If your company has problems filling orders, it will incur higher operating costs and will ultimately lose sales and customers to its competitors.

Order Fulfillment And Shipping	
What is your average time for order fulfillment?	11 days.
Do you expedite rush or special orders?	Yes.
Do you use a private carrier to handle rush or expedited orders?	Yes, Air Express.
Do you ever need to postpone order fulfillment because of production backlogs, out-of-stock inventory items, lack of equipment capacity, or other issues?	Yes, we are having problems scheduling print runs.
Do you have any sole source suppliers that can impact your ability to deliver your products or services?	Quick Save is the only local supplier for the type of 3-ring binders we use for our seminars. We are trying to locate another supplier out of state.
Do you have a contingency plan if your supply for critical products or services is interrupted temporarily?	We always arrange a second source for portable PC projection systems in case our normal supplier is unable to deliver the type of system that we need for one of our programs.
Are you vulnerable/at risk because of unfavorable business relations with any of your suppliers?	No, there are no competitive issues.

Have you implemented EDI to support any of your customers' or suppliers' order entry requirements?	We would like to implement an EDI system once we have our European and Asian distributors in place. However, this is not a high priority for us at this point.
Do seasonal or peak loads cause bottlenecks?	We have had problems in March, our busiest month.
Do you hire additional personnel to handle seasonal or peak loads?	Yes, we rely on our subcontractors.
Do you outsource work to handle peak loads?	We use our direct mail service to help us fulfill Requests for Information.
Do you have a formal bidding process in place with your subcontractors?	Orders are forwarded to our East and West Coast sales offices. Yes, we send out an RFP for all major projects.

PRIORITIZING LIMITED RESOURCES

It is often possible to handle sales and support problems before they damage customer relations by assigning extra resources or prioritizing delivery schedules. For example, if a major customer demands immediate delivery of a product that is on allocation, your company may weigh the value of its relationship with this customer and decide to delay a delivery to another customer.

Most salespeople are too biased and have too narrow a view of their company's operations to make objective decisions about which customer orders to expedite or delay. So in most companies, a senior marketing or operations manager is responsible for scheduling development and production resources. And decisions about prioritizing specific orders are based on a careful evaluation of how these decisions will impact the company's ability to achieve its objectives.

Customer Relations	Resource or Policy
Who is responsible for scheduling service resources?	Our VP of Sales is responsible for scheduling and prioritizing our sales support personnel's assignments.
Who is responsible for scheduling manufacturing and production resources?	Our VP of Operations manages and prioritizes all internal production resources. Our VP of Development manages and prioritizes all internal and subcontracted development work.
Is there a process in place to prioritize or expedite product deliveries?	We have monthly department managers' meetings to review all new business opportunities and outstanding projects.

Step 7: Evaluate your sales and support facilities.

Most companies that achieve total market domination provide local sales and support facilities.

Your company can use the "Facility" worksheet to help it evaluate its facilities requirements.

Facility	Location (Date Opened)	Satisfaction Level (Last Evaluation)	Current Status (Problems)
East Coast Sales Office	1999	Excellent	Need high-speed data link to main office, and Intranet server
Headquarters	May 1985	Acceptable	Redesign LAN Need new phone system
West Coast Sales Office	1998	Excellent	Need high-speed link to main office, and Intranet server
When was the last time you performed a facilities audit?	Last year		
Facilities Evaluation by:	Controller		

The Bottom Line: Do you have an effective customer service and support model?

If you have effective customer support programs in place, your company will be able to provide the level of service that it needs to differentiate it from its competitors, generate new business, reinforce customer loyalty, ensure repeat business, and earn referrals.

Companies that achieve total market domination treat their customers the way that they would like to be treated in their place. When a company treats it customers like friends, it is selling downhill. And when a company is selling downhill, it is easy to build the momentum that it needs to achieve its business objectives.

In the next chapter, you will learn how to create accurate sales forecasts and realistic marketing budgets to help your company focus its marketing resources on the selling activities that will enable it to achieve total market domination.

DO YOU HAVE AN EFFECTIVE PROCESS FOR DEVELOPING SALES FORECASTS AND MARKETING BUDGETS?

The future cannot be known. The only thing certain about it is that it will be different from, rather than a continuation of, today.

—PETER DRUCKER

Some business managers think that fluctuations in their company's cash supplies are too irregular and unpredictable to manage properly. But in fact, that is not true. Cash flow *is* predictable and manageable, because it is affected by a company's strategy and market position.

Of course, the more market data that your company has to make decisions about where and when to allocate its resources, the easier it will be to manage its cash supplies and to achieve its business objectives. This is why it is so important for your company to develop timely, accurate sales forecasts and realistic marketing budgets.

In this chapter you will learn how your company can use these tools to help it manage its resources and achieve its marketing objective.

Sales Planning	Client-Centered™ Training's Sales Planning Process
Who is responsible for generating your company's sales forecast?	Bob Nelson, VP of Sales.
Forecast Frequency	Monthly.
Forecast Accuracy	Our forecasts are usually within 35% of actual sales.
Who is responsible for generating your company's marketing budget?	Nancy Johnson, VP of Sales and Marketing, develops our marketing budget and presents it to our CFO and our President for approval.
Budget Frequency	Annual, with quarterly revisions based on sales revenues and cash flow.
Budget Accuracy	We stay within 15% of our budget. Our marketing budget is indexed to quarterly sales revenues.

Step 1: Evaluate your sales forecasting procedure.

In some parts of the world, shamans kill chickens to help them forecast future events. In the business world, marketing managers sift through sales and marketing data and use electronic spreadsheets and intuitions about market trends to help them predict the future sales of their company's products. Unfortunately, sales forecasting—like chicken sacrifice—is an inexact science.

Nevertheless, forecasting sales is an integral part of the planning process of every business. Sales forecasts are used to plan production, departmental budgets, and personnel requirements, and impact virtually every aspect of a company's operations.

Sales forecasts are usually based on a combination of factors, including:

- Market demand
- Competition
- Price sensitivity
- Product's life cycle
- Historical sales data
- Anticipated reorders
- Outstanding sales proposals
- Feedback from strategic accounts

Sales forecasts are usually expressed in dollar volumes and number of units, and often include the names of specific accounts that are expected to generate sales revenues in a specific time period.

Accurate sales forecasts enable your business to allocate its resources efficiently. But if your sales forecast is too high, excess production can tie up your company's operating capital and lead to cash-flow problems, and if your sales forecast is too low, unsatisfied customer demand may open your market to competitors.

Companies that achieve total market domination develop accurate sales forecasts to help them allocate their resources effectively.

CREATE AN ACCURATE SALES FORECAST

The accuracy of a sales forecast depends on the market data that is used to create it. If accurate, up-to-date market information is not available from market-research groups or other information sources, it will be necessary for your company to do its own market research to determine its customers' buying habits and key purchase factors.

Poll Your Customers

In most selling situations, questionnaires, market surveys, and focus groups are the most effective tools to help you obtain timely, accurate information about prospective customers' intent to purchase your products.

- Do you know about our product?
- Do you understand what our product is or does?
- Do you understand how it can be of value to your company?
- Do you plan to purchase our type of product?
- When do you plan to make a purchase decision?
- How much do you think our product is worth?
- Would your company be willing to purchase at least one of our products on a trial basis?

Poll Your Sales Force

Your sales force is usually the best source of information about its customers' intent to purchase your company's products.

However, sales forecasts that come from your sales force may be misleading. Your sales force may create pessimistic sales forecasts because it does not want its quotas raised, or it may create optimistic sales forecasts to justify additional marketing resources. In any case, sales forecasts from your sales force should never be dismissed. They reflect internal expectations, and they can easily become a self-fulfilling prophecy.

- □ How many units of each product do you expect to sell during the next sales period?
- □ How much revenue do you expect to generate over the next sales period?
- □ Are your strategic accounts reordering product?
- □ Are any issues, such as product delays, going to impact sales of this product?
- □ If a sales forecast has been revised recently, what event has precipitated this change?

If your sales manager's sales forecast is substantially different than your marketing department's sales forecast, it may indicate that your market research has not identified one or more key market factors that are influencing your customers' purchase process.

Poll Your Managers' Opinions

Many companies rely on a consensus of management opinions to track industry trends and to establish which key market factors should be addressed in their market research.

- □ What innovations or product introductions may impact this market?
- □ How will emerging technologies, such as e-commerce, impact our market?
- □ Why has a major competitor gone out of business?
- □ How much market share can we win if we sell our product for 25 percent less than the market leader?
- □ Do we need to change our pricing, service policy, or other business terms to meet our sales objectives?

Poll Your Resellers

Many companies base their sales forecasts on their resellers' sales forecasts for their products. This is an important data point to use in constructing a sales forecast. However, some resellers make overly optimistic sales forecasts because they want to ensure adequate product supplies, and because they believe that they will get better pricing and support if they are perceived as a major customer. Other resellers "sandbag" or release overly conservative sales forecasts so that they will be perceived as making a Herculean effort to beat their forecast. Unfortunately, resellers often fail to think through the long-term consequences of having overstocked suppliers or product shortages.

- □ Do you plan to stock our entire product line?
- □ How much of our product do you expect to sell this month, this quarter, this year?
- □ Do you expect your sales to increase over the next quarter? If so, how much? If not, why?

In new markets which are experiencing rapid growth, it may be very difficult to create an accurate sales forecast. When I was at Microsoft, we polled the top twenty PC manufacturers to help us determine how many copies of our operating system we could expect to ship over the next twelve months. Our customers' sales projections were so large that we reduced their estimates, for our own forecast, by about 50 percent. But to our surprise, the PC market was growing so rapidly that six months later we revised our own forecast to exceed our customers'!

Depending on your selling situation you may need to revise your sales forecast every quarter, every month, or every week.

Evaluate Similar Markets

In some selling situations it is helpful to evaluate how similar products have performed in similar markets. Of course, the more similar the market situation is, the more reliable conclusions based on this data will be.

- □ How is this market similar to ours?

□ What factors have impacted this market that may impact our market?

Evaluate Historical Sales Data

Many companies use historical sales data, particularly if their sales are seasonal, to forecast future demand for their products. However, historical sales data is not very helpful in new or volatile markets. For example, sales forecasts for computer products that are based on historical sales data are often obviated by the introduction of new products based on emerging technologies.

Research Published Market Information

The *Annual Survey of Buying Power* published by *Sales and Marketing Management* magazine is a good source of information about businesses' "intent to purchase" broken out by product type, industry, and geographical area. Industry analysts' reports, census data, data from government trade organizations, and data from industry associations are also valuable sources of market information.

DO MARKET RESEARCH

There are four key factors that will affect the reliability of your company's market research: the quality and objectivity of the survey process, the size of your market sample, the homogeneity of your sample, and the time frame for your questions.

As a rule, the larger your sample size is, the more reliable your market research will be. For example, if you poll every business in Redmond, Washington, you will be able to find out exactly how many of those businesses plan to purchase PCs. If you poll just ten businesses, your results will be much less reliable.

The more closely buyers in another market's demographics match those of your market sample, the more likely it is that those buyers will have the same purchase intent. For example, businesses in New York will very likely have similar purchase plans as businesses in Boston. However businesses in George, Washington, which is a very small town, will most likely have different purchase concerns.

The shorter the time frame for a market survey, the more reliable it will be. So a market survey of businesses' intent to purchase PCs in the next month will be more accurate than a market survey of businesses' intent to purchase PCs over the next year.

A Reality Check

Market data on sales of related products can help you identify profitable market opportunities and can provide a reality check for your sales forecast. For example, sales of digital cameras have generated demand for photo-quality color inkjet printers. Since customers that purchase digital cameras rarely need more than one photo-quality printer, this effectively limits the market for photo-quality printers to the number of customers that have purchased digital cameras.

BUILD A FORECAST MODEL

Sophisticated mathematical models can be created to help your company forecast future sales based on historical sales data. These models evaluate sales trends, sales cycles, seasonal purchase patterns, and other events, and use exponential smoothing and other mathematical procedures to calculate future sales performance. However, most companies create sales forecasts based on an analysis of key market factors.

The easiest, but rarely the most accurate, way to predict potential sales for a product is a *one-factor market analysis*. For example, if a PC needs a modem to transmit data, and virtually all PCs transmit data, it is reasonable to assume that the market for PC modems will be approximately equal to the number of PCs that have been sold.

A *multiple-factor market analysis* can provide a more accurate estimate of the potential market for a product. For example, if 20 percent of PCs are manufactured with modems, 15 percent of PCs are connected to local area networks, and 30 percent of PCs already have an after-market modem installed, 65 percent of PCs will not need an after-market PC modem.

□ If you assume that 10 million PCs have been sold, and that the market for PC modems is equal to 35 percent of the installed base of PCs, the total market for PC modems will be equal to 3.5 million units.

You can further refine this sales forecast by considering other key market factors. For example, if your company sells high-speed digital modems, or distributes modems through system integrators, you can use these factors to develop a more accurate forecast.

Your market research might reveal that:

□ 80 percent of modems are sold by system integrators and 20 percent of modems are sold through computer stores and mail-order.

□ 30 percent of modems are external modems, and 70 percent of modems are internal modems.

□ 20 percent of modems are high-speed digital modems, and 80 percent of modems are low-speed analog modems.

□ Five modem manufacturers produce high-speed digital modems, which are priced between $695 and $895.

□ 25 percent of high-speed digital modems sell for more than $800, 50 percent sell for between $700 and $800, and 25 percent sell for less than $700.

□ The price of PC modems is declining about 30 percent per year.

□ A customer "intent to purchase" study indicates that 30 percent of PCs will be upgraded with modems over the next twelve months.

□ Your company has priced its modem at $695 and supports it with a two-year unconditional warranty—besting the ninety-day warranty offered by your competitors.

□ Your modem has just received a "Best Buy" rating in a comparative review in a leading trade publication.

□ Your company has budgeted $285,000 to market its modem.

With this additional information you can calculate that the market for high-speed, external modems that are sold through system integrators is

3.5 million PCs
× 20% [high-speed]
× 30% [external]
× 80% [sold through system integrators]
= 168,000 modems
× 30% [intent to purchase this year]
= 50,400 modems.

At this point, you might poll your sales manager to determine how many modems he or she believes your company will sell over the next year.

- Based on preproduction sales orders of 1,300 modems to a major Internet Service Provider and positive feedback from customers at a trade show, your company's sales manager forecasts sales of 10,000 modems over your company's first year of production.

Now, you will need to evaluate all of the data that you have collected to predict how successful your company will be in launching its new modem.

Based on your company's modest marketing budget, your modem's competitive price, exceptional warranty and favorable product review, your sales manager's confidence, and your survey of customers' loyalty to their current suppliers, you *estimate* that your company will capture 12 percent of its PC modem market during its first year of production.

50,400 modems × 12% [market share] = 6,048 modems.

Assuming that your reseller price is 60 percent of your $695 retail sales price, your revenue forecast for your first year will be

$417 [Reseller Price] × 6,048 modems = $2.5 million.

In this example, your company could have relied on its sales manager's forecast and built 10,000 modems. But the price of modems is coming down 30 percent each year, and if your company became overstocked, it might be forced to sell some of its modems at a loss. Betting on a more conservative forecast may result in losing a few sales to competitors, but your company will reduce its investors' risk, and it may be able to meet additional demand for its modems by increasing its production facilities or subcontracting production to another manufacturer.

Total market for products or service[1]	Number of modems sold worldwide	Number of modems sold by company	Percent of world-wide market	Company's sales revenues
Last year	35,000	—	—	—
This year	50,400	6,048	12	$2.5 million
Next year	59,950	9,592	16	$3.5 million
Two years	75,372	14,389	19	$5 million
Three years	87,205	19,185	22	$6 million

Where do these market estimates come from?

(For example: customer survey, industry reports, internal analysis, government statistics, etc.)

Our forecast is based on user surveys and market estimates provided by the Computer Products Research Company. Our internal market data confirms these estimates.

Are you confident that the information that you have about your market is accurate and up to date?

Yes—we expect high-speed DSL access to drive demand for our digital modems.

Potential Pitfalls

If your market is immature, if new products are introduced during your product's life cycle, if a major competitor goes out of business, or if other *key market factors change*, your sales can be impacted substantially.

About ten years ago, a well-known Japanese electronics manufacturer ran a million-dollar advertising campaign to launch its new

---

[1] If you want to calculate the total market potential for a *consumable* product, you will need to determine its rate of usage, which is the quantity of the product that you are selling that is required or consumed by each customer.

> Total Market Potential =   [Total Number of Prospects in Market]
> × [Rate of Usage]
> × [Average Revenue Per Sale].

modem. The modem was of the highest quality and priced reasonably, but it sold poorly and was soon featured in liquidation ads. The reason the modem failed to win market share was very simple—it was not compatible with the emerging industry-standard Hayes modem command set. And no amount of advertising could overcome this key market factor.

HOW BIG IS YOUR MARKET?

Several years ago I consulted with a software company that had developed an accounting system for nonprofit radio and television stations. The term "nonprofit" always makes me a bit nervous, so I immediately calculated the total market potential for the company's product.

Unfortunately, my concerns proved to be well founded. My client did not believe that his company could raise its product's price and compete against a software package that had been developed at a university and was in the public domain. And, assuming my client held its price and achieved "total market domination," there just weren't enough nonprofit stations to justify staying in business.

I felt so bad delivering this news that I didn't charge my client for the hour that it took to consult them out of business.

Step 2: Create a sales forecast for your company based on your sales representatives' monthly sales forecasts.

Many companies build a "bottom-up" sales forecast based on their sales representatives' estimates of future sales.

Client-Centered™ Training's monthly sales forecast includes a column for "% confidence" to indicate how confident Thomas Butler, a salesperson who works in its Southern region, is that each one of his "Top 10" prospective customers' contracts will close during the month of June.

Sample Monthly Sales Forecast for June (Business Unit/Sales Team/Other)			

Salesperson: Thomas Butler

Territory: Southern Region

Date: May 31

Top 10 Prospects		Revenue	Month	Confidence
1	Tacoma Toy Co.	15,000	June	99%
2	Big Sky Hiking Co.	20,000	June	99%
3	Tee-Off Golf Co.	18,000	June	90%
4	Electronics Shack	15,000	June	90%
5	Acme Auto Repair	16,000	June	80%
6	Johnson Machine	10,000	June	80%
7	Seattle Movies	24,000	July	60%
8	Ace Plumbing	19,000	July	55%
9	Good Buys	11,000	July	50%
10	The Game Co.	14,000	August	40%
Revenue Forecast for June:		$68,000		

Client-Centered™ Training's sales manager for its Southern region compiles a monthly sales forecast for his region based on his sales representatives' monthly sales forecasts.

Sales Forecast for Southern Region	April	May	June	Second Quarter
Number of Seminars	14	17	12	43
Revenue Generated ($1,000s)	140	170	120	430
Profit Generated ($1,000s)	60	90	40	190
% Change Same Period Last Year.	+38	+45	-8	+31

Client-Centered™ Training's Vice-President of Sales and Marketing creates a sales forecast for the entire U.S. market based on his regional sales managers' sales forecasts.

Second Quarter Sales Forecast	North Region	East Region	South Region	West Region	U.S. Market
Sales Seminar	10,000	30,000	110,000	100,000	250,000
Trade Show Seminar	20,000	30,000	80,000	60,000	190,000
Presentation Seminar	2,000	3,000	105,000	10,000	120,000
Consulting Seminar	15,000	25,000	25,000	85,000	150,000
Manager Seminar	20,000	40,000	110,000	125,000	295,000
Total Seminar Opportunity	67,000	128,000	430,000	380,000	1,005,000

Client-Centered™ Training can use these reports to help it develop marketing budgets and to allocate its marketing resources between different territories.

Your company should compare different marketing opportunities within different segments of its market to help it focus its selling efforts.

Step 3: Evaluate your marketing budget.

A marketing budget defines how much money your company plans to spend on specific marketing activities, such as advertising and sales automation, over the course of your company's fiscal year. Most marketing budgets are divided between fixed-expense items, such as salaries and telephone expenses, and discretionary expenses. In some companies, special marketing budgets are developed for specific projects such as a major product launch or attendance at a national trade show.

Every marketing manager has an opinion about how large a marketing budget he or she needs to achieve total market domination. But in most companies, the total amount of money that is budgeted for marketing activities is tied to a percentage of the company's sales revenues. If sales revenues go up, additional marketing funds are allocated, and if sales go down, the company tightens its marketing budget.

Some companies allocate a disproportionate percentage of their sales revenues to marketing activities to help them "buy" market share. However, at some point a company must limit its marketing expenses if it wants to earn a profit for its shareholders.

There is no proven "formula" that your company can use to help it determine how much money it should invest to market its product. However, most companies that achieve total market domination invest 30 to 40 percent of their sales revenues to build and retain market share.[2]

CREATING A MARKETING BUDGET

In the past, most companies based their marketing budget on their previous year's budget; however, most companies today use zero-base budgeting or ZBB to help them control expenditures. ZBB involves allocating your company's resources on the basis of a cost-benefit analysis of each of your company's major marketing activities.

The ZBB process involves three steps:

1. *Break down each marketing activity into "decision packets," which include all of the information that your company needs to evaluate a marketing activity and compare its costs and benefits with other marketing activities.* Each decision packet should include the activity's purpose, costs, and estimated benefits, as well as the consequences that are expected if the activity is not funded.
2. *Evaluate each marketing activity and rank it in order of decreasing benefit to your company.* In a large company, the rankings for each marketing manager's activities should be passed along to his or her manager (or the manager's manager) and re-ranked until all activities have been evaluated and compared.
3. *Allocate your company's marketing resources on the basis of your senior managers' final evaluation.* As a rule, high-value marketing activities are funded immediately, while lower-priority items may be eliminated or may be funded if additional marketing funds become available.

The ZBB process makes it possible to compare the relative value of different marketing activities and can help your company identify and eliminate low-payback marketing activities. However, the value of the ZBB process depends on individual managers' honesty and candor. If your managers lose their objectivity, your budget

---

[2] According to *Selling Power* magazine, most companies invest up to 35 percent of their sales revenues in marketing expenses.

process will become political, and allocations will depend more on individual managers' ability to promote their pet projects than on the ability of specific marketing activities to help your company achieve its business objectives.

Benefits of ZBB Process

☐ Evaluate past performance

☐ Improve resource allocation

☐ Track progress toward specific objectives and key results

☐ Identify problems and learn from past mistakes

☐ Improve communication

☐ Positive impact on motivation and morale

☐ Develop managers' planning skills

Companies that achieve total market domination use ZBB to target their marketing resources to the marketing activities that will provide the greatest return on their investment.

REAL WORLD BUDGETS

One of the major assumptions in all sales forecasts is the amount of money to be spent on marketing. In most selling situations, the more money that a company invests marketing its products, the greater its sales will be. However, at some point, investing additional marketing dollars will continue to generate sales, but it will not increase a company's profits.

If your company's marketing budget, as a percentage of your company's sales revenues, is lower than your industry average, it may be that your company's sales force is more efficient and that your company has a lower cost of sales than its competitors. On the other hand, it may mean that your company is underspending and will eventually lose market share to companies that have more aggressive marketing budgets.

Sales and Marketing Management magazine publishes an *Annual Survey of Selling Costs* that compares total selling expenses as a percentage of company sales for virtually every industry. You can use this guide as a reality check to determine how your company compares to others in its industry.

Companies that achieve total market domination are willing to invest all of the marketing resources that are needed to achieve their long-term business objectives. It can be tempting to increase profits by cutting back on marketing expenses; however, this strategy can rarely work for very long. The key to building market share is to *continue funding* the marketing activities that yield the greatest positive return on your company's investment.

Of course, key market factors change over time, so it is critical to implement a zero-base budgeting process that will enable your company to track the success of each marketing strategy that it is funding.

Step 4: Evaluate your financial systems and your management reports.

An evaluation of your company's financial reports will help you determine whether enough capital is available to support ongoing marketing programs and to fund new business opportunities.

You can use the "Finance Department" worksheet to help your company evaluate its financial status.

Finance Department	Personnel
Chief Financial Officer/Controller	Nancy Smith
Treasurer	Terry Smith
Bookkeeper	Sandy Stone
Administration Manager	Linda Thomas
In-house Legal Counsel	Terry Smith
Outside Auditor/CPA Firm	Jones & Parker
Do you employ HR Counsel?	Robertson Agency
Attach your company's financial statements for the past three years.	
Attach additional financial reports for the current year, which describe your financial condition.	
□ Cash flow analysis	
□ A/R Report	
□ A/P Report	

☐ Inventory Report
☐ Sales/Bookings Report
Does your company have an adequate line of credit?   No, we are working with our banks to increase our limit to $500,000   Are you seeking additional credit sources?   Yes, we are working with a leasing company.
Are you seeking a private placement? No.
Are you planning to sell stocks or corporate bonds? No.
Are you planning to do an IPO? Yes.
Approximate date of announcement? June 1997.
What does your company plan to do with additional financing?   We want to acquire a multimedia production company.   We are also interested in acquiring a small book publisher in the business/financial/computer market.
Specify amount of financing.   We want to issue 1 million shares of private stock at $15 per share.
Do you have a fallback plan if you do not receive funding, or if your funding is delayed?   If we cannot complete an IPO, we will continue to finance our growth from retained earnings.
Have you developed a Financing Plan? If so, attach a copy.   No, we will be interviewing investment bankers in the near future.
Has your company's Financing/Business Plan been reviewed by an outside consultant or CPA to make sure that its assumptions are logical and consistent?   Our in-house counsel and controller have reviewed our business plan and agree that our company has the resources and that it is within the capabilities of our current management team to execute.   Our bank's Senior Vice President who handles business accounts has also reviewed our plan.
Do you have adequate insurance to cover your business, including key employee life insurance, errors and omissions, fire, theft, and other potential hazards? Yes.
Have you had an Insurance Audit in the last twelve months? No.

The "Business Status" report can help you manage your company by providing an "executive-level" view of how you expect your business to *change* over the next period. Having this information will make it easier to make decisions about how and where to allocate your resources.

Client-Centered™ Training's Business Status for the Next _6_ Months.	Decline	The Same	Increase
Sales			12%
Profits			8%
Production Costs			3%
Overhead		No change	
Marketing Expenses			15%
Cash Flow			28,000
Working Capital	30,000		
Inventory Level			175,000
Accounts Receivable			85,000
Pricing		No change	
Customer Support		No change	
Image/Quality			Improve
Staff Satisfaction		No change	
Customer Satisfaction		No change	

CHANGES IN FINANCIAL STATUS

Your company can use the "Financial Condition" worksheet to help it manage anticipated changes in its financial status over the next six, twelve, or twenty-four months.

The Bottom Line: Do you have an effective process for developing sales forecasts and marketing budgets?

It is impossible to prescribe a formula that can help your company predict how much money it must invest in its marketing strategies to achieve its marketing objectives. Every market is different and every company in every market has different capabilities. But by developing accurate sales forecasts, your company can plan production, set departmental budgets and personnel requirements, and control virtually every aspect of its operations. And by implementing a zero-based budgeting process, your company can prioritize the marketing activities that will enable it to achieve its marketing objectives.

Client-Centered™ Training's Financial Condition			
Rate as less than <, equal to =, or greater than > our current level.	Next 6 Months	Next 12 Months	Next 24 Months	Reason for Change
Sales	>	>	>	Referrals and new business
Profits	=	>	>	Near term profits will suffer because we are opening new offices in Europe. However next year, referrals and new business will increase sales and profits.
Production costs	=	<	<	We are bringing all printing in-house early next year.
Overhead	=	>	>	We are adding new sales personnel next year.
Employee compensation	=	=	=	We plan to maintain our current incentive and profit-sharing programs to sustain employee satisfaction.
Marketing expenses	>	>	>	Our marketing budget is indexed to our sales revenues.
Cash flow	<	=	=	We do not anticipate any cash flow problems over the next 24 months.
Working capital	=	<	>	We do not plan to increase our credit line to support our new business.
Inventory level	=	>	>	We will increase inventory levels when we bring production in-house.
A/R Collections	<	=	=	We believe that the economy will be stable next year.
Pricing	=	<	<	We plan to decrease the prices of our seminar workbooks to increase our market share and support our seminar business.
Customer support costs	<	=	>	We plan to implement an Internet-based call center to handle sales issues.

Some companies take calculated financial risks to help them build the market momentum that they need to overcome their competitors. For example, Apple Computer recently announced that it will spend over 100 million dollars to launch its new iMac PC. But companies in most markets are more conservative with their marketing resources and index their marketing budgets to their company's sales revenues.

It is difficult to identify any "rule" that your company can use to help it allocate its marketing resources. But there is one strategy that every company can use to help it dominate its market: *employ experienced financial managers with board-level influence over your company's strategic business decisions.* The more objective that your company is about its budget decisions, the easier it will be to achieve total market domination.

In the next and final chapter, you will learn how to identify and implement best Client-Centered™ sales practices that will help your company achieve total market domination.

CHAPTER 11

IDENTIFY AND IMPLEMENT BEST CLIENT-CENTERED™ SALES PRACTICES

Make it so!
—Jean Luc Picard

At this point, you should be prepared to identify best Client-Centered™ sales practices for your company and to develop specific recommendations that address the key objectives for implementing your sales evaluation process.

STRATEGIES FOR MANAGING CHANGE IN YOUR COMPANY

Implementing best practices in your company can help your company improve its sales team's performance and build the market momentum that it needs to achieve total market domination. But implementing best practices is about managing change. And, as you have read earlier in this book, managing change can be a difficult challenge.

Over the years, I have developed ten principles that your company can use to help it implement its best sales practices.

1. *Confront reality.* Every business is a "people" business. And it is the *impact on specific individuals in your company* that often obviates the possibility of ever implementing best practices.

288

Be honest about your company's strengths and weaknesses. If your managers don't have the skills that they need to do their job effectively, they must be trained. And if your managers don't understand their market, you must bring people into your organization who can articulate your customers' needs and concerns.

2. *Be prepared to address all of the issues that may need to be changed or re-engineered to implement best practices in your company.* Depending on your selling situation, it may be necessary to address key market factors, customer expectations, and personnel issues, as well as your company's business processes.

3. *Focus your company's resources on fixing problems that will provide the greatest payback.* There is no reward if you succeed at planning but fail at implementation! Focus your initial efforts on implementing best practices that will have a rapid payback, and then use those successes to rally support for implementing more ambitious changes.

4. *Be realistic about the scope of change that can be achieved with your company's resources.* If you reach beyond your company's capabilities and resources, your plan will fail, and if your expectations are too limited, it may not matter if you succeed. Focus your efforts on implementing best practices that can be achieved with your company's marketing resources.

5. *Use Client-Centered™ communication skills to build the understanding and the consensus that you need to implement best practices throughout your company.* If you fail to create a clear, concise, compelling story that explains how and when a best practice will impact your company's success, you will not be able to build the critical mass of support that you need to change your company.

It is often helpful to bring one or more customers into your internal selling process as advocates to confirm the importance of specific best practices.

6. *Develop a compelling case for implementing best practices and obtain senior management's mandate to implement those changes.* If you do not obtain senior management's support, you may be unable to secure the resources that you need to implement those practices throughout your company.

7. *Use objectives and key results to help you develop an action plan for each best practice that you plan to implement.* Objectives and key results can provide the infrastructure that your company needs to define, communicate, motivate, measure, and sustain change. By defining performance metrics and measuring key results, you can demonstrate the positive impact of implementing best practices and build support for future change.

8. *Use feedback from your customers to help your company refine its sales and marketing processes.* Use customer feedback to help your company identify its best practices, and use the First Law of Total Market Domination to measure the impact that implementing those best practices has had. Your customers may not always be right, but their opinions will define your company's success. Quality is what your customers say it is!

9. *Be honest about deploying whatever resources are necessary to implement best practices in your company.* If your sales team does not have the experience or motivation to implement best practices, hire new personnel who can seed those skills in your company. And if your managers are not able to think creatively about their selling situation, hire consultants to provide the perspective that your company needs to visualize how it can achieve its next level of success.

10. *Build diversity within your company.* Any time that your company implements major change is an ideal opportunity to recruit people with diverse backgrounds who can bring new experience and introduce fresh ideas into your company.

   Innovation depends on exploring unconventional points of view. And diverse groups are more likely to generate the "out of the box" thinking that will help your company uncover innovative ideas and help your company build momentum in its market.

The first step on the path to identifying best Client-Centered™ sales practices for your company is to identify your company's critical success factors.

Step 1: Identify your company's critical success factors.

The Client-Centered™ sales evaluation process can help your company re-energize and re-engineer its marketing strategies and improve its sales force's performance by helping your company identify its critical success factors.

As you go through the chapter-by-chapter outline in this section, try to identify the specific success factors, such as developing compelling pricing strategies and building a well-trained sales force, that are critical to *your* company's success.

Chapter 1—Do You Understand the Key Factors That Drive Your Customers' Purchase Decisions?

□ Confirm that your company has identified and prioritized your customers' needs and concerns.

□ Use your understanding of your customers' purchase factors to identify key customer benefits.

□ Document your customers' purchase process.

□ Identify any negative market factors that may influence your customer's purchase process.

□ Confirm that your Marketing Information System provides the information that your sales team needs to make informed business decisions.

Chapter 2—Are Your Company's Resources Allocated in a Way That Is Consistent with Achieving Its Marketing Objectives?

□ Identify your company's long- and short-term business objectives.

□ Evaluate your company's value equation.

□ Evaluate where your market, your company, and your company's products are in their life cycle, and confirm that you have aligned your company's marketing strategies to leverage its position in its market.

□ Evaluate the performance of each product that your company is selling, and confirm that your company's marketing resources are focused on the products that have the greatest sales potential.

□ Confirm that your company is using market and product integration strategies to leverage its resources.

□ Confirm that your marketing strategies are aligned with your company's objectives by tracking the outcome of every marketing program, and by taking any corrective action that is necessary to reengineer, reenergize, or replace unsuccessful programs.

Chapter 3—Have You Developed a Clear, Concise, Compelling Marketing Story That Defines "Who, What, Where, When and Why" Customers Should Do Business with Your Company?
- □ Evaluate your company's position in the market.
- □ Evaluate your competitors' position in the market.
- □ Evaluate your product's strengths and weaknesses.
- □ Develop a marketing story that answers "who, what, when, where and why" a customer should do business with your company.
- □ Map the elements of your marketing story to your customers' needs and concerns.
- □ Confirm that your marketing communications arouse interest, provide information, and create a preference for your company's products.
- □ Confirm that your company's marketing communications are clear, concise, and compelling.

Chapter 4—Does Your Marketing Plan Provide the Focus Your Company Needs to Leverage Its Selling Efforts?
- □ Evaluate your short- and longer-term marketing strategies to determine whether they will enable your company to achieve its marketing objectives.
- □ Evaluate your sales plan to confirm that it provides a road map to the specific sales objectives that you have specified in your marketing plan.
- □ Confirm that your sales kit communicates your marketing story and addresses all of your customers' questions about your company's products and services.
- □ Confirm that you are leveraging your customer relationships by selling products *horizontally*, across your customers' companies, divisions, and workgroups, and *vertically*, within the company, division, or workgroup that they are selling to.
- □ Confirm that your business relationships provide access to the customers, product promotions, financing, technical expertise, and other resources that your company needs to help it achieve its marketing objectives.

- □ Confirm that your company and its resellers have invested the money and other resources that are necessary to achieve success.
- □ Confirm that your pricing strategy maximizes your company's market share and profitability.

Chapter 5—Do You Have Effective Programs in Place to Identify Prospective Customers?

- □ Confirm that you are using the most effective marketing programs to identify prospective customers.
- □ Evaluate the payback on your prospecting activities by tracking the number of sales leads generated by each promotion and the amount of sales revenue that is generated from those leads.
- □ Confirm that your advertising is influencing your customers' perception of your company's quality with questionnaires and focus groups that measure changes in your customers' brand preference.
- □ Evaluate the effectiveness of trade shows, newsletters, user groups, electronic bulletin boards, and other marketing activities.

Chapter 6—Do You Have Effective Programs in Place to Qualify Prospective Customers?

- □ Confirm that you have adopted a Client-Centered™ selling methodology to make it easier for your sales force to communicate effectively and to help its customers move through their purchase process.
- □ Evaluate your company's use of innovative marketing techniques, which rely on creativity, visibility, and memorability to create a preference for your company's products.
- □ Confirm that your company is using contact forms to collect customer information.
- □ Evaluate your company's ability to win major accounts.
- □ Evaluate whether team selling is the most cost-effective way for your company to represent its products.
- □ Confirm that your sales force is using territory, account, and sales call plans, and periodic account reviews to help it manage its selling efforts.

Chapter 7—Is Your Sales Force Prepared to Present Your Company in a Professional, Client-Centered™ Way?

- ☐ Review your organization's personnel policies.
- ☐ Map your sales representatives' skills to specific business opportunities.
- ☐ Confirm that your sales managers are spending as much of their time as possible training, coaching, motivating, and evaluating your sales force.
- ☐ Confirm that your sales manager's objectives and key results are in line with your company's marketing objectives.
- ☐ Evaluate the programs that you have in place for goal setting, motivation, and personnel appraisals.
- ☐ Confirm that your company's managers have the planning and reporting systems that they need to support their decision process.
- ☐ Confirm that your sales training program is Client-Centered™.
- ☐ Confirm that your compensation program will enable you to recruit and motivate a world-class sales force.
- ☐ Evaluate the system that you have implemented to review your sales personnel.
- ☐ Evaluate your Sales and Marketing Department's workload to determine whether you should increase or decrease its personnel.

Chapter 8—Is Your Company Using Computers and Communication Technologies to Leverage Its Sales Efforts?

- ☐ Identify areas of your sales infrastructure that should be automated.
- ☐ Evaluate your sales automation system.
- ☐ Evaluate your customer information system.
- ☐ Evaluate your communication systems.
- ☐ Evaluate your use of e-mail marketing.
- ☐ Evaluate your accounting systems.
- ☐ Confirm that your sales team is comfortable working with your sales automation system, and that it has timely, competent technical support.

□ Confirm that your company is using the Internet and network computing to help it support its sales process and market its products.

Chapter 9—Do You Have an Effective Customer Service and Support Model?

□ Confirm that your company is using customer satisfaction questionnaires to measure its customers' satisfaction with your company's sales, service, and support.

□ Identify any production and quality control issues that may impact your customer service level.

□ Evaluate your ability to respond with "zero-latency" to business events such as transactions and customer interactions.

□ Determine whether your company is having any problems filling customer orders.

□ Confirm that your corporate facilities enable your company to be as close as possible to your customers.

Chapter 10—Do You Have an Effective Process for Developing Sales Forecasts and Marketing Budgets?

□ Evaluate your sales forecasting procedure to confirm that your company is generating accurate sales forecasts.

□ Evaluate your budgeting procedure to confirm that your marketing budget is efficient, objective, and tied to sales performance metrics.

□ Determine whether your marketing budget is in line with your competitors' marketing budgets.

□ Evaluate your financial systems and your management reports to determine whether your company's managers have all of the information that they need to make informed business decisions.

Step 2: Use the worksheets from your Client-Centered™ sales evaluation to identify your company's best sales practices.

After identifying your company's critical success factors, you can review your company's sales evaluation worksheets to help you determine what your company is doing well—its best sales practices—and to identify the policies, processes, and procedures that need to be re-engineered to help your company achieve its sales objectives.

The "Key Objectives for Client-Centered™ Training's Sales Evaluation" worksheet presents a summary of its coordinator's evaluation and recommendations. You can create a sales evaluation worksheet to identity best sales practices that need to be implemented throughout your company.

Key Objectives for Client-Centered™ Training's Sales Evaluation	Evaluation	Recommendation
Determine whether our marketing story is clear, concise, and compelling. (Chapters 1 and 3)	Client-Centered™ Training has identified its customers, needs and concerns, and has developed a clear and concise marketing story. However C-CT has not done a good job of differentiating its seminars from those of its competitors.	Client-Centered™ Training needs to do a better job of articulating the *value* of using custom-tailored training modules, to make its marketing story more compelling. Client-Centered™ Training can help build its brand by emphasizing its *"today's marketing technology"* tagline in its sales collateral and media advertising.
Evaluate whether our marketing budget is in line with other businesses in our industry. (Chapter 10)	Client-Centered™ Training's budget is equal to 29% of its total sales revenues. The industry average for sales training companies is 31%. C-CT's marketing budget is in line with its competitors'. However, C-CT should begin promoting its Web site as soon as possible, to create awareness of its Internet-based training services. C-CT will also need to increase its marketing budget to support future expansion into Europe, Asia, and South America.	C-CT should increase its Web marketing budget by at least 50%. The amount of market development funds necessary to enter foreign markets will depend on the business partners that C-CT works with in each country. In any case, C-CT should work with its bank to increase its line of credit, and to help implement the internal systems it needs to support its international business.

Determine whether our company should enter any new markets. (Chapters 2 and 3)	Client-Centered™ Training's development personnel are working at 115% of capacity to complete already scheduled projects.	Unless C-CT raises additional capital and hires additional development personnel, it should remain focused on achieving its current marketing objectives.
Identify emerging market factors, such as online training, that may affect our business over the next three years. (Chapter 8)	Client-Centered™ Training has identified multimedia training and the Internet as key technology challenges.	The Internet and multimedia training technologies will begin to have a major impact on C-CT's customers' expectations (and its business opportunities) over the next twelve months.
Evaluate our sales training program. (Chapter 6)	Client-Centered™ Training's sales and marketing personnel have exceeded quota for each of the last five quarters. However, C-CT is not good at developing accurate sales forecasts.	C-CT should ask its sales representatives to provide a monthly sales forecast based on their best estimate of when their most active accounts will close. C-CT's sales representatives who are overly pessimistic about closing new business opportunities should be counseled about how their reports are used to establish marketing and product development budgets.
Determine the most cost-effective way to use the Internet to market our services and provide customer support. (Chapter 8)	Client-Centered™ Training plans to hire a Web guru as soon as it finds the right individual. Client-Centered™ Training plans to enhance its Web site to support e-commerce. Client-Centered™ Training is developing new products for the Internet, and plans to market these products through its Web site early next year.	Client-Centered™ Training is taking the right steps to incorporate Internet marketing and e-commerce into its business strategy. C-CT could implement an Internet gateway on its LAN to support e-mail and videoconferencing with its subcontractors, business partners, and customers.

| Determine whether our company's value equation is in balance. (Chapter 3) | Shareholders: Client-Centered™ Training's sales have risen over 40% for each of the last five years, and profit margins have remained over 25%. C-CT has used its retained earnings to fund growth. Employees: C-CT has experienced extremely low turnover, and its employees consider the company an "exceptional place to work." Customers: C-CT has consistently ranked "very good" or "excellent" in every category that is tracked in its customer questionnaires. However, C-CT has generated very few customer referrals. | Client-Centered™ Training's management team has done a good job of balancing its company's value equation. However, because of the tight employment market, C-CT should plan to increase its employees' salaries and offer stock options to key personnel. C-CT should be more proactive about soliciting referrals from its customer base. |

Step 3: Develop an action plan, including objectives and key results (performance metrics), for each best sales practice that you plan to adopt within your company.

After you have identified your company's best sales practices, you should evaluate which best practices will provide the greatest return on your company's investment of time and money. Then you can use the "Management by Objectives" worksheet to help you develop action plans to implement your highest priority best sales practices within your company.

Management by Objectives: Nine Steps to Improving Productivity	Client-Centered™ Training Equips Its Sales Force with Notebook PCs
1. Define your goals.	Provide our salespeople with notebook computers so that they can work out of their homes, save commute time, and increase the amount of selling time that they spend with customers.
2. Define your key results.	Each salesperson should spend four days each week making sales calls. Each salesperson should make at least 8 customer calls each week. Each salesperson should close nine new accounts this quarter. *What gets measured gets done!*
3. Evaluate your strengths and weaknesses.	Most of our sales force has had experience using a PC, but two of our salespeople are older and are apprehensive about making mistakes. Our sales manager has had no previous computer training, but our IS manager is an excellent teacher.
4. Determine a course of action.	Our IS manager is installing our new sales automation system on our new computers this Friday. He will distribute them to our sales force on Tuesday and will present a training class on our sales automation system on Wednesday. After our salespeople are comfortable working with their computers, we will allow them to work out of their homes three days each week.
5. Budget your resources (time, personnel, and capital).	The PO for the computers has been approved, and we have budgeted time for training classes. All of our sales personnel have promised that they will attend training.
6. Determine completion date.	Our salespeople will be trained by the end of next week.
7. Write down your plan.	We have written down our plan and incorporated it into our sales personnel's objectives.
8. Monitor results.	We will review our progress with our VP of Sales at our monthly meeting.
9. Implement rewards.	We are putting a bonus plan in place to ensure that our salespeople make at least 8 customer calls each week. If our salespeople sell 15 systems this quarter, they will earn a free trip for themselves and their spouses to New Orleans.

The most important factor in predicting the success of change is the support of senior management.

Step 4: Validate your company's best sales practices with your customers.

Use your company's sales results (and other performance metrics), customer comments, and feedback from your sales force to help you evaluate the impact that implementing specific best sales practices, re-engineering sales processes, and automating sales systems has had on your company's ability to move business forward and close sales.

Step 5: Evaluate new marketing opportunities.

Most companies do not have any difficulty identifying new business opportunities. The problem that most companies face is evaluating the constellation of business opportunities that are competing for its limited resources and identifying the opportunities that are most likely to help it achieve its business objectives.

Fortunately, there are a few heuristics that your company can use to help it evaluate new business opportunities and predict which opportunities are likely to help it achieve its objectives.

1. *Is your new opportunity consistent with the strategic goals of your company?* One of the keys to success is remaining focused on the core competencies that have led to success in your market. The farther away from your core competencies your new opportunity takes you, the greater the risk your company has of channeling its resources into its new venture at the expense of its core business.

2. *Does your new opportunity extend or expand an existing product line or service?* Opportunities that provide your customers with additional capabilities or services are the easiest to market and the most likely to succeed. For example, a company that manufactures precision cutting tools might introduce a computer-controlled milling table to augment its product line and demonstrate that it remains on the "cutting edge" of new technology.

   Developing custom products can be a tempting business opportunity. However, it is rarely profitable to lose focus on your company's primary business objective unless your company can leverage its custom work in its regular product line.

3. *Does your new opportunity leverage your current business operation?* It is less costly and less risky to develop a new product if it uses technologies and components that are used in your company's other products. It is also less risky to sell a new product to existing customers than to have to develop a new customer base.

4. *Does your new opportunity support a coherent marketing strategy?* Many companies fail to achieve total market domination because they never formulate a coherent marketing strategy, but instead develop and launch a "string" of products. More profits come from finding new applications for existing products and technologies than from launching new products or evangelizing new technologies.

   Sales representatives often demand new products to "fill the holes" in their company's product line or to match competitive products. And one-stop purchasing can provide a competitive advantage. But it is usually very costly for a company to promote a "complete" line of products. Most companies make over 80 percent of their profits from less than 20 percent of the products that they sell, and offering a "complete" product line rarely increases profitability.

5. *Is your new opportunity self-funding?* Companies can often convince their customers or business partners to help them fund their research and development costs. This arrangement can be advantageous to customers, if it is the most cost-effective way to solve their problems, and it can be advantageous to business partners if it results in an equitable opportunity to share new profits.

6. *Does your new opportunity meet the profit requirements of the company or profit center that will be financing the project?* No business opportunity is worth financing unless it will ultimately lead to significant profits for your company. In manufacturing companies, gross profit generally must be no less than 35 percent and preferably well over 45 percent to earn a profit of 10 percent EBIT (Earning Before Income Tax).

7. *Will your new opportunity enable your company to bring the first product of its type to market?* It is easier to build market share as the

first company to market with a new product or technology. But the only sure way to win a race is to stay in the lead. If your product is flawed, or if you fail to support your customers, your company may lose the advantage that it has gained by being first to market.

8. *Will you be able to do a limited rollout before "betting your company" on your new opportunity?* The more experience your company has introducing similar products, the more aggressive it can afford to be when it introduces new products.

9. *Give new opportunities a chance to prove themselves—but be objective about evaluating your success.* Use objectives and key results to track each marketing activity, and review all marketing activities on a quarterly basis.

Your company can use the "New Product Planning" questionnaire to help it evaluate new business opportunities.

New Product Planning Questionnaire	Client-Centered™ Training's *Seminar-In-a-Box* Programs
Is your new opportunity consistent with the strategic goals of your company?	Seminar-In-a-Box programs enable us to provide courseware to large organizations that have in-house training departments.
Does your new opportunity extend or expand an existing product line or service?	We can use our seminar workbooks as the basis for each Seminar-In-a-Box program.
Does your new opportunity leverage your current business operation?	Absolutely—we can use our existing channels to resell this product.
Does your new opportunity support a coherent marketing strategy?	Our new Seminar-In-a-Box programs are consistent with our strategy of delivering high-quality cost effective multimedia training materials to our clients.
Is your new opportunity self-funding?	We would like to launch a Seminar In-a-Box program that covers Client-Centered™ Communication Skills. Our development budget is $25,000. If this product does well, we would like to create Seminar-In-a-Box products based on each one of our basic selling skill seminars.
Does your new opportunity meet the profit requirements of the company or profit center that will be financing the project?	If we market Seminar-In-a-Box seminars at $395, they will have a gross profit margin of 82%. Our other seminar materials have a gross profit margin of 64%.

Will your new opportunity enable your company to bring the first product of its type to market?	No, but we think it will be among the best-quality programs available.
Will you be able to do a limited rollout before "betting your company" on your new opportunity?	We will introduce the Communications module in the Northwest region. If it does well, we will sell the product through our national channels.
Have you given your new opportunities a chance to prove themselves? Have you been objective about evaluating your success?	We have a $55,000 marketing budget for our promotion. Our pilot test will take three months. If we do not sell at least 2,000 units during our test promotion, we will redesign our product.

Step 6: Engineer creativity into your company.

Many of the most innovative and successful companies have begun with a moment of inspiration. The founders of Compaq Computers, for example, drew a picture of what would become their company's first portable PC on a coffee-stained napkin in a café. This moment, captured with a photograph of the napkin lying on a café table, was featured in an advertising campaign as a testament to Compaq's realization of the American dream.

Not every successful company begins with a moment of inspiration, and not every inspiration leads to a successful business. But it is important to learn how to think creatively and how to engineer creativity and innovation into your corporate culture.

1. *Get in touch with whatever enables you to focus your creative energy on developing new ideas and solving business problems.*
   - Break out of your routines. Many people are most creative when they break out of their normal daily routine and engage in different activities during the day.
   - Try working on your problem very intensely for a period of time to absorb the material that you need in order to understand every facet of your problem, and then force yourself to engage in a different activity to enable your sub-conscious mind to work on your problem.
   - Write down good ideas immediately. Some of the best ideas tear loose from short-term memory at the most inconvenient times, such as when there isn't a pen or pencil in sight.

- ☐ Write down all of your creative ideas, even if you do not see any immediate use for them. Some of the best ideas take a bit of time to digest before you realize their true value.

2. *Use brainstorming and focus sessions to facilitate the sharing of ideas.*
   - ☐ There are two rules for successful brainstorming: first, allow yourself plenty of time to brainstorm, and second, try not to set an unrealistic level of expectation for the time that you invest at your meeting.
   - ☐ OK, I have two more suggestions; don't be too organized, and don't be judgmental about other people's ideas. If you are too organized, you will engineer the creativity out of your meeting. And if you are judgmental, no one will want to brainstorm with you, as the star witness or the prosecution!

3. *Study other businesses and meet with creative people in allied industries.*
   - ☐ One of the best ways to get new ideas is to analyze a completely different business to learn how it addresses the problem that your own company is dealing with. For example, if your company is having a difficult time convincing retailers to stock your line of PC products, you might study how consumer products companies compete for retail shelf space.
   - ☐ Participation on standards committees and participating in joint technology ventures can have a profound impact on the success of your company. Sharing information can help your company stay abreast of new market opportunities and can help your company bring products to market more quickly.

4. *Meet with your customers.*
   - ☐ Remember the First Law of Total Market Domination. Meeting with customers can help you discover new product ideas and catch new market trends. Customers love to tell their suppliers about their problems, their successes, and their concerns. But most companies don't take the time to listen!

5. *Never overlook an unusual finding as accidental or random.*
   - ☐ Your curious piece of data may be a gold nugget hidden in a mountain of the obvious.

6. *Continually explore how your products can be refined and adapted to new markets.*
   - Any research that your company has done or proprietary technology that your company has developed is an ideal place to begin formulating new product plans and marketing ideas.
7. *Solve your own business problems, and then use your experience to develop new products and new marketing strategies.*
   - The best ideas are often the most simple and obvious ones. If your company has a problem, there is a good chance that many other companies are concerned with the same issue. And if a sales promotion is compelling to you, it will probably appeal to other customers as well.
8. *Be agnostic about great ideas—it doesn't matter where they come from!*
   - Being an expert at deriving solutions from other people's ideas is a wonderful skill. There is no need to reinvent the wheel if you can figure out how to get somebody else's wheel to roll down your path!
9. SUGGESTION BOX + INCENTIVES = CREATIVE IDEAS + PROFITS
   - IBM awards millions of dollars each year to employees who submit suggestions that save IBM money or enable it to address new business opportunities. The amount of IBM's awards is determined by the savings or benefits that the company derives from its employees' suggestions. IBM's suggestion box has helped drive IBM's success for decades.
10. *Use emerging computer and communication technologies to facilitate communication and dialog, and to encourage creative problem solving.*
    - Use e-mail and videoconferencing to facilitate meetings, share ideas, and manage time.
11. *Use your company's "learning experiences" to drive its future success.*
    - Many creative people do not handle stress very well. And many people who are extremely ambitious may compensate by becoming depressed, insecure, or overly aggressive if they fail to meet their goals. If you can't accept your employees' failures, fire them. Otherwise be positive about their "learning experience" and encourage them to continue doing the job that your company hired them to do.

Step 7: Develop a process for handling sales and marketing problems.

Most business managers learn how to accomplish specific tasks, such as creating budgets and calculating demand curves, in school. In the classroom, business problems are usually straightforward, and decisions are either right or wrong. But in the real world, business problems are often extremely complex, and managers must make decisions without having enough information to make informed decisions, and with no feedback process to enable them to evaluate whether or not, in retrospect, they have made the best choice.

Selling is fun when sales and profits are up. But it is no fun to come to work when sales are down, profit margins are eroding, the company's best salespeople are quitting, and shareholders are demanding change. This "real world" can be very stressful.

Over the years, I have developed a few heuristics that may help you get your marketing strategies back on track *when things go wrong*.

1. *Focus on your customers' key market concerns.* Failure to map specific elements of your marketing story to specific customer needs and concerns is the reason the vast majority of all marketing strategies run aground.
2. *What difference would it make to your customers if your company went out of business tomorrow?* Is there a *compelling* reason for customers to purchase your product today?
3. *Assume that everyone in your organization is doing a perfect job, and then work backward to see what can be done to improve your situation.* The less your managers' egos are involved, the better chance they will have of resolving your company's problems.
4. *Have your managers switch roles with one another.* Schedule an off-site planning session where your managers can assume—just for your meeting—different roles. Assuming a new role can give your managers a fresh perspective on their problems.

   This technique is especially helpful when a company has endured a bad situation for a long period, and individuals have strong opinions about how problems have developed and why they have not been resolved.
5. *Take two days off.* Thinking in circles will tire you out; it will not move your business forward. If you have "gone over everything a dozen times" and are feeling overwhelmed, take

a couple of days off. If you are able to relax, you may be able to regain your sense of humor and begin thinking about your situation more objectively and more creatively.

6. *Bite the bullet and seek outside help.* Don't wait too long to call in an outside consultant. Great advice won't help you if you don't have any resources left to restart your business.

My phone number is in the book!

Step 8: Take responsibility for your company's success.

You can hire people to help you accomplish almost any business task, but you can only count on your own intuition and judgment when it comes to making the fundamental decisions that will ultimately determine your company's success. One of these fundamental decisions is whether or not your company will be ethical and work with its customers in a Client-Centered™ way.

According to a 1997 survey by the Ethics Resource Center and the Society for Human Resources Management, 84 percent of surveyed companies have codes of conduct. But a recent study[1] of two hundred sales managers by *Sales and Marketing Management* magazine reported:

- □ 49 percent of the surveyed sales managers say that their sales representatives have lied on sales calls
- □ 34 percent say that they have heard their sales representatives make unrealistic promises
- □ 22 percent say that their sales representatives have sold products that their customers didn't need
- □ 30 percent say that customers have demanded kickbacks for buying their product or service
- □ 54 percent say that the drive to meet sales goals does a disservice to customers

Many major corporations have been caught in high-visibility scandals that have had grave consequences such as costly lawsuits, a deluge of negative press, and a weakened market position.

---

[1] Michele Marchetti, "Whatever it takes," *Sales and Marketing Management*, December 1997.

Prudential Insurance Company, for example, recently paid $425 million to settle a class-action suit. Prudential Insurance's agents convinced its customers to purchase new policies, promising that they would virtually pay for themselves, while unbeknownst to customers, these agents were using up the cash value of their older policies to pay for the new ones. As a consequence of this action, Prudential Insurance's share of the U.S. life insurance market fell from 7.78 percent to 6.59 percent in 1996.

Although many companies espouse a Client-Centered™ approach to marketing their products, *Sales and Marketing Management* magazine's study indicates that the *stress* caused by quotas, incentive compensation plans, and a fiercely competitive selling environment is eroding the morality of many sales professionals.

Companies that want to achieve total market domination can mitigate this stress by developing compensation plans and sales objectives that balance their desire for their sales force to be as aggressive as possible, with their concern about maintaining a Client-Centered™ relationship with their customers.

1. Educate your sales force about the implications of unethical behavior and discipline any employees who violate your company's code of conduct.
2. Develop compensation plans that provide a high enough base salary to cover your sales representatives' basic living expenses.
3. Tie some portion of incentive compensation to customer satisfaction and retention.
4. Develop a "bottom-up" sales forecasting process, which includes input from your company's sales force, to help your company set realistic sales quotas.

10 Steps to Ethical Client-Centered™ Selling

Customers want to do business with suppliers that are ethical and that provide a high level of customer service.

1. Never misrepresent your products.
2. Answer your customers' concerns honestly and completely.
3. Provide accurate, timely information.
4. Inform your customers of issues that are critical to their success.
5. Don't pursue business that is bad for your customer.
6. Don't pursue business that is bad for your company.
7. Don't disparage your competitors.
8. Work with people who you believe are ethical.
9. Take responsibility for your customers' satisfaction.
10. Follow the "Golden Rule."

TEN LAWS OF TOTAL MARKET DOMINATION

The 10 Laws of Total Market Domination are not shortcuts to success. The truth is, there is no lazy path to success. The only way to win customers and earn their loyalty is to be a good business partner. But by taking a Client-Centered™ approach to marketing, you can *engineer* your company's success. And, like other great entrepreneurs, you can drive your company to achieve total market domination.

10 Laws of Total Market Domination

1. The easiest and most reliable way to learn about your customers' needs and concerns is to ask them.

2. Don't roll out your marketing program until you have tested your marketing story.

3. Before you can influence your customers' purchase process, you must establish your credibility.

4. Your company's mission statement, like any other marketing communication, should be clear, concise, and compelling, and should communicate the value that your company provides to its customers.

5. Companies that stay close enough to their customers to anticipate what their customers must do to remain competitive are the companies that will ultimately dominate their industry.

6. The success of a distribution channel hinges on the ability and willingness of both partners—the supplier and the reseller—to invest the money and other resources that are necessary to achieve success.

7. Virtually every problem selling situation can be traced back to incorrect assumptions about a customer's needs and concerns, and a failure to verify communications during the qualification process.

8. Diversity drives creativity in an organization and can be the catalyst that enables a company to address new markets and business opportunities.

9. Early technology adopters can gain a competitive advantage against companies that are unwilling or unable to adapt their marketing strategy to leverage new computer and communication technologies.

10. It is ten times more expensive to acquire a new customer than to retain a current customer.

A FINAL NOTE

If you are interested in obtaining blank copies of the worksheets in this book in electronic form, or you would like to request information about Client-Centered™ sales presentations and consulting services, please visit our Web site at www.daytonassociates.com, or contact:

Dayton Associates
477 123rd Place NE
Bellevue, Washington 98005
Voice: (425) 451-1140
E-mail: info@daytonassociates.com
Internet: www.daytonassociates.com

I love to hear from readers, and I would be delighted to learn how your company has used the Client-Centered™ sales evaluation process to help it re-engineer its sales infrastructure and achieve total market domination.

Thanks again for your support!

—Doug Dayton

SALES AUTOMATION SOFTWARE— EVALUATION GUIDE

The "Sales Automation Software Evaluation" worksheet was adapted from the format used in Information Systems Marketing, Inc.'s annual *Guide to Sales, Customer Service and Marketing Automation*. ISM publishes individual product reviews from this guide on its Web site at www.ismguide.com. You can use this worksheet to help your company identify its sales automation requirements and evaluate sales automation software products from different companies.

Sales Automation Software Evaluation Worksheet	Services/Capabilities
General Information	
Company	Sales Automation System, Inc. (example)
Contact	Robert Nelson
Address	123 Main St. Bellevue, WA 98005
Telephone	800-555-1212
Fax	425-555-2121
E-mail	info@salesauto.com
Internet	http://www.salesauto.com
Years in business	10
Number of employees	215

Number of resellers	141
Total user base	2,800
Languages/localization	English, Spanish, French Supports $Euro
Local system integrators	□ Network PC, Inc. □ Seattle Sales Systems
Price	$995 for the first user, plus $500 for each additional user
Enterprise license	Negotiable

Application Overview

Sales Automation System (SAS) is a powerful enterprise-wide solution that provides customer, sales, and marketing management modules. SAS is available in English, Spanish, and French and runs on MS-Windows 95, 98, NT, and CE. SAS is supplied with MS-Access, and may be used with SQL Server or Sybase SQL.

SAS displays customer and sales information in a tree view, which offers a hierarchical display of contacts within an account, and in a folder, which sits on the desktop or the main screen. Information can also be displayed in a grid with the ability to drill down (move from a summary report to a source document) for more detail with a mouse click.

Users can seamlessly toggle between account and contact screens. Leads are tracked within a folder and may be attached to items as objects in the note section of the screen. An unlimited number of contacts can be attached to a lead or a sales opportunity.

SAS includes a proposal generator that is integrated with MS Word. The proposal generator supports drag-and-drop price configuration and can be interfaced to a tax table.

Users can configure different account and contact views on a spreadsheet-style grid by selecting a field from a drop-down field list and then dragging and dropping that field into the view. Users can save a file as an object onto the MS Windows desktop using ActiveX technology.

SAS provides a basic time management module and integrates with Microsoft Schedule+ and MS Outlook. SAS also integrates with MS Office, Lotus Notes, and most other MS Windows applications.

Contact Management

Contact information	□ Can store and access contact information by contact name, company name, and twenty user-defined fields
	□ Complete account history is available with query by example and text search
	□ E-mail and Internet access is available through icons located on the left-hand side of the home screen

	□ Can select a new field from a drop down list and add it to contact and account screens by dragging and dropping the field into place
	□ Can drill-down into any line item or folder item for contact information
Contact history	□ Can track contact history, including all events, proposals, sales, notes, and letters
	□ Automatic telephone log
	□ Can view all contact events in a tree or grid view
	□ Can drill-down in grid view to access event details including type of contact, date, time, status, priority and description
	□ Can customize view with user-defined fields to display additional contact information

Account Management

Activities	□ Can track accounts and related information such as addresses, customer contacts, and E-mail and Internet address
Contact history	□ Can track contact history on all activities and events associated with an individual contact or account
Order entry	□ SAS integrates with any accounting package that supports ActiveX technology (e.g., Great Plains Software)
	□ User can save a proposal as an MS Word or HTML document (if installed with MS Office)
Order history	□ Can track account history with custom fields
	□ Integrates with third-party accounting package
Lead tracking	□ Can create any number of contact/prospect lists
	□ Can configure contact lists to track source, marketing activities, promotional events, literature fulfillment, status, territory, and user-defined criteria
	□ Can prioritize leads using various systems, (e.g., A, B, and C priority rating)
	□ Can sort leads by activity completed, time since last action, and other user-defined criteria
	□ Can attach note fields to individual contacts
Proposals and contracts	□ SAS offers a separate Proposal Generator to create sales proposals and contracts

	☐ The proposal generator can be customized to accommodate a unique sales infrastructure and interface with compatible accounting systems
	☐ Proposal templates can be stored as MS Word template files
Sales analysis	☐ SAS includes over 50 predefined reports
	☐ Reports may be created or customized with Crystal Reports
Sales Force Management	
Expense reporting	☐ Can track and report on expenses through a time and expense form that is integrated with MS Excel
	☐ Can import and export time and billing information from third-party applications using SAS Interface Wizard
Territory assignment	☐ Can reassign accounts by dragging and dropping a selection from a list
Activity reporting	☐ Can generate sales reports on demand and create new reports with MS Excel and MS Access, and Crystal Reports
Special events	☐ Can track results for specific marketing activities
	☐ Can create and summarize customer survey results
Time and Activity Management	
Scheduling	☐ Basic scheduling functionality is supported—can schedule defined activities for a single user
	☐ Multiuser and resource scheduling (e.g., rooms and machines) are supported with third-party applications such as MS Schedule+
To-do lists	☐ Can generate a list of to-dos and schedule due dates
Tickler/Alarm	☐ Can set automatic tickler/alarm
	☐ Can integrate with a third-party package, such as MS Schedule+ or MS Outlook
Electronic mail	☐ Supports MAPI and VIM-compliant e-mail products
	☐ Supports Microsoft Mail and Lotus Notes
Fax/Modem	☐ Supports TAPI
Notes	☐ Can attach an unlimited number of notes to any field on any screen

Transaction log (time stamp)	□ Supports automatic date and time stamping of all activities
Telemarketing/Scripting	
Call lists	□ Can assemble call lists using a simple database search (query-by-example)
Auto-dialing	□ Supports auto-dialing, speed dial, and redial abilities
Scripting	□ Supports limited scripting using electronic notes
Call recording	□ Can automatically capture a call and its associated activities
Call planning	□ Can attach a call outline as a note to a telephone activity
Call statistics/reporting	□ Can track the duration, purpose, effectiveness, and results of each customer contact
Customer Service	
Incident assignment	□ Can record and assign a support call (incident) to an appropriate support representative □ Incidents can be tracked by priority, type of action to be taken, and objective of the support call □ Can configure the customer activity/contact box by adding an incident assignment button
Incident escalation	□ Can customize an action plan for an incident with a manual escalation procedure
Incident tracking	□ Can record and query incidents by example
Incident reporting	□ Can track incidents by contact, by company, by assigned support representative, and by status of response
Marketing Services	
Product/Price configurator	□ The system automatically uses price and quantity information to generate a quote □ SAS supports standard tax tables
Campaign management	□ Can track completed activities related to a sales campaign with a graphical status display
Opportunity management	□ Can track status, type, sales amount, and likelihood (percentage) to close □ Can query opportunities based on ranges, representatives, forecasted sales, and closure percentages

Marketing databases	◻ Can access a marketing database on the Internet or locally through an Intranet or CD
Electronic lead generation	◻ Can download a lead and classify it in order to route it directly to a sales representative
Competitive information	◻ Can download information from the Internet and attach it to a contact or company
Letter-writing capabilities	◻ Integrated with MS Word
Mail merge	◻ Automatically creates merge lists ◻ Integrated with MS Word
Label creation	◻ Integrated with MS Word

Decision Support Services

Ad hoc query generator (QBE)	◻ All fields support query-by-example
SQL generator/capability	◻ Supports SQL Server and Sybase Server
Forecasting/Planning tools	◻ Integrated with MS Excel ◻ Can integrate with ODBC compatible third-party applications
Graphical or statistical modeling tools	◻ Integrated with MS Excel and MS Access ◻ Can integrate with third-party applications via OLE support
EIS module with advanced graphical tools	◻ Integrated with MS Excel and MS Access
Predefined reports	◻ Includes 50 predefined reports
User-defined reporting	◻ Can integrate with third-party applications that support MS SQL Server or Sybase Server.

Technical Features

Operating systems supported	◻ MS Windows 95, 98, and NT
Handheld platforms supported	◻ MS Windows CE and US Robotics Pilot
Network operating systems supported	◻ MS Windows NT, Novell Netware, TCP/IP
Define software architecture	◻ Supports MS Windows interfaces. APIs are published, but source code is not available
Scalability	◻ Unlimited number of users
Direct integration with other systems	◻ Integration with any systems that incorporate ActiveX

Software programming language(s) used for development	☐ MS Visual Basic 5 and C++
First software release date and platform(s)	☐ 1996—SFAP v. 2.0, Wintel platform
Last software release date and platform(s)	☐ 1997—SFAP v. 2.0, MS Windows 95, MS Windows NT
Minimum hardware requirements for clients	☐ 16MB RAM, 100MB hard disk space, Pentium processor
Customization toolkit available	☐ Optional Configuration and Customization System is available ($5,000—includes 3-day training class)
Toolkits used in software development	☐ MS Visual Basic 5 and C++ used with ODBC
Work flow process can be configured	☐ Yes
Database servers directly supported	☐ Any ODBC compliant database
OLE supported	☐ Client and server
DBMS supplied with package	☐ MS Access 97
SQL supported	☐ MS SQL Server, Sybase
Distributed database support	☐ Yes
Client/Server databases supported	☐ Yes
ODBC compliant	☐ Yes
Database replication	☐ The RBMS vendor defines supported method.
Data synchronization	☐ Record level, bidirectional synchronization available (3Com Palm Pilot)
Server-to-server database synchronization supported	☐ Yes ☐ N-tiered synchronization supported
Wireless options offered	☐ Supports latest CDPD standards
Internet connectivity for synchronization and replication	☐ Web browser, e-mail, and import/export data
Internet connectivity	☐ Internet browser interface is available ☐ HTML files can be transmitted via e-mail
Thin-client support	☐ Business components can be downloaded from the Internet and launched from a Web browser
Source code available	☐ System integrators can purchase source code

Seamless integration of third-party development tools at the field level	□ Yes. MS Visual Basic
Security features	□ Ability to restrict data access at the form, field, and content levels, to individual users and groups of users.
External software packages that can be integrated	□ MS Office □ ActiveX applications
Integrated Mail Transport	□ MS Exchange
Help function	□ Windows-compatible Help menu is available □ Help is context sensitive □ User may add text to help database
Training and Support	
Training	□ Recommend five days of training for system manager □ Recommend one day of training for system users □ $600 per day at SAS
On-site support	□ On-site support is available through a local SAS system integrator □ On-site support is also available directly from SAS for $1,200 plus expenses per day
Telephone support	□ Free for the first 90 days □ Telephone support may be purchased for $125 per hour (first 90 days from installation are free) □ A support contract that covers all telephone support for one year is available for $1,500 □ A toll-free support number is available: (800) 555-1234
System documentation	□ An indexed system guide and an easy-to-understand user manual is provided on a CD-ROM
Electronic bulletin boards and online forums	□ FAQs and e-mail to support group are available on the SAS Web site
Maintenance agreement	□ A Customer Maintenance Agreement is available at 15% of the suggested retail price
Product warranty	□ 90 days

Product Strengths:	Product Weaknesses:
Contact management	Marketing automation
Account management	Time management
Sales force management	Group Scheduling
Customer support	Planning Tools (requires Crystal Reports)
Call statistics	Order Status & tracking (depends on accounting application)
Predefined sales reports	Sales forecasting
User-friendliness	
OLE, ODBC, and SQL support	

APPENDIX B

LEADING SALES AUTOMATION COMPANIES

This list of sales automation software companies is for information purposes only. It is not intended to be an endorsement or a recommendation by the author or by Adams Media.

Aurum Software (Enterprise CIS)
Aurum is a subsidiary of Baan Software.
2350 Mission College Boulevard, Suite 1300
Santa Clara, CA 95054-1535
Telephone: 408-986-8100
FAX: 408-654-3400
Toll Free: 800-683-8855
www.aurum.com

GoldMine Software Corp. (Entry SFA)
17383 Sunset Boulevard, Suite 301
Pacific Palisades, CA 90272-4138
Telephone: 310-454-6800
FAX: 310-454-4848
Toll Free: 800-654-3526
www.goldminesw.com

Moss Micro, Inc. (Mid-level SFA)
36 Executive Park
Irvine, CA 92614
Telephone: 714-260-0300
FAX: 714-260-0325
www.mossmicro.com

Onyx Software (Internet CIS)
330 120th Avenue NE, Suite 210
Bellevue, WA 98005-3014
Telephone: 425-451-8060
FAX: 425-990-3343
www.onyx.com

Oracle Corporation (Enterprise CIS)
500 Oracle Parkway
Redwood Shores, CA 94065
Telephone: 650-506-7000
FAX: 650-506-7200
www.oracle.com

Pivotal Software Inc. (Mid-level SFA)
260 W. Esplanade, Suite 310
North Vancouver, BC V7M 3G7
CANADA
Telephone: 604-988-9982
FAX: 604-988-0035
www.pivotal.com

Platinum Software Corporation (Help Desk)
8100 SW Nyberg Road
Tualatin, OR 97062
Telephone: 503-612-2800
FAX: 503-612-2600
Toll Free: 800-883-4587
www.clientele.com

Sage U.S., Inc. (Entry SFA)
17950 Preston Road, Suite 800
Dallas, TX 75252-5793
Telephone: 972-818-3900
FAX: 972-733-4251
Toll Free: 800-835-6241
www.telemagic.com

SalesLogix, Inc. (Mid-level SFA)
8800 N Gainey Center Drive,
Suite 200
Scottsdale, AZ 85258
Telephone: 602-368-3700
FAX: 602-368-3799
Toll Free: 888-643-6400
www.saleslogix.com

Siebel Systems (Enterprise CIS)
1855 South Grant Street
San Mateo, CA 94402-2667
Telephone: 415-295-5000
FAX: 415-295-5111
www.siebel.com

Symantec Corporation (Entry SFA)
10201 Torre Avenue
Cupertino, CA 95014-2132
Telephone: 408-253-9600
FAX: 408-252-4694
Toll Free: 800-441-7234
www.symantec.com

UpShot (Internet SFA)
400 Convention Way
P.O. Box 5267
Redwood City, CA 94063
Telephone: 650-482-3730
FAX: 650-482-3737
Toll Free: 888-700-8774
www.upshot.com

Vantive Corporation (Enterprise CIS)
2455 Augustine Drive
Santa Clara, CA 95054-3002
Telephone: 408-982-5700
FAX: 408-982-5710
Toll Free: 800-582-6848
www.vantive.com

NON-DISCLOSURE AGREEMENT

Your company can use a Non-Disclosure Agreement to help it protect its "Confidential and Proprietary Information." Many companies, for example, ask prospective investors and employees to sign a non-disclosure agreement before disclosing their business plans to them.

Your company should check with its attorney before disseminating any company confidential information or executing any non-disclosure agreements.

Sample Non-Disclosure Agreement

Agreement made June 19, 200X, between Acme Corporation, a corporation organized and existing under the laws of the State of California, with its principal place of business at 123 Main Street, San Francisco, California, herein referred to as Corporation, and Client-Centered™ Training, Inc., a corporation, with its principle place of business at 477 123rd Place NE, Bellevue, Washington, herein referred to as Consultant.

CONFIDENTIAL AND PROPRIETARY INFORMATION

Each party acknowledges and agrees that any and all information concerning the other's business is "Confidential and Proprietary Information," and each party agrees that it will not permit the duplication, use, or disclosure of any such "Confidential and Proprietary Information" to any person (other than its own employee, agent, or representative who must have such information for the performance of its obligations hereunder), unless such duplication, use, or disclosure is specifically authorized by the other party. "Confidential and Proprietary Information" is not meant to include any information which, at the time of disclosure, is generally known by the public or any competitors of the parties to this Agreement.

1. Any modifications or addendum to this contract shall be made only in writing. Such modifications or addendum will not become valid until signed by all parties to this Agreement.

2. The laws of the state of Washington shall govern this Agreement.

3. If either Corporation or Consultant employs attorneys to enforce any rights arising out of or relating to this Agreement, the prevailing party shall be entitled to recover attorney's fees.

4. If any term or provision of this Agreement shall be found to be illegal or unenforceable, then, notwithstanding any such illegality or lack of enforceability, this Agreement shall remain in full force and effect and such term or provision shall be deemed to be deleted.

Corporation: _____   Date: _____

Consultant: _____   Date: _____

INDEX

A

Account focus meetings, 146
Accounting system, evaluating, 230–31
Account plans, evaluating, 142–45
Account review process, evaluating, 145–46
Accounts, preparation of company in selling to major, 135–37
Action plans, developing for best sales practice, 298–300
Activity-based planning, 8–9
Advertising
  banner, 241
  Internet, 241
  key to creating effective, 107
  mistakes in, 108
  results, 108–13
  reviewing budget for, 110–11
Advertising communications, 196
  evaluating plan for, 106–7
Airplane marketing, 122–23
Ambrex Accounting software, 49

B

Background checks, 178–83
Backward product integration, 33
Banner advertisements, 241
Best sales practices
  developing action plans for, 298–300
  identifying company's, 295–98
  validating company's, with customers, 300
Breakeven pricing, 94
Budgeting, zcro-base, 281, 282–85
Budget(s)
  developing, for sales automation project, 248–49
  developing for sales automation systems, 248–49

marketing, 280–82
  in marketing plans, 58–59
  reviewing advertising, 110–11
Burger King, 12
Business concerns, influence of, on purchase decisions, 5
Business cycle, evaluation of company position in, 27–31
Business objectives, 22
  evaluating short- and longer-term, 23–26
  evaluation of primary, 20
  tailoring compensation plan to meet, 182–83
Business partners, evaluating relationships with, 73–75

C

Change
  preparing for, xi–xx
  strategies for managing, in your company, 288–308
Channel conflict, 82
Client-Centered™ approach to marketing, 1–5
Client-Centered™ customer support, 254–55
Client-Centered™ sales evaluation process, xii–xiii
Client-Centered™ sales practices, 125
  identifying and implementing best, 288–310
Client-Centered™ training, mission statement of, 20
Coaching, 163
Combination plan, 181
Commission, 181
Communications
  advertising, 106–7, 196
  corporate, 106–7, 111–13, 196
  technologies in leveraging sales

efforts, 201–53
wireless, 224–25
Company
    allocation of resources by, and
        achievement of marketing
        objectives, 19–35
    engineering creativity into, 303–5
    evaluating market position of,
        39–40
    evaluating pricing strategy of, 88
    identifying most significant
        accomplishments of, 41
    representation of, by sales force,
        153–200
    reviewing personnel policies of,
        158–59
    taking responsibility for success of,
        307–8
Compaq Computers, 39, 303
Compensation. *See also* Sales
    compensation plan
    communication of plan, 187–93
    incentive, 183–87
    for members of sales team, 185–87
    reseller, 82–84
    total target, 181–83
Competitive advantage and
    survival, 252
Competitive intelligence, 43–44
Competitor, evaluating strengths and
    weaknesses of, 42
Computers
    in leveraging sales efforts, 201–53
    role of, in virtual office, 245–46
    security procedures for, 235–39
Computer telephony, 222–24
Computing, network, 201, 236–39
Consultants
    dilemma of, xviii
    evaluating, 87
    working with, xvii
Cookies, 241
Corporate communications, 196
    evaluating, 111–13
    evaluating plan for, 106–7
Corporate culture, describing,
    157–58
Creativity, engineering, into
    company, 303–5
Credibility, 259–60
Crime, 235–39

Critical success factors, identifying
    company's, 290–95
Customer communication,
    naming your company and your
    products, 114
Customer contact form, 129–31
Customer demand, 91–92
Customer information systems
    (CIS), 217. *See also* Marketing
    information systems (MIS)
    benefits of, 218
    deploying, 219–20
    evaluating your, 216–18
    on Internet, 221
Customer requirement analysis,
    131–39
Customers
    describing your, 2–4
    documenting purchase process for,
        10–11
    effective programs for qualifying
        prospective, 124–52
    effective programs in identifying
        prospective, 98–123
    evaluating relationships with, 73
    expectations of, 92–93
    factors driving purchase decisions
        of, 1–18
    identifying key purchase factors
        for, 4–6
    knowing, in prospecting, 99–101
    managing information for, 216–18
    new ways of reaching, 224–30
    support call centers for, 221–22
Customer satisfaction survey,
    performing, 257–59
Customer service, web-based,
    221–22
Customer service and support model
    effectiveness of, 254–67
    evaluating, 255–56

D
Database marketing, 216
Data mining tools, 230
Decision support, 219, 231–35
Delta Airlines, 264–65
Demand-oriented pricing, 92
Direct prospecting methods, 98
Distribution channels, 197
    benefits of, 77–78

identifying most profitable, 83–84
in marketing plans, 57
multiple, 80–81
Distribution strategy
developing coherent, 78–80
evaluating, 75–77
Document conferencing, 225–26
DoubleClick, Inc., 229, 241

E
Eddie Bauer, 260
Ego, 194
Electronic bulletin boards, 117–21
Electronic commerce, 201, 242–44
Electronic Data Interchange (EDI),
227
Electronic forms and workflow
computer applications, 226–27
Electronic mail, 228–30
Employees
attitudes of, 194–95
excessive turnover in, as warning
signal, 162
self-evaluation of, 194–95
Exclusive distribution, 78

F
FasFax Corporation, 12
Financial statements, in marketing
plans, 58–59
Financial status, changes in, 285–87
Financial systems, evaluating, 283–85
Flowchart, creating, for sales process,
204–11
Focus groups, 91–92
Forward marketing integration, 33
Forward product integration, 32

G
Gartner Group, 264
Gates, Bill, 177
Government regulation of Internet
suppliers and users, 244

H
Hertz, 254
Hiring process
background checks in, 178–83
psychological testing in, 178
Historical analysis, 91
Honesty, xiv–xvii

I
IBM, 163–64
Impression, making first, 255
Incentives, 181
as compensation, 183–87
Indirect prospecting methods, 98
Industry standards, 260–62
Information systems. *See also*
Customer information systems
(CIS); Marketing information
systems (MIS)
evaluating, 232–35
Innovative marketing, 121
Integration
backward product, 33
forward marketing, 33
forward product, 32
Intensely competitive markets, 92
Intensive distribution, 78
International Data Corporation, 242
Internet, 201
advertising on, 241
customer information systems
on, 221
evaluating use of, 236–39
future use of, 245
government regulation of
suppliers and users on, 244

J
Just in time (JIT) inventory
management, 137

K
Kaypro Corporation, xix–xx

L
Leader pricing, 93
Leads
evaluation of prospecting methods
for generating, 98–99
prioritizing your, 105
quality, 101–3
Litigation, 86–88

M
Management by Objectives
worksheet, 298–99
Management reports, evaluating,
283–85
Marginal analysis, 94–95

Marginal cost, 94
Marginal revenue, 94
Market, determining size of, 278–81
Market decline, 29
Market factor identification
　in differentiating company and
　　project, 37–39
　negative, 11–12
　and purchase decision, 12–14
Market growth, 28
Marketing. *See also* Sales and
　marketing
　airplane, 122–23
　aligning strategy with company
　　objectives, 33–34
　Client-Centered™ approach to, 1–5
　database, 216
　evaluating new opportunities for,
　　300–303
　innovative, 121
　test, 92
　web sites, 239
Marketing budget
　creating, 281–82
　developing, 268–87
　evaluating, 280–81
Marketing department, evaluating,
　117–21
Marketing information systems
　(MIS), 217
　definition of, 15
　evaluation of, 15–18
Marketing objectives
　allocation of resources consistent
　　with, 19–35
　tailoring compensation plan to
　　achieve, 184–85
Marketing plans
　definition of, 53
　developing clear, concise, 53–54
　distribution, pricing, and
　　promotion strategy in, 57
　evaluating, 61–63
　executive summary in, 54–55
　financial statements, budgets and
　　revenue forecasts in, 58–59
　identifying risk factors to, 95–96
　information and competitive
　　strategy in, 55–56
　management team in, 59
　objectives of, 53–54

　operations in, 57–58
　product strategy in, 56
　in providing focus needed to
　　leverage selling efforts, 52–97
　reasons for stopping, 97
　risks in, 58
　template for, 54–60
Marketing story
　defining elements of, 45–47
　development of clear, concise,
　　compelling, 36–51
　finding time to test, 49–51
　mapping elements of, to your
　　customer's needs and concerns,
　　47–49
Market maturity, 28
Market research, 273–74
Markets
　normal competitive, 92
　prestige, 92
Market start-up/product
　introduction, 28
Market surveys, 91
Microsoft, 254
　and activity-based planning, 8–9
　Client-Centered™ approach of,
　　1–5
　golden handcuffs of, 183
　hiring process at, 177
　investment in strategic planning
　　of, 52
Mission statement of Client-
　Centered™ Training, 21–31
Motivating, 163–64
Multiple distribution channels, 80–81

N
Network computing, 201
　evaluating your use of, 236–39
Newsletter, 117
Non-disclosure agreement, 323–24
Nordstrom, 254, 260
Normal competitive markets, 92

O
Objectivity, xiv–xvii
Oligopolies, 92
Online application processing
　applications, 230
Order fulfillment issues, identifying,
　265–66

Organization chart, reviewing, to improve productivity, 159–61

P

Penetration pricing, 89
Personal concerns, influence of, on purchase decisions, 5
Personal networking, 122
Personnel policies, reviewing, for company, 158–59
Pet rock, 107
Portals, 242
Praise, 194
Press relations, managing, 113–14
Prestige market, 92
Price barriers, psychological, 93
Pricing
    breakeven, 94
    demand-oriented, 92
    evaluating strategy of, 88
    leader, 93
    in marketing plans, 57
    penetration, 89
    strategy in, 196
Problem solving, 196–200
Productivity, reviewing organization chart to improve, 159–61
Products
    evaluating demonstrations, 131–33
    evaluating strengths and weaknesses of, 44
    evaluation of sales, 31
    performance of, 32–34
Product strategy, changing, 197
Profit, 88–90
Profit maximization strategies, 88–89
Promotion, in marketing plans, 57
Prospecting
    choosing winning strategy for, 99
    evaluation of methods for generating leads, 98–99
    know your customer in, 99–101
    low-risk, 104
    managing press relations, 113–14
    newsletters in, 117
    and prioritizing your leads, 105–7
    qualifying in, 103–4
    quality leads in, 101–3
    sales formulas in, 104–5
    trade shows in, 114–16
    user groups and electronic bulletin boards in, 117–21
Prudential Insurance, 308
Psychological price barriers, 93
Psychological testing, 178
Pull strategy, 106
Purchase factors, identifying, in competitors positioning of products, 14–15
Push strategy, 106

Q

Qualification questionnaire, 128–29
Quality image, promoting, 262–66
Quality leads, 101–3

R

Real world problems, 34–35
Resellers
    changing, 86
    compensation for, 82–84
    evaluating, 84
    recruiting best, 85
Resources, prioritizing limited, 266–67
Return on Investment (ROI), 31
Revenue forecasts, in marketing plans, 58–59

S

Sales and marketing
    developing process for handling problems, 306–7
    evaluating effectiveness of group, 198–200
    evaluating workload of department, 197–98
    identifying key players in organization, 155–57
Sales and support facilities, evaluating, 267
Sales automation software, evaluation guide for, 312–20
Sales automation systems
    developing budget for project, 248–49
    evaluating, 209–11
    functional requirements capabilities, 211–12
    identifying areas in, 206–9
    leading companies in, 321–22
    successful adoption of, 212–15

Sales call plans, evaluating, 149–50
Sales call reports, reviewing, 150–52
Sales compensation plan
  evaluating, 180–81
  redesigning, 197
Sales efforts, use of computers and
  communication technologies to
  leverage, 201–53
Sales evaluation worksheets, xiii–xiv
Sales force automation (SFA), 217
  key to effective, 201–2
Sales forecasts
  building model, 274–78
  creating accurate, 270–73
  effectiveness of process for
    developing, 268–87
  evaluating procedure, 269–70
Sales formulas and real world results,
  104–5
Sales infrastructure
  documenting your, 202–4
  identifying areas for automating,
    206–9
Sales kit
  accessories and ancillary
    products, 68
  assembling, 65–66
  competition, 71
  configuration information, 69
  customer education, 70–71
  distribution support, 72
  employee programs, 72
  evaluating, 65
  of expansion capabilities, 69
  general product information in, 67
  implementation/conversion
    strategy, 70
  market information in, 66–77
  product availability and delivery
    schedules, 72
  product ordering and distribution
    information, 71
  product/technical specifications, 68
  prospecting information in, 67
  support strategy, 69–70
  system architecture, 68
  system functions in, 67–68
  template for, 66–77
  terms and conditions of sale, 72
  third-party suppliers, 68–69
  training, 70
Sales managers

coaching duties of, 163
defining objectives and key results,
  165–66
evaluating duties of, 164
motivating duties of, 163–64
and time management, 164–65
training duties of, 162
Sales order process, evaluating,
  263–64
Sales organization, reorganizing, 196
Sales plan, 140–46
  evaluating, 63–65
Sales process, creating flowchart for,
  204–11
Sales proposals, evaluating your,
  133–34
Sales qualification questions,
  175–77
Sales recruiting process, evaluating,
  170–74
Sales representatives
  coaching, 163
  cost of replacing, 161–62
  evaluating, 164, 189–93
    aptitude, experience and
      motivation in, 174
  mapping skills of, to specific
    business opportunities, 160–61
  motivating, 163–64
  representation of company by,
    153–200
  reviewing sales call reports of,
    150–52
  sales revenue needed to cover
    direct costs of, 148–49
  time spent working with
    customers, 147–48
  training, to improve selling
    skills, 162
Sales teams
  compensation for members of,
    185–87
  effectiveness of, 138–39
  evaluating qualifications process
    of, 126–28
Sales training programs, evaluating,
  167–68
Selective distribution, 78
Selling downhill, xii
Selling efforts, leveraging, 52–97
Selling methodology, adopting
  specific, 166

Selling price, determining your, 90–91
Skimming, 90
Spam, 229–30
Strategic planning, Microsoft's investment in, 52
Strategic positioning, 197
Subcontractors, evaluating, 87
Supplier performance evaluation and review (SPEAR), 137
Supply strategies, 137
System suppliers, evaluating, 249–52

T
Team selling. *See* Sales teams
Technologies, concerns about adopting, 247–48
Teledesic, 245
Territory plans, evaluating, 140–41
Test marketing, 92
Time, value of, 146–50
Time management for sales managers, 164–65
Total market domination, 310
    1st law of, 6
    2nd law of, 14
    3rd law of, 21
    4th law of, 50
    5th law of, 83
    6th law of, 120–21
    7th law of, 128
    8th law of, 156–57
    9th law of, 215
    10th law of, 257

Total target compensation, 181
    determining, 181–83
Trade shows, 114–16
Training. *See also* Sales training programs
    duties of sales managers in, 162
    of sales representatives, 162
Turnkey solutions, 33

U
User groups, 117–21

V
Value equation, evaluation of, 26
Vendor analysis, 137–39
Videoconferencing, 225
Virtual office, 245–46
Visitors, tracking, to Web site, 239–40

W
Web-based customer service, 221–22
Web sites
    marketing your, 239
    tracking visitors to, 239–40
    and use of cookies, 241
White knight, 196–97
Wireless communications, 224–25

Z
Zero-base budgeting (ZBB), 281
    real world, 282–85
Zero-latency enterprise, 264–65

Selling Microsoft

Put the sales techniques that worked at Microsoft to work for you! Microsoft insider Doug Dayton shows how innovative sales tactics helped drive the company to its unprecedented "total domination" of the personal computer software market, and how you can use the same techniques to increase your own sales. As an account manager for Original Equipment Manufacturers (OEMs) for Microsoft, Dayton was responsible for closing over 40 percent of the company's OEM contracts involving millions of dollars in sales to major high-tech businesses. In *Selling Microsoft*, he shares his powerful, unique sales system known as "Client-Centered Selling" that helped him transform the OEM sales organization into one of the most successful and effective in the business.

Available in:
Hardcover, 1-55850-821-X, $20.00, 320 pages
Trade paperback, 1-58062-052-3, $9.95, 320 pages

Available Wherever Books Are Sold

If you cannot find these titles at your favorite retail outlet, you may order them directly from the publisher. BY PHONE: Call 1-800-872-5627. We accept Visa, MasterCard, and American Express. $4.95 will be added to your total order for shipping and handling. BY MAIL: Write out the full titles of the books you'd like to order and send payment, including $4.95 for shipping and handling, to: Adams Media Corporation, 260 Center Street, Holbrook, MA 02343. 30-day money-back guarantee.